Medical Communication

in Clinical Contexts

Benjamin R. Bates
Ohio University-Athens

Rukhsana Ahmed
University of Ottawa

Kendall Hunt
publishing company

Cover images © Shutterstock, Inc.

www.kendallhunt.com
Send all inquiries to:
4050 Westmark Drive
Dubuque, IA 52004-1840

Copyright © 2012 by Kendall Hunt Publishing Company

ISBN 978-1-4652-0829-3

Printed in the United States of America
10 9 8 7 6 5 4 3 2 1

Medical Communication in Clinical Contexts

Table of Contents

1 Introduction to Medical Communication in Clinical Contexts. 1
  Benjamin R. Bates and Rukhsana Ahmed

2 Moving Across Disciplines and Genres:
  Reading Identity in Illness Narratives and Reflective Writing Texts **17**
  Franziska Gygax, Regula Koenig, and Miriam A. Locher

3 Building a Case for Centered Patient-Physician Communication:
  Standardizing Genuine Interaction in the Medical Context. **37**
  Jennifer Malkowski

4 Hassan, Ami, and Dalia's Mom: Narrative Medicine in Pediatrics **59**
  Eva Berger and Isaac Berger

5 Breaking Bad News in the Provider-Recipient Context:
  Understanding the Hesitation to Share Bad News from the Sender's Perspective. . **77**
  Jayson L. Dibble

6 Side Effects Talk in General Practice Consultations **95**
  Kevin Dew, Maria Stubbe, Anthony Dowell, and Lindsay Macdonald

7 Hearing That Doesn't Help:
  An Evaluation of Appraisal Support During High-Risk Pregnancies **125**
  Jennifer Hall

8 Assessing Baseline Cultural Sensitivity Among Employees at a Hospital System:
  A Mixed-Methods Approach **143**
  Jay Baglia, Anthony Nerino, Judith N. Sabino, and Jarret R. Patton

9 Physicians' Views of Interpersonal Communication Training,
the Importance of Communication in Their Medical Practices,
and the Delivery of Bad News. **167**
   Patricia Amason, Cortney Smith, Samantha Romanin, and Melissa Horvath

10 Effective Health Communication in the Management of Chronic Conditions:
Theoretical Considerations for a Multicultural Framework **187**
   Zhenyi Li, Elizabeth Dean, and Jennifer Walinga

11 "Diabetes Conversation": A Dialogue Among Métis, First Nations
Community Members, and Professionals to Understand Type 2 Diabetes **207**
   Hasu Ghosh

12 Communicating About Childhood Immunization:
New Insights from Aotearoa/New Zealand **229**
   Margie Comrie, Elspeth Tilley, Bronwyn Watson, and Niki Murray

About the Authors **251**

Acknowledgements

We are grateful to the contributions, hard work, and peer-strengthening that the authors in this book provided. Their contributions ensured that this volume could exist on a conceptual plane, and their commitment to helping us through each stage was invaluable. We would also like the thank Dr. Ted Avtgis for introducing us to Kendall Hunt, Paul Carty for his reading of and comments on the proposal, and the production staff at Kendall Hunt for bringing the text into material existence.

— Ben and Rukhsana

It has been a great pleasure to work with my co-editor, Dr. Rukhsana Ahmed. She first suggested the idea of a co-edited volume, and it has been a delight to see the idea become a reality. Thank you to my colleagues at Ohio University for a collegial and cooperative work environment in which co-editing a book is considered as valuable a contribution to scholarship as writing one's own; and to my School Director, Dr. Jerry Miller, and the Dean of the Scripps College of Communication, Dr. Scott Titsworth, for their support of my work on this book. I deeply appreciate Dr. Celeste Condit, who introduced me to the intersections between, among, and through the multiple paths of scholarship that inform the practice of health and medical communication. Finally, I want to acknowledge the ongoing and always generous support of Betsy Morley, both in my life in the university and beyond it.

— Ben

First, I earnestly thank my co-editor, Dr. Benjamin R. Bates, for his dedication, collaboration, and guidance in producing this volume. I also thank my colleagues and students at the University of Ottawa for providing an intellectually stimulating learning environment that enables further exploration of issues in medical communication. I particularly acknowledge the continued encouragement and support of Dr. Martine Lagacé, the Chair at the Department of Communication, and Dr. Antoni Lewkowicz, the Dean of the Faculty of Arts, in my professional growth that makes projects like this successful. Finally, I am deeply grateful to my family for always providing a supportive environment for learning and personal growth. A special thank you to my husband, Dr. Zahirul Hasan Khan, our daughter, Zerin Mahzabin Khan, my father, Dr. Momtaz Uddin Ahmed, and my mother, Momena Ahmed, for their encouragement, patience, and understanding during the course of this work.

— Rukhsana

Chapter 1

Introduction to Medical Communication in Clinical Contexts

Benjamin R. Bates and Rukhsana Ahmed

Introduction

In the past 20 years, there have been increasing calls for practitioners in the medical professions to adopt what is called a "patient-centered" model of care (General Medical Council, 2003; Institute of Medicine, 2001). As part of this patient-centered model, there is growing agreement that patient-centered medical communication is an important skill for healthcare providers to adopt (Epstein, 2000; Levinson & Roter, 1993; Platt & Gordon, 1999). These patient-centered medical communication skills include appropriate diagnostic interviewing techniques, incorporating the patient's view and voice in the treatment phase, and placing patients at the center of a medical communication culture. In addition to asking practitioners to become more patient centered, many of the accrediting medical college boards are beginning to explicitly require patient-centered communication be incorporated into the classroom and into clinical rotations (Commission, 2011; Liaison Committee, 2011). Although it is clear that interviewing techniques are an important skill and a skill that many practitioners are beginning to embrace in the medical communication (Boyle, Dwinnel, & Platt, 2005; Noble, Kubacki, Martin, & Lloyd, 2007; O'Keefe, Robertson, Sawyer, & Baghurst, 2003), the adoption of patient-centered medical communication in the health and allied professions is still limited.

To be sure, many health practitioners are patient-centered medical communicators. Indeed, many agents in the healthcare and medical system seek to become more patient centered (Lambert et al., 1997; Wanzer, Booth-Butterfield, & Gruber, 2004). Too many practitioners, however, think that they are patient-centered medical communicators when they are not. When patients are asked to recall their physicians' communication, for example, the patient's recollection of how patient-centered the interaction was differed significantly from the physician's recall (Olson & Windish, 2010). These are not only differences in style, but differences in understanding the content of medical communication. Although medical communicators report developing shared understanding of the patient's health difficulty and negotiating a treatment plan, when the patients were asked about the diagnosis and treatment, they often had a different understanding than their provider (Makaryus & Friedman, 2005; Maniaci, Heckman, & Dawson, 2008). Indeed, despite many hospitalists' claims to practice patient-centered communication, many patients claim that the depth and engagement of their interaction was so slight that they were unable to name any member of their healthcare team when they were discharged from the hospital (Arora et al., 2009). This limited practice of patient-centered communication did not only include attending physicians, but also residents, interns, nurses, and support staff. Physicians, nurses, therapists, and other medical communicators are becoming increasingly expert in the biomedical sciences; yet, their ability to apply this expertise in the context of patient care is challenged by difficulties in communicating with patients. Patients tend to be less familiar with biomedical processes, less conversant with the technical terminology of healthcare, and less accustomed to scientific standards of care than providers are, and thus, less able to participate fully in medical communication. At the same time, providers are less likely to recognize the life processes of their patients, be less conversant with local lay vocabularies, and less accustomed to narrative and experiential standards for evaluating medical communication.

These gaps between the patient and the provider in creating a shared space for patient-centered medical communication may be due to a need for both theories supporting patient-centered medical communication and empirical evidence for specific interventions to promote patient-centered medical communication. The difficulties in enacting theoretically informed and empirically supported patient-centered medical communication are threefold. First, there may not be a shared understanding of what patient-centered medical communication is, particularly given the strong biomedical orientation toward healthcare supported by current education models. Second, the advantages of adopting patient-centered medical communication may not be readily apparent to either patient or practitioner. And, finally, there is a lack of practical models for enacting patient-centered medical communication to provide a foundation for future medical education. Although the authors of each chapter in this book clarify their understanding of patient-centered medical communication in clinical contexts, we offer a brief overview of our collective understanding of patient-centered medical communication as well as the advantages of adopting a patient-centered approach in clinical contexts. After this overview, we provide a summary of the three themes of this book and offer a brief synopsis of the chapters that our authors have contributed.

What Is Patient-Centered Medical Communication?

One significant challenge to patient-centered medical communication is creating shared understanding of what it is. Patient-centered medical communication, conceptually defined, is an approach that seeks to place the patient and his or her understanding of health, healing, and illness at the center of the clinical communication encounter. In this definition, patient-centered medical communication stands in opposition to what Swenson, Zettler, and Lo (2006) call "a biomedical, or 'doctor-centered' communication style, which encompasses a disease-oriented approach to patient problems and a doctor-centered orientation to decision-making" (p. 200; see also Taylor, 2009). Although Swenson and her colleagues focused on physicians, many other medical communicators also adopt a biomedical communication style when they focus first on mechanical injury or biological causation of ill health rather than on the patient as a person.

It should also be noted that it is not only the healthcare providers who use biomedical communication. Many patients and their families enable a biomedical communication in their clinical encounter. Great effort has gone into helping providers adopt patient-centered medical communication. It is nonetheless vital to encourage patients try to place themselves in the center of this communicative interaction. Advocates of patient-centered medical communication hold that the patient's experience matters on both a practical level and a philosophical level (see Vanderford, Jenks, & Sharf, 1997 for a review). Practically, the patient should ask for their experience to be placed at the center of the clinical encounter because it is their body that is healed or not. If the patient's lifestyle, capabilities, and worldviews are not included in the clinical consultation, easily addressed barriers like allergies, ability to pay, or constraints on lifestyle change recommendations may be neglected. More philosophically, because the patient's identity is often more strongly implicated in these communicative interactions than is the physician's identity, and because each patient is a unique agent whose identity is comprised of a unique confluence of cultural, age, ethnic, gender, and other factors including, effective clinical communication must, at some level, be patient centered.

In this conceptual distinction between patient-centered medical communication and biomedical communication, there are five primary dimensions on which biomedical and patient-centered medical communication differ (Mead & Bower, 2001, pp. 1088–1091; see also Homstrom & Roing, 2010; Sparks, Villagren, Parker-Raley, & Cunningham, 2007).

1. Rather than adopting a focus on the biological causation of disease or the mechanics of injury as is done in the biomedical model, patient-centered care adopts a biopsychosocial perspective in which the biological, psychological, and social perspectives on sickness, illness, and disease are integrated.

2. Whereas the biomedical model adopts a focus on gold standards and generalizable treatment that would apply to all patients, the patient-centered model adopts a view of the "patient-as-person" in which the medical communicator seeks to understand the individual's unique illness-related experience.

3. The patient-centered model of medical communication would also see the "doctor-as-person," holding that the affective experience of communicating with the provider can contribute to (or detract) from the healthcare experience just as much as, if not more than, the biomedical model's framing of the "doctor-as-technician."

4. The biomedical model of medical communication tends to focus on power and responsibility for health outcomes in the physician's ability to correctly diagnose and treat the patient. In the patient-centered model, however, there is a focus on sharing power and responsibility so that the patient's perspective on illness is accounted for, there is mutual provision of information, and in turn, mutual decision making.

5. The biomedical model tends to treat medical communication from a task orientation, in which the primary goal of communication is to diagnose and treat, but in the patient-centered model, a relational orientation is also present. In the patient-centered model, both the provider and patient use medical communication to form a "therapeutic alliance" perspective and seek to promote rapport and the perception of genuine caring in the communication encounter.

As a practical matter, patient-centered medical communication requires that healthcare providers as medical communicators both adapt their affective behaviors toward their patients (Eide, Grauggard, Holgersen, & Finset, 2003; Ong, de Haes, Hoos, & Lammes, 1995; Ong, Visser, Lammes, & Haes, 2000) and solicit participatory behaviors by their patients (Gordon, Street, Sharf, & Sousek, 2006; Street & Gordon, 2006, 2008; Street & Millay, 2001). Patients, as medical communicators, should then accept their provider's affective behaviors and respond to these solicitations. For adaptations in affect, patient-centered medical communication calls for healthcare providers to make displays of empathy, offer appropriate reassurance, and show concern for their patients as individuals. In response, the patient should accept this empathy, reassurance, and concern. To solicit participatory behaviors, patient-centered medical communication encourages healthcare providers to ask open-ended questions in the diagnostic interview, elicit questions from patients regarding diagnoses and treatment recommendations, and invite disclosure of challenges and opportunities for improving care from the patient's perspective. The patient, then, has a complementary responsibility to answer these questions, follow up with their own inquiries, disclose their views, and otherwise become full participants in their own care.

In these adaptations, patient-centered medical communication should not be confused with simple patient choice or deference to the patient (Arora, 2003; Kiesler & Auerbach, 2006). Rather, the essential point of patient-centered medical communication is to perform communication in clinical contexts that matches the patient's preferred style for communication as fully as possible (Aita, McIlvain, Backer, McVea, & Crabtree, 2005; Auerbach, 2000, 2001; Deadman, Leinster, Owens, Dewey, & Slade, 2001; Zanbelt, Straets, Oort, & de Haes, 2005). These matches in communication preference can be on many dimensions. Some patients prefer that the provider take the lead role in the clinical conversation, while other patients prefer to share leadership over the conversation. Some patients may want to control the flow of information, but others want the provider to control the flow. Some patients want the physician to choose treatment options, and other patients want to be given a menu of options to choose from. These and many other dimensions offer providers and patients many ways to adapt to one another's styles and to create a medical communication environment in which the patient's communication preferences can be placed at the center of the interaction.

Why Have Patient Centered Medical Communication?

This call for patient-centered medical communication assumes, however, that patients and providers recognize the value of patient-centered medical communication. There is strong agreement that patient-centered medical communication is valuable for both patients and providers. There is equally strong evidence, however, that current efforts to promote patient-centered medical communication through medical training and education are insufficient.

Patient-centered medical communication overwhelmingly has been shown to be better for both patient and provider than biomedical communication. Not only can patient-centered medical communication be justified from moral and ethical grounds (Duggan, Geller, Cooper, & Beach, 2006), but empirical and conceptual meta-analyses show the overall positive effects of patient-centered care for the patient (Holmstrom & Roing, 2010; Venetis, Robinson, Turkiewicz, & Allen,

2009), as well as for the provider and the provider's business (Rundle-Thiele & Russell-Bennett, 2010).

In the immediate clinical encounter, patient-centered medical communication, because it invites greater levels of disclosure by patients to providers, leads to more correct diagnoses than does biomedical communication (Dyche & Swiderski, 2005; Marvel, Epstein, Flowers, & Beckman, 1999). In follow-up visits, patient-centered medical communicators find that patients are more likely to adhere to treatment recommendations because the patient's views on the acceptability, desirability, and practicality of treatment and treatment outcomes have been addressed in the patient-centered visit (Marinker, 1997; Schneider, Kaplan, Greenfield, Li, & Wilson, 2004; Marinker, 1997). Because of this enhanced disclosure, as well as building agreement on what constitutes a better health outcome between patient and provider, patient-centered medical communication leads to better immediate outcomes for health among patients with acute conditions (Stewart, 1995; Werner & Malterud, 2005), as well as better long-term outcomes for patients with chronic health conditions (Stewart, 1995; Kaplan, Greenfield, & Ware, 1989). In addition to better outcomes overall, patients who experience patient-centered medical communication with providers also attain these positive health outcomes more quickly than do patients who experience only biomedical communication with their providers (Rao, Weinberger, & Kroenke, 2000; Stewart et al., 2000).

Not surprisingly, because patient-centered medical communication is associated with all these positive health outcomes, patients who receive this kind of care also report much higher levels of patient satisfaction (Kinnersley, Stott, Peters, & Harvey, 1999; Little et al., 2001b). On the contrary, patients who receive only biomedical communication tend to experience worse outcomes, receive more unnecessary tests, and are more likely to be readmitted for recurrence or complications of their original condition than patients who experience patient-centered medical communication (Epstein et al., 2005; Little et al., 2001a; Stewart et al., 2000). And, if these positive outcomes for the patient were not enough, healthcare providers who regularly use patient-centered medical communication are far less likely to be sued by their patients for medical malpractice (Beckman, Markakis, Suchman, & Frankel, 1994; Levinson, Roter, Mullooly, Dull, & Frankel, 1997; Lyles, Dwamena, Lein, & Smith, 2001).

Although there is a substantial evidence base for the value of patient-centered medical communication, current models for training healthcare providers to enact it are insufficient. Overall, there are few empirically supported guidelines for teaching patient-centered medical communication to future health practitioners (Veldhuizen, Ram, van der Weijden, Wassink, & van der Vleuten, 2007) and there is a lack of consistency among courses in how patient-centered medical communication is taught (Cegala & Lenzmeier Broz, 2002; Gysels, Richardson, & Higginson, 2005; Weissman, Haidet, Branch, Gracey, & Frankel, 2010). Perhaps most disconcerting is that, as a physician reaches the end of her or his schooling, there is a significant drop-off in enacting patient-centered medical communication skills (Cantwell & Ramirez, 1997; Eisenthal, Stoeckle, & Ehrlich, 1994; Haidet et al., 2002). Moreover, as doctors enter their residency training the enactment of patient-centered medical communication declines further (Hafferty, 1998; Haidet, Kelly, & Chou, 2005). The same decline has been found in other health and allied professions; as a person gains additional medical training, their enactment of patient-centered medical communication decreases (Benbassat & Baumal, 2004; Rouf, Chumley, & Dobbie, 2009).

The solution to promoting more patient-centered medical communication in clinical contexts is likely not additional education. Classroom education on patient-centered medical communication has significant short-term effects in promoting more patient-centered medical communication in simulated patient and laboratory settings (Beach, Rosner, Cooper, Duggan, & Shatzer, 2007; Rosen et al., 2004; Ho, Yao, Lee, Beach, & Green, 2008). The long-term efficacy of simply having more in-class sessions on patient-centered medical communication is, however, doubtful, as patient-centered medical communication tends to decline after one leaves school and is no longer directly tested for their patient centeredness (Ho, Yao, Lee, Hwang, & Beach, 2010). Similarly, although continuing medical education classes have some short-term effect, in the long run providers often default to their original biomedical training (Brown, Boles, Mullooly, & Levinson, 1999; Jenkins & Fallowfield, 2002; Levinson & Roter, 1993). What may be needed instead of additional classes are empirically supported models for enacting patient-centered medical communication that are both theoretically informed and clinically effective. Instead of telling healthcare providers how to be patient-centered medical communicators, it may be more useful to show how patient-centered medical communication has been performed as a model for the desired behaviors.

About This Book

This edited collection is an attempt to show, not only tell, how patient-centered medical communication can be performed in clinical contexts. In this showing, three primary themes present themselves. First, although many medical communication scholars treat original theoretical research and practical applications as separate and non-intersecting efforts, we believe the most powerful health interventions often seek to expand theoretical ground, and the best communication theories are often enhanced by their demonstration in practical contexts.

Therefore, this collection offers an integrated view of health communication in applied clinical contexts. We have chosen to feature chapters that both discuss the findings of and remaining communication questions in recently completed or on-going research projects in clinical health contexts. Rather than attempting to build a practical, how-to manual for communicating in the clinic or seeking to erect theoretical/explanatory models for how clinical medical communication should work, the first theme of this edited volume discusses how medical communication is practiced in applied clinical contexts and how it should reflect an integrated view of research, theory, and application.

Second, this collection reflects medical communication's nature as a multi-disciplinary, yet specialized field of study. That is, rather than attempting to study in-depth clinical health communication as the study of doctor-patient interaction, or as the cultivation of social support, or as some other focused slice of health communication in applied clinical settings, this volume portrays the breadth of applied clinical medical communication. We feature medical communication research and applications in clinical contexts, including experiences in the formal clinic and in clinical outreach to communities. The contributions draw insights and experiences from health programs and interventions from around the world. In doing so, we seek to address key crosscutting issues that are central to applied clinical communication in preventing diseases, promoting health, and shaping personal practices. The following contributions employ a variety of methodological approaches, including quantitative, qualitative, mixed-method, rhetorical, interpretive, case study, discourse analytic, and critical analytic approaches. As such, the second theme of this book is that the topical and methodological diversity of applied clinical health communication research is a strength; we believe that "good" clinical health research need not follow a single methodological paradigm.

Finally, we believe the study of medical communication is simultaneously social scientific, humanistic, and professional in orientation. Accordingly, this collection features contributions from both established and emerging scholars and practitioners in communication studies and allied fields as well as those in the health professions and allied health fields. Collectively, the contributions also provide readers with:

- An understanding of how patient-centered medical communication can be effectively used to improve the health of individuals, communities, and populations
- Pertinent health communication information, analysis, and instruction in clinical contexts
- An outline of past successful research projects and practical applications in patient-centered medical communication

- A review of best theories and practices in practical medical communication interventions in applied clinical contexts
- A demonstration of how medical communication practice and medical communication research in clinical contexts inform one another

In examining these ongoing and completed projects, the third and final theme of this volume is that exemplars of applied clinical and communication projects offer strong models for health practitioners and medical communicators to improve the delivery of patient-centered medical communication.

Toward demonstrating these themes, the collection is divided into four sections. In the first section, the contributors to this volume argue for the importance of placing patients in the center of a medical communication culture and demonstrate a variety of methods and theories for doing so. Franziska Gygax, Regula Koenig, and Miriam Locher open this section in chapter 2. They offer a demonstration of how life writing and reflective writing help medical communicators create patients and providers, respectively, and help articulate their identities in the clinical setting. These narratives, constructed through reflective discourse, show how language shapes our clinical identity as medical communicators. Gygax, Koenig, and Locher show that learning how to "read" an "other" (illness narratives) and to reflect on "self" (reflective writing) are vital skills for successful patient-centered medical communication.

In chapter 3, Jennifer Malkowski moves us from reflection on previous communication acts to an examination of medical interviewing. Malkowski argues that, in the patient intake interview, vernacular rhetorics used by patients to describe personal experiences of health come into contact with official rhetorics of medicine used by healthcare providers. This chapter seeks to interrogate the current patient-centered model of medical interviewing to assess how well standardized patient interviews prepare future physicians for real-time patient communication when they need to negotiate these competing rhetorics. Malkowski illuminates how standardized training and evaluation practices might better prepare future physicians for the situationally dependent nature of patient interviewing, and further, she theorizes about the ways the medical curriculum might better conceptualize, incorporate, promote, and assess effective patient-centered medical communication.

Closing this section, in chapter 4, Eva Berger and Isaac Berger show that patient-centered medical communication is further complicated when communication is challenged by differences not only between a medically trained individual and a lay patient, but also when there are significant differences in age and other statuses. They show that, in pediatrics, communication is shaped by three parties (the physician, the child, and the parents), with varying degrees and characteristics of parent involvement. Their chapter uses the method of participatory ethnography to present an analysis of three real cases (rather, life stories) out of hundreds encountered by Isaac Berger over a 50-year pediatric career. These stories serve as basis for the analysis of the potential of patient-centered narrative medicine to bring back direct, humane, and unmediated communication to the doctor-patient relationship and to aid healing.

Having placed patients in the center of the medical communication culture, the second section shows providers coming to that same center to meet their patients through medical communication. In chapter 5, Jayson Dibble opens this section with a discussion of breaking bad news or of sharing undesirable information with healthcare recipients. In their efforts to account for patient needs, Dibble argues that there is a strong bias on the part of providers to hesitate and/or fail to adequately convey negatively valenced information. Although research has long attended to the issue of competently communicating bad news when necessary, Dibble shows that our dominant view, a perspective that acknowledges the well-being of the recipient only, is insufficient to creating a true patient-centered medical communication environment. Through this critical review, Dibble offers both suggestions for practitioners and directions to guide future research.

Picking up on similar themes, Kevin Dew, Maria Stubbe, Anthony Dowell, and Lindsay Macdonald use chapter 6 to investigate one common context where potential bad news may be broken to the patient: side effects of recommended treatment. Dew and his colleagues focus on general practitioners' initiated side effects talk and patient talk associating side effects with symptoms in the consultation. Their analysis focuses on the ways in which general practitioners and patients talk about side effects in the consultation, and also considers the consequences of these interactions for the doctor-patient relationship, use of prescribed medicines, and patient safety. It argues that the outcomes can in part be understood as a consequence of the interactional dilemmas that doctors and patients face in relation to the medical consultation. Dew and his colleagues conclude there is a need for GPs to consider ways to better recognize and respond to patient expressions of concern about side effects in the interests of patient safety if they are to meet the patient as part of a patient-centered medical communication culture.

Closing this section, chapter 7 by Jennifer Hall investigates how women who experienced high-risk pregnancies were influenced by the narratives they heard and read as they attempted to create their own narratives during the sense-making and decision-making processes. Hall argues that positive and negative social support is a critical component of health and medical professionals' communication during high-risk pregnancies. Further, she claims that health communication research can be used to identify techniques that make supportive communication as effective as possible. After determining patient-centered communication patterns that result in positive reappraisals of pregnancy risk, Hall offers practical applications for medical personnel and friends and family members who are trying to offer comfort and social support.

Sections 1 and 2 are primarily concerned with using theories and methods to examine acts of communication to understand when medical communication has been patient-centered and when it has needed improvement. Sections 3 and 4 are focused on theoretically and methodologically informed communication interventions that seek to promote patient-centered medical communication. Within the walls of the clinic, Jay Baglia, Anthony Nerino, Judith Sabino, and Jarret Patton use chapter 8 to discuss how they helped a large hospital system's efforts to increase cultural competence as part of patient-centered medical communication. The network established a Cultural Awareness Implementation Team charged with developing a comprehensive plan to enhance cultural competence and improve patient healthcare experiences. Baglia and Nerino describe the plan implementation and discuss the results of a baseline assessment of cultural competence. They conclude with a description of educational programs for both the hospital staff and the surrounding community that they have developed.

In chapter 9, Patricia Amason, Cortney Smith, Samantha Romanin, and Melissa Horvath discuss a communication intervention for increasing trust between physicians and patients in the context of breaking bad news. After assessing the role interpersonal communication plays in their practices, their preparedness for effectively communicating with their patients, and the communication strategies they employ while delivering bad news, Amason and colleagues presented physicians with a model for breaking bad news, known as S-P-I-K-E-S. The S-P-I-K-E-Sprotocol features methods to use during the discussion of bad news and how to handle obstacles that arise during such conversations. When asked specifically about their use of strategies similar to those in the S-P-I-K-E-S model, Amason and colleagues found that physicians were able to compare their actual nonpatient-centeredcommunication acts to more effective options for creating a patient-centered communication environment. Amason and colleagues conclude with opportunities for physician training and patient education.

Concluding this section, chapter 10 reflects Zhenyi Li, Elizabeth Dean, and Jennifer Walinga's efforts to build a multicultural framework for patient-centered medical communication. Li and her colleagues sought to maximize the effectiveness of health communication based on the multiculturalism developed in Canada and elsewhere. They hold that a consideration of theories of effective multicultural communication offers a rational basis for targeted management focused on lifestyle behavior change and potentially superior health outcomes. Li and colleagues provide examples of the application of a multicultural framework in health communication research and practical applications of the framework to enhance health education outcomes.

The final section in this collection considers clinical contexts outside of the clinic. That is, this section offers examples of when healthcare providers enact patient-centered medical communication in community health applications. When clinical options are offered in the field, these chapters show that patient centeredness is still necessary. Hasu Ghosh uses chapter 11 to discuss an ongoing community-based research project that aims to contribute to better understanding of the causes of and ways to reduce the impact of Type 2 diabetes among First Nations in Canada. Ghosh argues that, while the biomedical model would attribute the causes of diabetes to diet and lifestyle shifts, the biomedical focus on risk factors cannot convey the social, cultural, and personal dimensions of susceptibility to contracting a disease. Ghosh demonstrates the potential and urgency of deriving mutual language of multiple stakeholders for framing people's and professionals' understandings of susceptibility to develop diabetes; and negotiating common solutions to inform culturally appropriate health service delivery that are equitable, sustainable, and culturally appropriate.

Finally, in chapter 12, Margie Comrie, Elspeth Tilley, Niki Murray, and Bronwyn Watson discuss the findings of and remaining questions in an ongoing research project to explore communicative phenomena in the childhood immunization context in Aotearoa/New Zealand. Using a detailed grounded qualitative analysis of focus group and in-depth interview transcripts with 107 immunization decision makers, themes about the indigenous understanding of immunization were derived. These themes revealed patient and parent preferences for visual aspects and content of immunization communication, and these were applied to modify the design of a communication intervention to promote immunization. Comrie and colleagues document the grounded research approach from start to finish, showing how applying an emic process enabled generation of new ideas that broadened the range of possible solutions currently being considered for immunization communication challenges in New Zealand.

Altogether, we believe that these 11 chapters demonstrate the power of communication to create or interfere with the creation of a patient-centered medical communication environment. We hope that these research interventions and applied projects can serve as models for health communication practitioners, medical communication scholars, and clinical practitioners to improve their understanding of theories, methods, and models for promoting patient-centered medical communication.

Aita, V., McIlvain, H., Backer, E., McVea, K., & Crabtree, B. (2005). Patient-centered care and communication in primary care practice: What is involved? *Patient Education and Counseling, 58,* 296–304.

Arora, N. K. (2003). Interacting with cancer patients: The significance of physicians' communication behavior. *Social Science and Medicine, 57,* 791–806.

Arora, V., Gangireddy, S., Mehrota, A., Ginde, R., Tormey, M., & Meltzer, D. (2009). Ability of hospitalized patients to identify their in-hospital physicians. *Archives of Internal Medicine, 169,* 199 201.

Auerbach, S. M. (2000). Should patients have control over their own health care? Empirical evidence and research issues. *Annals of Behavioral Medicine, 22,* 246–259.

Auerbach, S. M. (2001). Do patients want control over their own health care? A review of measures, findings, and research issues. *Journal of Health Psychology, 6,* 191–203.

Beach, M. C., Rosner, M. B., Cooper, L. A., Duggan, P. S. A., & Shatzer, J. (2007). Can patient-centered attitudes reduce racial and ethnic disparities in care? *Academic Medicine, 82,* 193–198.

Beckman, H. B., Markakis, K. M., Suchman, A. L., & Frankel, R. M. (1994). The doctor-patient relationship and malpractice: Lessons from plaintiff depositions. *Archives of Internal Medicine, 154,* 1365–1370.

Benbassat, J., & Baumal, R. (2004). What is empathy and how can it be promoted during clinical clerkships? *Academic Medicine, 79,* 832–839.

Boyle, D., Dwinnel, B., & Platt, F. (2005). Invite, listen, and summarize: A patient-centered communication technique. *Academic Medicine, 80,* 29–32.

Brown, J., Boles, M., Mullooly, J., & Levinson, W. (1999). Effects of clinician communication skills training on patient satisfaction. *Annals of Internal Medicine, 131,* 822–829.

Cantwell, B. M., & Ramirez, A. J. (1997). Doctor-patient communication: A study of junior house officers. *Medical Education, 31,* 17–21.

Cegala, D. J., & Lenzmeier Broz, S. (2002). Physician communication skills training: A review of theoretical backgrounds, objectives and skills. *Medical Education, 36,* 1004–1016.

Commission on Osteopathic College Accreditation. (2011). *Accreditation of colleges of osteopathic medicine: COM accreditation standards and procedures.* Retrieved from http://www.osteopathic.org/inside-aoa/accreditation/predoctoral%20accreditation/Documents/COM-standards-of-accreditation-effective-7-1-2011.pdf

Deadman, J. M., Leinster, S. J., Owens, R. G., Dewey, M. E., & Slade, P. D. (2001). Taking responsibility for cancer treatment. *Social Science and Medicine, 53,* 669–677.

Duggan, P. S., Geller, G., Cooper, L. A., & Beach, M. C. (2006). The moral nature of patient-centeredness: Is it 'just the right thing to do?' *Patient Education and Counseling, 62,* 271–276.

Dyche, L., & Swiderski, D. (2005). The effect of physician solicitation approaches on ability to identify patient concerns. *Journal of General Internal Medicine, 20,* 267–270.

Eide, H., Grauggard, P., Holgersen, K., & Finset, A. (2003). Physician communication in different phases of a consultation at an oncology outpatient clinic related to patient satisfaction. *Patient Education and Counseling, 51,* 259–266.

Eisenthal, S., Stoeckle, J., & Ehrlich, C. (1994). Orientation of medical residents to the psychosocial aspects of primary care: Influence of training program. *Academic Medicine, 69*, 48–54.

Epstein, R. M. (2000). The science of patient-centered care. *Journal of Family Practice, 49*, 805–807.

Epstein, R. M., Franks, P., Shields, C. G., Meldreum, S. C., Miller, K. N., Campbell, T. L. et al., (2005). Patient-centered communication diagnostic testing. *Annals of Family Medicine, 3*, 415–421.

General Medical Council. (2003). *Tomorrow's doctors: Recommendations on undergraduate medical education.* London: General Medical Council.

Gordon, H. S., Street, R. L., Sharf, B. F., & Sousek, J. (2006). Racial differences in doctors' information-giving and patients' participation. *Cancer, 107*, 1313–1320.

Gysels, M., Richardson, A., & Higginson, I. J. (2005). Communication training for health professionals who care for patients with cancer: A systematic review of effectiveness. *Support Care Cancer, 13*, 356–366.

Hafferty, F. (1998). Beyond curriculum reform: Confronting medicine's hidden curriculum. *Academic Medicine, 73*, 403–407.

Haidet, P., Dains, J., Paternitti, D., Hechtel, L., Chang, T., Tseng, E. et al. (2002). Medical student attitudes toward the doctor-patient relationship. *Medical Education, 36*, 568–574.

Haidet, P., Kelly, A., & Chou, C. (2005). Characterizing the patient-centeredness of hidden curricula in medical schools: Development and validation of a new measure. *Academic Medicine, 80*, 44–50.

Ho, M.-J., Yao, G., Lee, K.-L., Hwang, T.-J., & Beach, M. C. (2010). Long-term effectiveness of patient-centered training in cultural competence: What is retained? What is lost? *Academic Medicine, 85*, 660–664.

Ho, M.-J., Yao, G., Lee, L.-L., Beach, M. C., & Green, A. (2008). Cross-cultural medical education: Can patient-centered cultural competency training be effective in non-Western countries? *Medical Teacher, 30*, 719–721.

Holmstrom, I., & Roing, M. (2010). The relation between patient-centeredness and patient empowerment: A discussion on concepts. *Patient Education and Counseling, 79*, 167–172.

Institute of Medicine. (2001). *Crossing the quality chasm: A new health system for the 21st century.* Washington, DC: National Academies Press.

Jenkins, V., & Fallowfield, L. (2002). Can communication skills training alter physicians' beliefs and behavior in clients? *Journal of Clinical Oncology, 20*, 765–769.

Kaplan, S. H., Greenfield, S., & Ware, J. E., Jr. (1989). Assessing the effects of physician-patient communication on the outcomes of chronic disease. *Medical Care, 27*, S110–S127.

Kiesler, D. J., & Auerbach, S. M. (2006). Optimal matches of patient preferences for information, decision-making and interpersonal behavior: Evidence, models and interventions. *Patient Education and Counseling, 61*, 319–341.

Kinnersley, P., Stott, N., Peters, T. J., & Harvey, I. (1999). The patient-centeredness of consultations and outcome in primary care. *British Journal of General Practice, 49*, 711–716.

Lambert, B. L., Street, R. L., Cegala, D. J., Smith, D. H., Kurtz, S., & Schofield, T. (1997). Provider-patient communication, patient-centered care, and the mangle of practice. *Health Communication, 9*, 27–43.

Levinson, W., & Roter, D. (1993). The effects of two continuing medical education programs on communication skills of practicing primary care physicians. *Journal of General Internal Medicine, 11*, 147–155.

Levinson, W., Roter, D. L., Mullooly, J. P., Dull, V. T., & Frankel, R. M. (1997). Physician-patient communication: The relationship with malpractice claims. *Journal of the American Medical Association, 277*, 553–839.

Liaison Committee on Medical Education. (2011). *Functions and structure of a medical school: Standards for accreditation of medical programs leading to the MD degree.* Retrieved from http://www.lcme.org/functions2011may.pdf

Little, P., Everitt, H., Williamson, I., Warner, G., Moore, M., Gould, C. et al. (2001a). Observational study of the effect of patient-centeredness and positive approach on outcomes of general practice consultations. *British Medical Journal, 323*, 908–911.

Little, P., Everitt, H., Williamson, I., Warner, G., Moore, M., Gould, C. et al. (2001b). Preferences of patients for a patient-centered approach to consultation in primary care: Observational study. *British Medical Journal, 322*, 468–472.

Lyles, J., Dwamena, F., Lein, C., & Smith, R. (2001). Evidence-based patient-centered interviewing. *Journal of Clinical Outcomes Management, 8*, 28–34.

Makaryus, A. N., & Friedman, E. A. (2005). Patients' understanding of their treatment plans and diagnosis at discharge. *Mayo Clinic Proceedings, 80*, 991–994.

Maniaci, M. J., Heckman, M. G., & Dawson, N. L. (2008). Functional health literacy and understanding of medications at discharge. *Mayo Clinic Proceedings, 83*, 554–558.

Marinker, M. (1997). From compliance to concordance: Achieving shared goals in medicine taking. *British Medical Journal, 314*, 747–748.

Marvel, M. K., Epstein, R. W., Flowers, K., & Beckman, H. B. (1999). Soliciting the patient's agenda: Have we improved? *Journal of the American Medical Association, 281*, 283–287.

Mead, N., & Bower, P. (2001). Patient-centeredness: A conceptual framework and review of the empirical literature. *Social Science and Medicine, 51*, 1087–1110.

Noble, L., Kubacki, A., Martin, J., & Lloyd, M. (2007). The effect of professional skills training on patient-centeredness and confidence in communicating with patients. *Medical Education, 41*, 432–340.

O'Keefe, M., Robertson, D., Sawyer, M., & Baghurst, P. (2003). Medical student interviewing: A randomized trial of patient-centeredness and clinical competence. *Family Practice, 20*, 213–219.

Olson, D. P., & Windish, D. M. (2010). Communication discrepancies between physicians and hospitalized patients. *Archives of Internal Medicine, 170*, 1302–1307.

Ong, L. M. L., de Haes, I. J. C. J. M., Hoos, A. M., & Lammes, F. B. (1995). Doctor-patient communication: A review of the literature. *Social Science and Medicine, 40*, 903–918.

Ong, L. M. L., Visser, M. R. M., Lammes, F. B., & Haes, J. (2000). Doctor-patient communication and cancer patients' quality of life and satisfaction. *Patient Education and Counseling, 41*, 145–156.

Platt, F. W., & Gordon, G. H. (1999). *Field guide to the difficult patient interview.* Philadelphia: Lippincott, Williams, & Wilkins.

Rao, J. K., Weinberger, M., & Kroenke, K. (2000). Visit-specific expectations and patient-centered outcomes: A literature review. *Archives of Family Medicine, 9*, 1148–1155.

Rosen, J., Spatz, E. S., Gaaserud, A. M., Abramovitch, H., Weinreb, B., Wenger, N. S. et al. (2004). A new approach to developing cross-cultural communication skills. *Medical Teacher, 26*, 126–132.

Rouf, E., Chumley, H., & Dobbie, A. (2009). Does patient-centered interviewing correlate with global student performance in clinical skills examination? *Patient Education and Counseling, 75*, 11–15.

Rundle-Thiele, S., & Russell-Bennett, R. (2010). Patient influences on satisfaction and loyalty for GP services. *Health Marketing Quarterly, 27*, 195–214.

Schneider, J., Kaplan, S. H., Greenfield, S., Li, W., & Wilson, I. B. (2004). Better physician-patient relationships are associated with higher reported adherence to antiretroviral therapy in patients with HIV infection. *Journal of General Internal Medicine, 19*, 1096–1103.

Sparks, L., Villagren, M. M., Parker-Raley, J., & Cunningham, C. B. (2007). A patient-centered approach to breaking bad news: Communication guidelines for health care providers. *Journal of Applied Communication Research, 35*, 177–196.

Stewart, M. (1995). Effective physician-patient communication and health outcomes: A review. *Canadian Medical Journal, 152*, 1423–1433.

Stewart, M., Brown, J. B., Donner, A., McWhinney, J. R., Oates, J., Weston, W. W. et al. (2000). The impact of patient-centered care on outcomes. *Journal of Family Practice, 49*, 796–804.

Street, R. L., & Gordon, H. S. (2006). The clinical context and patient participation in post-diagnostic consultations. *Patient Education and Counseling, 64*, 217–224.

Street, R. L., & Gordon, H. S. (2008). Companion participation in cancer consultations. *Psychooncology, 17*, 244–251.

Street, R. L., & Millay, B. (2001). Analyzing patient participation in medical encounters. *Health Communication, 13*, 61–73.

Swenson, S. L., Zettler, P., & Lo, B. (2006). 'She gave it her best shot right away': Patient experiences of biomedical and patient-centered communication. *Patient Education and Counseling, 61*, 200–211.

Taylor, K. (2009). Paternalism, participation and partnership—The evolution of patient centeredness in the consultation. *Patient Education and Counseling, 74*, 150–155.

Vanderford, M. L., Jenks, E. B., & Sharf, B. F. (1997). Exploring patients' experiences as a primary source of meaning. *Health Communication, 9*, 13–26.

Veldhuizen, W., Ram, P. M., van der Weijden, T., Wassink, M. R., & van der Vleuten, C. P. M. (2007). Much variety and little evidence: A description of guidelines for doctor-patient communication. *Medical Education, 41*, 138–145.

Venetis, M. K., Robinson, J. D., Turkiewicz, K. L., & Allen, M. (2009). An evidence base for patient-centered cancer care: A meta-analysis of studies of observed communication between cancer specialists and their patients. *Patient Education and Counseling, 77*, 379–383.

Wanzer, M. B., Booth-Butterfield, M., & Gruber, K. (2004). Perceptions of health care providers' communication: Relationships between patient-centered communication and satisfaction. *Health Communication, 16*, 363–384.

Weissman, P. F., Haidet, P., Branch, W. T., Jr., Gracey, C., & Frankel, R. (2010). Teaching humanism on the wards: What patients value in outstanding attending physicians. *Journal of Communication in Health Care, 3*, 291–299.

Werner, A., & Malterud, K. (2005). 'The pain isn't as disabling as it used to be': How can the patient experience empowerment instead of vulnerability in the consultation? *Scandinavian Journal of Public Health, 33*, 41–46.

Zanbelt, L., Straets, E., Oort, F., & de Haes, H. (2005). Coding patient-centered behavior in the medical encounter. *Social Science and Medicine, 61*, 661–671.

Chapter 2

Moving Across Disciplines and Genres: Reading Identity in Illness Narratives and Reflective Writing Texts

Franziska Gygax, Regula Koenig, and Miriam A. Locher

Introduction

For this chapter, we propose to discuss the concept of identity within the two text genres of life writing and reflective writing, situated within the larger field of illness narratives. We consider the concept of identity construction an ideal entry point for our analyses since both the reading of narratives and the creation of reflective writing texts crucially rely on recognizing and acknowledging self and other. These skills have been recognized as vital for the development of future doctors to ensure successful interaction between them and their patients.

Narratives are omnipresent in our lives and play a crucial role in doctor-patient communication, in literature, and in everyday linguistic situations. The rapid development during the past few years of the new field of narrative medicine (as coined by Rita Charon, 2006) demonstrates the importance and necessity of paying heed to the power of narratives that deal with the experience of illness. Arthur Kleinman observes that talking with patients about their illness is a kind of "witnessing" and this narrative encounter can help patients "order that experience" and can thus be of "therapeutic value" (Kleinman, 1988, p. xii). However, most doctors are not trained to be susceptible to specific linguistic and literary uses in their patients' stories. Thus, it is necessary to integrate literary and linguistic issues into the curriculum at medical schools to approach illness more holistically.

In addition, numerous recent illness narratives by patients/writers provide new insights that go beyond the biomedical dimension of an illness, and with their aesthetic impact express additional aspects of human experience. Since many of these texts are autobiographical, the field of autobiography studies has become influential regarding theorizing and exploring the specificities of illness narratives. Literary texts dealing with illness often challenge medical discourse and practices, although their writers are usually nonmedically trained laypersons. Although there are various reasons why they decide to write about their illness experience, the powerful effect of helping "to relieve the suffering of the self" (Couser, 1997, p. 289) is always acknowledged. Thus, telling one's experience of illness is always intricately linked to identity and to the continuously changing process of constituting identities. Self-invention and the formation of identity are at the core of all autobiographical, if not of all narratives in general.

A linguistic analysis of reflective writing texts by medical students from the University of Nottingham (UK) on an encounter with a memorable patient offers crucial information on the ways in which future doctors interpret a patient's narrative and reflect their own situations. In the field of medicine, reflective writing is acknowledged to be an important part of the learning process in medical studies (Bolton, 2010; Brady, Corbie-Smith, & Branch, 2002; Mann, Gordon, & Mac Leod, 2009; Shapiro, Kasman, & Shafer, 2006; Wald & Reis, 2010; Wald, Reis, Monroe, & Borkan, 2010). It provides future doctors with ways to evaluate their behavior and it encourages self-criticism. The students' texts are ideal for the study of linguistic identity construction with the qualitative framework of positioning theory within interactional sociolinguistics (Bucholtz & Hall, 2005; Davies & Harré, 1990; c.f., De Fina, 2003, 2010) since the students face several dilemmas. For example, they are medical students but have to construct an expert identity when interacting and communicating with their patients. In addition, they are addressing the teacher for whom they write the text and, thus, create a student identity. We argue that the tensions between these different roles shape their texts, and we illustrate that the students create different personas in their texts to meet the specific expectations entailed in the task of reflective writing.

Both life writing and reflective writing texts lend themselves to study and theorize identity construction from a linguistic and literary perspective by using our own disciplinary concepts, but at the same time, having them engage in a dialogue with concepts from other disciplines. It is our intention to show that we can approach the concept of identity from a transdisciplinary approach and can, thus, enhance our insight into constructions of identity. Moving across disciplines on the one hand means to find similarities between our theoretical concepts of identity and to integrate them into our disciplinary analysis on the other hand. The methodology chosen is a qualitative content analysis combined with discourse analytical tools as well as theoretical concepts from literary and cultural studies. Our findings then flow back into the teaching of communication skills at the University of Nottingham to improve current and future communicative training of medical students.

This project is part of a larger interdisciplinary project funded by the Swiss National Science Foundation (c.f., illness-narratives.unibas.ch). The project, Life

(Beyond) Writing: Illness Narratives, involves the fields of literature, linguistics, and medicine. It was developed to provide new insights into illness (narratives) by collaborating across disciplines. The outcome should contribute to literary and linguistic studies, medical student training, and the training of communication skills and didactics in the medical curriculum.

Definitions of 'Identity'

Definitions of Identity by Cultural and Literary Critics

In the field of literary and cultural studies it is common knowledge that *identity* is always a construction, and neither innate nor essential and, to a considerable extent, constructed through language. Particularly in autobiography studies, the concept of identity has been theorized, reconceptualized, and even contested. Autobiographers are known to identify themselves through their name on the cover of their book, yet we know that we cannot trust this convention as a number of autobiographies demonstrated. (Gertrude Stein's famous autobiography, *The Autobiography of Alice B. Toklas*, (1933) is a case in point.) Many theoreticians have contributed to the discussion of identity (c.f., Smith & Watson, 2010) and in the recent past even neuroscientific research has become influential in autobiography studies through John Paul Eakin (2008) with his reliance on Antonio Damasio's work. While Eakin is attracted by Damasio's claim of an "autobiographical self" (Damasio, 1999, pp. 17–18), others criticize this role of neuroscience in literary studies: Narratologists, they claim, can offer more insight into the role of consciousness, in particular with regard to witnessing our own experiences (c.f., Butte, 2005). Although there has been some intriguing new work in cognitive poetics (c.f., Keen, 2007) and even autobiographical illness narratives such as Siri Hustvedt's *The Shaking Woman* (2010) explore the role of neuroscientific research, we do not want to enter this debate nor do we have enough sophisticated knowledge in the field of neuroscience; instead, we draw on the field of interactional sociolinguistics as specified below to apply a concept of *identity* that shares similarities in the two disciplines.

In the relatively new field of affect studies with its "affective turn" (Ticineto Clough & Halley, 2007) in cultural studies and its focus on subject identity and trauma, Emmanuel Levinas has become an authority regarding "the ethical imperative in the face of suffering" (Diedrich, 2007, p. 148). Illness narratives in particular, with their rendering of suffering, are bound to affect readers in a variety of ways. For Levinas, identity is always engagement with otherness: "The strangeness of the Other, his irreducibility to the I, to my thoughts … is precisely accomplished as a calling into question of my spontaneity, as ethics" (Levinas, 1969, p. 43).

Alterity and language are intricately intertwined because "language is already an address to and from the other" (Wyschogrod, 2002, p. 191); we could even state that only through language does the other come into being. Although Levinas' philosophical explanations and definitions of self, other, ethical, and ethics are not without contradictions and restrictions (c.f., Bernasconi, 2002, p. 234), his definition of identity and the consequential ethical response are useful for our discussion of Gillian Rose's illness narrative since this text addresses the unavoidable encounter between self and other. Yet, one must emphasize that Levinas' ethics do not provide any norms of action nor can they be related to a moral responsibility as may be expected in a clinical or therapeutic context (c.f., Perpich, 2008, pp. 2–16).

Definitions of Identity in Interactional Sociolinguistics

The discussion of identity in linguistics has a long tradition and ranges from approaches in neuroscience, stylistics, and conversation analysis to interactional sociolinguistics (for overviews, see Mendoza-Denton, 2002; De Fina, 2010). We focus here on the field mentioned last. In interactional sociolinguistics, as in the field of literary and cultural studies, it has become acknowledged that in any encounter involving two or more participants "we are forever composing impressions of ourselves, projecting a definition of who we are, and making claims about ourselves and the world that we test and negotiate in social interaction" (Riessman, 1990, p. 1195). Thus, *identity* is a concept inherent to all social interactions and narratives of such interactions.

Similar to literary studies, interactional sociolinguistics considers the concept of *identity* no longer to be a fixed entity assigned to people in an a priori fashion, but an emergent product of interaction (*the emergence principle*, Bucholtz & Hall, 2005). In interaction, language is only one—albeit an important—means of constructing identity. As Davies and Harré (1990, p. 46) argue, "an individual emerges through the processes of social interaction, not as a relatively fixed end product but as one who is constituted and reconstituted through the various discursive practices in which they participate." Individuals do not assume stable identities that are anchored in their psyche or fixed by their membership in specific social categories. Hence, identities are "intersubjectively rather than individually produced and interactionally emergent" (Bucholtz & Hall, 2010, p. 18).

Within positioning theory, identity construction is understood as "the social positioning of self and other" (Bucholtz & Hall, 2005, p. 586). Thus, Davies and Harré (1990) hold that "positioning" and "subject position"

> permit us to think of ourselves as a choosing subject, locating ourselves in conversations according to those narrative forms with

which we are familiar and bringing to those narratives our own subjective lived histories through which we have learnt metaphors, characters and plot. (p. 52)

Thinking about identity as an act of positioning can help us to explain "discontinuities in the production of self with reference to the fact of multiple and contradictory discursive practices and the interpretations of those practices that can be brought into being by speakers and hearers as they engage in conversations" (Davies & Harré, 1990, p. 62). In addition, positioning theory can help us see how individuals create coherence and reinforce their sense of self by choosing to position themselves in certain ways. This is particularly useful when considering how illness can disrupt an individual's life story and how illness brings about discontinuities.

By positioning ourselves and others in interaction, "we are thus agent (producer/director) as well as author and player and the other participants co-author and coproduce the drama. But we are also the multiple audiences that view any play" (Davies & Harré, 1990, p. 52). However, the act of positioning does not have to be intentional. Positioning involves four major processes (Davies & Harré, 1990): Learning of the categories that include and exclude some people, thus creating in-groups and out-groups; participating in the various discursive practices through which meanings are assigned to these in-group/out-group categories; positioning self in terms of these categories and storylines; and the recognition of oneself as belonging to certain categories and not others, i.e., developing a sense of oneself and, thus, seeing the world from that perspective (or point of view, as used in literary studies).

To sum up, our brief excursion into the fields of interactional sociolinguistics and literary and cultural studies shows that we can find a direct connection between the concept of *the other*, as proposed by Levinas, and *acts of positioning*, since these are inherently relational and involve a self and an other (c.f., the *positionality principle* and the *relational principle* proposed by Bucholtz & Hall, 2005). In addition, identity construction is interactionally and intersubjectively produced and can be seen as an act of positioning oneself and others in different ways, both in literary illness narratives as well as in first-person narratives written by medical students. The following discussion of Gillian Rose's illness narrative focuses on this interaction between self (autobiographer/philosopher/patient) and the other (readers). This is followed by a study of the acts of positioning employed by students in reflective writing texts.

Gillian Rose's *Love's Work:* Illness, Me, and the Other

Gillian Rose, a British philosopher and professor of social and political thought at the University of Warwick, wrote a memoir as she was dying of cancer in 1995. Her text illustrates that any illness narrative, regardless of the author's expertise in writing, shares a personal experience of illness with us readers, and therefore, contributes to (our) understanding of patients. If the autobiographer/patient is an academic or/and professional author, his or her text may represent illness in a more complex and elaborate way and sometimes even on a meta-level, but the additional insights gained from such a representation enhance our ways of responding to a patient's suffering. Thus, reading and discussing literary illness narratives can have a crucial impact on communication in clinical practice and improve it.

In a lecture in 1994 on time and death, Rose referred to Levinas (among others) in to emphasize that death is inseparable from life and from writing, and thus also from the other reading it (Wood, 2011, pp. viii–ix). It is this positioning of self and "the engagement with radical otherness" that is at the core of identity (Shildrick, 2002, p. 89). As mentioned above, cultural and literary critics in the field of illness narratives have emphasized the ethical imperative underlying these texts. We as readers are addressed in an unusually imploring way: If the patient/narrator will not live on, we (and/or the person present at the moment of death) are the ones to either imagine or utter the sentence, "*You* died" (Belling, 2004, p. 154; her emphasis), and are "called upon to respond to the vulnerability, destitution and nakedness of the other" (Shildrick, 2002, p. 88).

Greenhalgh (2006) also raises ethical issues in her approach to illness narratives, claiming that reading narratives makes us respond to specific situations and positions. Thus, illness narratives are bound to make us respond in a manner similar to the way medical doctors are expected to react to their patients, namely performing what Rita Charon calls "narrative ethicality" which "endows the practitioner with an eternal awareness of the vulnerability and the trust of self and other" (Charon, 2006, p. 34). Davies and Harré (1990) emphasize that the concept of positioning can be compared to reading a narrative, i.e., "any reader may, for one reason or another, position themselves or be positioned as outside the story looking in. Such positioning may be created by how the reader perceives the narrator and/or the author to be positioned" (p. 50).

With regard to identity construction we need to explore the specific position of the writing subject vis-à-vis his or her readership and to focus on the ways in which discourse affects both autobiographer/patient and reader. At the same time constructions of illness through language must be addressed (what does language do to illness?), so, too, must be the specific language used by the autobiographer (which again is influenced by illness). Focusing on the use of metaphors provides insight into the way an autobiographer/patient transforms experience into language and positions himself or herself, both vis-à-vis his or her readers as well as in relation to his or her illness.

Besides taking into account the intricate relationship between individual autobiographers/patients and readers, the issue of genre also plays a crucial role in the discursive construction of illness. Indeed, illness narratives encompass more than one particular genre. In fact, in many illness narratives, above all by authors who are also cultural and literary critics, we find a combination of autobiographical account and a more theoretical exploration of cultural and social constructions of illness (see, e.g., Stacey, 1997). Therefore, deciding to label one's text a specific genre as, for example, autobiography, memoir, diary, or/and cultural study also contributes to the positioning of the author and, thus, is part of the process of constructing identity. Our reading of Rose's illness narrative demonstrates that she uses different genres in a creative and challenging way. As mentioned above, Rose's illness narrative is about the relationship between the one being terminally ill and the other responding, thus positioning herself as one who is different from the other. By directly addressing the reader as "you" the author invites the reader to engage in an explicit dialogue. More than once she addresses the reader in a pleading way and asks him or her to engage in what might become a difficult undertaking. This explicit positioning of the reader vis-à-vis herself or himself is a narrative strategy other autobiographers writing about their illness employ as well. Rose even expresses her doubts whether her readers may have the patience and willingness to keep on reading since she is astounded by people's general difficulty in dealing with her "renewed vitality":

> Dare I continue? Are you willing to suspend your prejudices and judgment? Are you willing to confront and essay a vitality that overflows the bumble mix of average well-being and ill-being—colds and coughs and flu, periodic lapses in the collaboration with culture, or headachy days? (Rose, 1995, p. 72)

Besides her concern about her readers' responses Rose expresses consideration for a potential distancing on the side of the readers: Referring to cultural and social implications made with AIDS, she makes us aware of our uncritical associations with AIDS and thereby judges us as prejudiced:

> Suppose that I were now to reveal that I have AIDS, full-blown AIDS, and have been ill during most of the course of what I have related. I would lose you. I would lose you to knowledge, to fear and to metaphor. Such a revelation would result in the sacrifice of

the alchemy of my art, of artistic "control" over the setting as well as the content of your imagination. A double sacrifice of my elocution: to the unspeakable (death) and to the overspoken (AIDS). (Rose, 1995, p. 70)

Similar to the concept of frames[1] used by linguists to describe speakers' or readers' expectations, Rose makes assumptions about how readers will react once they learn that she has *cancer*, namely for them it means "judgment, condemnation" (1997, p. 72). Yet, Rose's main concern is language and literature/philosophy ("my art") and her role as autobiographer since she explicitly states her narrative strategy while corroborating the "autobiographical pact"[2] in an ironical way ("twist in the telling"). As a philosopher and writer she discusses the double-bind of language on a meta-level while at the same time implicating the reader in this pact:

Not that I haven't been wooing you continually by the moods of metaphor; but we have kept the terms of our contract: you have given me free rein, and I have honored my share of the obligation by not using up that freedom, by leaving large tracks of compacted equivocation at every twist in the telling. (Rose, 1995, p. 70)

But in spite of the double-bind of language Rose insists on the act of narrating/writing and links it to death/dying as in her lecture on time and death: "I must continue to write for the same reason I am always compelled to write, in sickness and in health: for, otherwise I die deadly, but this way, by this work, I may die forward into the intensified agon of living" (1997, p. 71). Writing about her illness here explicitly becomes life writing and death: Writing "beyond" what we do not know.

Rose's illness narrative is not only about illness, life, and death; it also links medical thought, philosophical thought, and literature (c.f., Diedrich, 2007, p. 159). It becomes illness narrative, life writing, and philosophical inquiry at the same time. In addition to these subgenres, Rose invents her own genre aimed to designate both her illness and her autobiographical writing. She labels her text a "colostomy ethnography" (1997, p. 87), incorporating minute descriptions of what

---

[1] The notion of *frame* refers to "structures of expectation based on past experience" (Tannen, 1993, p. 53) that are acquired over time in social practice when interactants categorize the experiences of similar past situations, or draw conclusions from other people's experiences. A frame can contain expectations about action sequences (such as the doctor taking the patient's history), but also about role and identity issues (such as the roles of doctors and patients in a consultation).

[2] C.f., Philip Lejeune's definition of this pact between author and reader assuming that there is an identity of name among author, narrator and the character talked about in the text (Lejeune, 1971, p. 12). Lejeune has modified this absolute statement in more recent publications on the autobiographical pact (c.f., Lejeune, 1989).

it means to live with a stoma and to "handle [her] shit" (1997, p. 89). "To handle shit" is no longer a metaphor, but instead refers to Rose's everyday life with cancer. Her body has changed and is no longer describable as before; her way of inscribing it into a text must be invented. Thus, the experience of illness triggers new forms of expressions on the one hand, and the reader/listener must respond to a hitherto-unknown discourse on the other hand.

Acts of Positioning in Reflective Writing Texts of Medical Students

Acts of positioning in reflective writing texts by medical students of the University of Nottingham are at the heart of our analysis in this section. In the field of medicine, reflective writing is acknowledged to be an important part of the learning process (e.g., Bolton, 2010; Brady, Corbie-Smith, & Branch, 2002; Mann, Gordon, & Mac Leod, 2009; Shapiro, Kasman, & Shafer, 2006; Wald & Reis, 2010; Wald et al., 2010). It provides future doctors with ways to evaluate their behavior and it encourages self-criticism. Thus, we deal with a text genre different from the literary text discussed above. Nevertheless, we argue that the texts still contain a core narrative and that the same analysis tools help us to understand processes of positioning in connection with narrating illness.

The 80 texts that are part of our corpus stem from the communication skills course taught at the University of Nottingham in 2010 (Victoria Tischler). After an internship with a general practitioner or in a hospital, second-year medical students are required to write a text on a memorable encounter with a patient, reflecting on their use of communicative strategies and problems, in order to pass the communication skills course. In particular the students had to describe the patient (age, diagnosis, language, etc.), state the context and reason for the encounter, use reported speech to reflect what they talked about in the form of drama dialogue, write about how they felt after the encounter and how the patient might have felt, and reflect on their use of communicative skills, their learning effect, and possible future behavioral changes. The students were informed about our study by their communication skills tutor and, if they wished to participate, they completed a written questionnaire and consent form.

We were interested in the dilemmas with respect to identity construction that this text type creates for the students. The text is written for evaluation by the communication skills tutor. This poses a dilemma for the students, since they should reflect on a past experience that might reflect badly on their skills, but they nevertheless might wish to project a competent identity for evaluation (i.e., a student who has learned from the past experience). We were interested in how the students solve this dilemma and what types of identities they evoke.

To systematically tag our corpus for acts of positioning, we first conducted a qualitative content analysis of the texts to develop a catalogue of types of identities that the students evoked. Once this list was complete, the texts were systematically categorized. To ensure inter-rater reliability, two coders analyzed the texts individually and the following comparison confirmed high reliability (95%).

Within the 80 texts of the Nottingham corpus, students positioned themselves in eight ways, as illustrated in Table 2.1. A sentence could be labeled as containing more than one positioning act.

Table 2.1

Identity categories and examples from the Nottingham corpus

Identity category: Narrator as …	Examples from the corpus
"medical student" in his/her second year (vis-à-vis his/her general practitioner and patients)	After greeting her, the GP proceeded to ask her if it was alright for me, a medical student to sit in during the consultation and ask her a few questions about her condition.
"student of the communication skills course" (vis-à-vis his/her communication skills tutor and conversational partners)	I was quite surprised by how much I could empathize with Mr. X and how I was able to sustain a conversation with him until the GP joined us. [mention of communication skills strategies]
"individual in the past" (before or during the encounter)	I was surprised by how I felt the care of Mr. X was one of my main concerns at the time and I realized the importance of establishing and maintaining a good relationship for the optimum care of Mr. X.
"individual in the present" (at the time of writing the text)	I think that I remember this encounter well as it was very successful and was one of the first times that I'd seen a patient on my own and feel that I'd actually completed the full process as a qualified doctor would, as opposed to when taking a history getting stuck at the diagnosis stage. It was also in a field that I am particularly interested in so this added to my personal interest in the patient.
"individual projecting alternative actions in past or future" (vis-à-vis what really happened in the encounter)	Therefore I should have been more patient and used more non-lexical utterances and adjusted my language in addition to my body language such as leaning towards the patient and smiling to create a relaxed and friendly atmosphere where the patient could express his views. … Next time I will be more careful when I want to show sympathy towards the patient and not use the first word that comes to mind necessarily.

continued

"individual projecting alternative actions in past or future" (vis-à-vis what really happened in the encounter)	Therefore I should have been more patient and used more non-lexical utterances and adjusted my language in addition to my body language such as leaning towards the patient and smiling to create a relaxed and friendly atmosphere where the patient could express his views. … Next time I will be more careful when I want to show sympathy towards the patient and not use the first word that comes to mind necessarily.
(novice) "doctor" (vis-à-vis his/her patients, the patients' relatives or nurses)	This particular consultation has stood out in my mind, as I have never encountered a patient that was so unwilling to communicate with me during a consultation. [emphasizing professional experience]
"private individual" (vis-à-vis his/her professional self)	Also, the fact that he was only a few years older than my own parents really hit home as well. … I had expected to feel fairly comfortable talking to her because I enjoy spending time with young children; however, I found it difficult to engage with her … it was much harder to make conversation than I had expected.
"cultural individual" (embedded within a specific cultural background)	Being a non-English speaker has put me in dilemma to choose the right word to the right person in the right situation. Cultural difference between my hometown and United Kingdom has somehow posed a constraint in my communication skills.

Table 2.2 shows the distribution of the types of identities evoked in the 80 texts. The third column lists the number of texts that contained one or more acts of positioning of a particular type. The fourth column shows how often this type occurred in percent, and the fifth column shows how important the category was in the overall distribution in percent.

What is immediately striking is that the students all use different acts of positioning in their texts. Categories 1–4 appear in all 80 texts; categories 5 and 6 in more than 69 percent. The remaining two (private individual and cultural individual) are less frequent.

To discuss these results and to illustrate a number of these categories in context, we draw on one particular text, which made use of six of the eight categories. (The two categories *private individual* and *cultural individual* are missing in this discussion, since they were not evoked by the narrator in this particular text). However, examples of these positioning acts are shown in Table 2.2. In this text the female narrator encounters a patient at the general practice showing severe symptoms of "excruciating chest pain, fatigue and loss of breath." During the encounter she feels intimidated by the suffering that the patient endures. In her discussion of the situation, she notes that she has not given justice to the severity of the symptoms. She writes that the encounter made her "realize the importance of learning to cope with a real patient's anxiety as well as one's own trepidation in dealing with

Table 2.2

Identity acts of positioning in 80 reflective writing texts, ranked according to most frequent occurrence to least frequent

Cat.	Narrator as …	#	% presence in text (N=80)	% of positionings overall (N=484)
1	medical student	80	100	17
2	student of communication skills course	80	100	17
3	individual in the past	80	100	17
4	individual in the present	80	100	17
5	individual projecting alternative actions in past or future	75	94	15
6	(novice) doctor	55	69	11
7	private individual	28	35	6
8	cultural individual	6	8	1
	Total	484		101

such situations." She adds that this encounter was a crucial eye-opener for her and that she has greatly improved her communication skills since.

In example 1, which occurs at the beginning of the text, the narrator positions herself as a "medical student" as well as a "student of the communication skills course." In addition, she uses the past tense to indicate the difference between her "past" self (her position as a character in her own narrative) and her "present" self (her reflective self at the time of writing). Furthermore, the positionings occur in the form of a meta-comment within the narrative (in the following, the identity positionings are numbered according to the categories in Table 2.2):

> It is said that experience is a substantial source of knowledge. This has been reflected personally through the valuable skills acquired throughout clinical visits [1] in improving my communication [2] as a medical student [1]. (emphasis added)

The narrator chooses identity positionings that correspond with the expectations entailed in the instructions to the reflective writing assignment, as well as the demands of the situation about which she writes. She thus positions herself as an "autobiographer" who recognizes her double role as medical student and student of communication skills, as well as her target audience (i.e., the communication skills teacher). In addition, she manages to adhere to the restrictions of the genre from within which she writes (reflective writing) by choosing to think back on her past self from her present position.

Example 2 is taken from the part in the narrative where the narrator reconstructs the dialogue between herself and the patient. She again positions herself as a "medical student" by assigning the speaker tag "student" to herself in the stage directions of the constructed dialogue and by referring to herself as "medical student" in the dialogue.

> Student [1]: Hi my name is <NAME>, I'm a first year medical student[3] [1] and I would like to take a clinical history [1;6]. Is that ok?
>
> Mr. X: (coughs) That's fine.
>
> Student: So what seems to be the problem? [6]
>
> Mr. X: I can't go on duck ... I've got this really bad pain in my chest ... it's unbearable (emphasis added)

By using the standard introduction with the open question "What seems to be the problem?" she also takes on the position of (novice) "doctor" since she is dealing with a patient on her own. She thus takes on the position of expert vis-à-vis her patient. It is understood, of course, that she is still an unqualified doctor (thus "novice"), as indicated by her self-labeling as student.

The student goes on to report that despite of feeling a lot of sympathy for the patient, she had failed to show this and thus feels that she has failed:

> Though I truly felt sympathy for the patient and his situation, I couldn't express it very well. I felt guilty and inept for not being able to do so [1,2,6]. This was enhanced by the intensity of Mr. X's symptoms and emotional distress. When Mr. X exhibited his frustration for not being able to exercise I should have conveyed my true emotions of empathy [2] to build up a better rapport with him.

The narrator already recognizes at this early stage of her medical career that it is one of the main tasks of health professionals to "respond to the vulnerability, destitution and nakedness of the other" (Shildrick, 2002, p. 88). This engagement with her patient, the other, from a "professional" position creates a dilemma for the narrator in the episode described, as she becomes aware that she cannot entirely fulfill the expectations that are entailed with that role: She fails in being unable to offer

---

[3] Although the student writes here that she is 'a first year medical student,' at the time of writing the text she was in the second year of her studies. Usually, students wrote about patient encounters in their second year.

the medical and emotional assistance that the patient needs and is overwhelmed with the overall situation.

The communication problem described in the text could not be resolved at the time of the encounter. It is later, at the stage of the reflective writing process, that the student offers an analysis and a solution. The narrator deals with the dilemma of having to write about a memorable and, thus potentially problematic, encounter, while at the same time having to present herself in a favorable light to the communication skills tutor by framing her narrative with the means of different identity positionings. In the introduction to her narrative (example 1 above), she presents herself as a former and inexperienced self "in the past." Following this short introduction, her actual narration of the encounter starts when she writes about her meeting with a patient. At the end of her text, she concludes by returning to her initial positioning of an inexperienced "past me" and wraps up her discussion.

> Looking back [4] on this scenario I would definitely express more empathy and acclimatize myself with the situation and its meaning [1,2]. Additionally it was a good indicator of the level of skill in communication I had at the time [1,2,3] and pointed out areas in which I needed to improve. It also demonstrated the role of a doctor [6] in supporting patients both medically and emotionally during the prognosis of a condition. Overall it proved to be an important lesson learned [1,2,3] in dealing with real patients and real clinical scenarios. Since it has also helped me improve on skills that were originally lacking [1,2,3] and now that I reminisce about it in my second year [4], I feel as though I have progressed [4] a lot with the valuable aid of the communication skills module.

In her first sentence, the narrator starts out by indicating future action in the form of the conditional (*I would*). In addition, the narrator not only refers to her past inexperienced self (*the level of skill in communication I had at the time; skills that were originally lacking*), but she also emphasizes that she has *progressed*. She positions herself as a current and more experienced "present me," which allows her to save face vis-à-vis her communication skills tutor. The tension arising from the fact that she chose to write about an encounter that potentially shows her in a negative light is resolved by the framing of the narrative with different identity positionings. This framing allows the student to merge conflicting identity positionings within the narrative in a productive and meaningful way.

Overall, we can state that the students do not, of course, position themselves in an empty space. Their acts of positioning always occur in the light of who is present and with whom they interact in the episode chosen. As shown above, they often take on two or more positionings at the same time to adapt to the situation. For example, in an encounter with a patient where the general practitioner is also present, students may choose to position themselves as medical students vis-à-vis their tutor, but at the same time position themselves as (novice) doctors when talking to their patients. In addition, there are many other aspects of a student's identity that may normally not overlap with the professional setting, but that nevertheless influence some of the positions that the student may choose to evoke in the text depending on the topic chosen. We labeled these occurrences as *private person* and as *cultural individual.*

To summarize, the students address the challenging reflective writing task by drawing on a range of positioning acts and thus create different projections of themselves. They use their linguistic skills to counteract potential negative evaluations that might arise in connection with the reported event by carefully crafting several learner identities and a difference between the past (uninformed) and present (informed) persona. In addition, the reflections on these different identity positionings have an impact on the overall text construction. In contrast to illness autobiographies, in the reflective writing texts it is the students who are healthy and their patients who are ill. Nevertheless, the narrators (students) still position themselves in accordance to *the other*, hence the patients, relatives, or the general practitioner present in the interaction described. In addition, the task of writing a reflective text requires the students to take on further roles (e.g., communication skills learner, reflective practitioner). Furthermore, the audience they write for is a mixed one: they not only have to address their communication skills tutor (who will eventually evaluate their narrative), but they also (potentially) address their general practitioners and fellow medical students. Therefore, some of their different roles may clash or will be difficult to be coherently presented within one narrative.

Conclusions and Implications

Our objective was to establish a dialogue between our two disciplines, linguistics and literature, by using similar concepts in an analysis of two different texts has been rewarding and has generated new insights into the specific ways in which identities are constructed. Our transdisciplinary exchange and dialogue enabled us to become aware of striking similarities in identity constructions both in Gillian Rose's illness narrative as well as in students' reflective writing texts. Rose, as autobiographer/narrator/patient, attempts to reach *the other* (the reader) by continuously constructing new ways of finding a language/discourse that may serve to express her suffering and may reach her reader/audience. The same creative and dialogic process can be found in the students' texts when we focus on identity; indeed, in both cases the writer struggles with the expectations of the listener/recipient/reader of their text. To meet these expectations the writer develops new narrative strategies and, at the same time, new and different identities, or, as it were, a multilevel discourse. Taking into consideration that the literary text mirrors a person's suffering and that the reflective writing text by a future doctor depicts an encounter with a suffering person, we realize the enormous task language has to fulfill: The *other* has to be reached despite the unbridgeable distance between the self and the other (c.f., Lyotard, 1988, p. 13), and, we might add, even more so if human suffering is involved.

The insights into the complex identity constructions in illness narratives and reflective writing texts by medical students provide possibilities of teaching future doctors to listen to *the other* and to be able to reflect on the self and its positions/identities when being engaged in a dialogue with patients. Furthermore, reflecting on their own different positions and on the ones of the patients vis-à-vis enables future medical doctors to "empathize with the patient's perspective, [and] ... to adopt patient-centered approaches in the delivery of medical care" (Khorana, Shayne, & Korones, 2010, p. 468). Confronting medical students with illness narratives and teaching them some basic narrative tools to make them "listen" to the narrative voice of suffering equally enhances their capability to interpret patients' illness narratives.

In addition, the task of reflective writing is useful for medical students as they are required to think about their communication skills. Often they reflect on a situation where their own skills have failed and they, thus, become aware that there is room for improvement. Reflective writing also encourages students to remain self-critical beyond the writing task and to adopt a reflective practice in their professional lives (Epstein, 1999). They are "enabled to let go and rewrite assumptions, taken for granteds [sic], ossified notions of themselves, and take greater responsibility for actions, thoughts and feelings, even ones of which they were previously unaware" (Bolton, 2010, p. 252). Furthermore, students have the opportunity to give "voice" to other characters and to explore their relationship with those characters in different ways. This process encourages students to adopt their patients' perspectives and to look at doctor-patient interactions from another point of view. Finally, reflective writing texts can be used to teach communication skills to medical students, as they can profit from the experiences and reflections of previous students. The texts themselves thus serve as a teaching tool.

In this chapter we have dealt with two types of texts and studied them in light of identity construction. We have shown that analyzing literary texts on illness, as well as encouraging students to engage in a reflective writing process, is a valuable tool for medical practitioners, as proposed by the medical humanities—a position that we fully endorse. Further research on representative texts in the domains of linguistics and literature/cultural studies and on the link to the domain of didactic transfer is needed so that future doctors may engage in a rewarding and fruitful dialogue not only across their patients but also across identities.

Acknowledgments

This paper was funded by the Swiss National Science Foundation and written in the context of the interdisciplinary project entitled "Life (Beyond) Writing": Illness Narratives (illness-narratives.unibas.ch). We wish to thank Victoria Tischler for giving us access to the reflective writing texts of her students.

References

Belling, C. (2004). The death of the narrator. In B. Hurwitz, T. Greenhalgh, & V. Skultans (Eds.), *Narrative research in health and illness* (pp. 146–155). Malden, MA: Blackwell.

Bernasconi, R. (2002). What is the question to which 'substitution' is the answer? In S. Critchley & R. Bernasconi (Eds.), *The Cambridge companion to Levinas* (pp. 234–251). Cambridge: Cambridge University Press.

Bolton, G. (2010). *Reflective practice: Writing and professional development*. London: Sage Publications.

Brady, D. W., Corbie-Smith, G., & Branch, W. T., Jr. (2002). 'What's important to you?': The use of narratives to promote self-reflection and to understand the experiences of medical residents. *Annals of Internal Medicine, 137*(3), 220–223.

Bucholtz, M., & Hall, K. (2005). Identity in interaction: A sociocultural linguistic approach. *Discourse Studies, 7*, 585–614.

Bucholtz, M., & Hall, K. (2010). Locating identity in language. In C. Llamas & D. Watt (Eds.), *Language and identities* (pp. 18–28). Edinburgh: Edinburgh University Press.

Butte, G. (2005). I know that I know: Reflections on Paul John Eakin's 'What are we reading when we read autobiography?' *Narrative, 13*(3), 299–306.

Charon, R. (2006). *Narrative medicine: Honoring the stories of illness*. New York: Oxford University Press.

Couser, G. T. (1997). *Recovering bodies: Illness, disability, and life writing*. Madison, WI: University of Wisconsin Press.

Damasio, A. R. (1999). *The feeling of what happens: Body and emotion in the making of consciousness*. New York: Harcourt.

Davies, B., & Harré, R. (1990). Positioning: The social construction of self. *Journal for the Theory of Social Behavior, 20*(1), 43–63.

De Fina, A. (2003). *Identity in narrative: A study of immigrant discourse*. Amsterdam: John Benjamins.

De Fina, A. (2010). The negotiation of identities. In M. A. Locher & S. L. Graham (Eds.), *Interpersonal pragmatics* (pp.205–224). Berlin: Mouton.

Diedrich, L. (2007). *Treatments: Language, politics, and the culture of Illness*. Minneapolis: University of Minnesota Press.

Eakin, J. P. (2008). *Living autobiographically: How we create identity in narrative*: Ithaca, NY: Cornell University Press.

Epstein, R. M. (1999). Mindful practice. *JAMA, 282*(9), 833–839.

Greenhalgh, T. (2006).*What seems to be the trouble? Stories in illness and healthcare*. Oxford: Radcliffe.

Hustvedt, S. (2010). *The shaking woman*. New York: Henry Holt.

Keen, S. (2007). *Empathy and the novel*. New York: Oxford University Press.

Khorana, A. A., Shayne, M., & Korones, D. N. (2010). Can literature enhance oncology training? A pilot humanities curriculum. *Journal of Clinical Oncology, 29*, 468–471.

Kleinman, A. (1988). *The illness narratives: Suffering, healing, and the human condition*. New York: Basic Books.

Lejeune, P. (1971). *L'autobiographie en France*. Paris: Armand Colin.

Lejeune, P. (1989). The autobiographical pact. In J. P. Eakin (Ed.), *On autobiography* (pp. 119–137). Trans. K. Leary. Minneapolis: University of Minnesota Press.

Levinas, Emmanuel. (1969). *Totality and infinity: An essay on exteriority*. Trans. A. Lingis. Pittsburgh: Duquesne University Press.

Lyotard, J.-F. (1988). *The differend: Phrases in dispute*. Trans. G. Van Den Abbeele. Minneapolis: University of Minnesota Press.

Mann, K., Gordon, J., & Mac Leod, A. (2009). Reflection and reflective practice in health professions education: A systematic review. *Advances in Health Science Education, 14*, 595–621.

Mendoza-Denton, N. (2002). Language and identity. In J. K. Chambers, P. Trudgill, & N. Schilling-Estes (Eds.), *Handbook of language variation and change* (pp. 475–499). Oxford: Blackwell.

Perpich, D. (2008). *The ethics of Emmanuel Levinas*. Stanford, CA: Stanford University Press.

Riessman, C. (1990). Strategic uses of narrative in the presentation of self and illness: A research note. *Social Science and Medicine, 30*, 1195–1200.

Rose, G. (1995). *Love's work: A reckoning with life*. London: Chatto & Windus.

Shapiro, J., Kasman, D., & Shafer, A. (2006). Words and wards: A model of reflective writing and its uses in medical education. *Journal of Medical Humanities, 27*, 231–244.

Shildrick, M. (2002). *Embodying the monster: Encounters with the vulnerable self*. London: Sage.

Smith, S., & Watson, J. (2010). *Reading autobiography: A guide for interpreting life narratives*, 2nd rev. ed. Minneapolis: University of Minnesota Press.

Stacey, J. (1997). *Teratologies: A cultural study of cancer*. London: Routledge.

Stein, G. (1933). *The autobiography of Alice B. Toklas*. New York.Y.: Harcourt, Brace and Company.

Tannen, D. (1993). What's in a frame?: Surface evidence for underlying expectations. In D. Tannen (Ed.), Framing in discourse (pp. 14–56). Oxford: Oxford University Press.

Ticineto Clough, P., & Halley, J. (Eds.). (2007). *The affective turn: Theorizing the social*. Durham, NC: Duke University Press.

Wald, H. S., & Reis, S. P. (2010). Beyond the margins: Reflective writing and development of reflective capacity in medical education. *Journal of General Internal Medicine, 25*, 746–749.

Wald, H. S., Reis, S. P., Monroe, A. D., & Borkan, J. M. (2010). 'The loss of my elderly patient': Interactive reflective writing to support medical students' rites of passage. *Medical Teacher, 32*, e178–e184.

Wood, M. (2011). Introduction. In G. Rose. *Love's work: A reckoning with life* (pp. vii–xiv). New York: New York Review of Books.

Wyschogrod, E. (2002). Language and alterity in the thought of Levinas. In S. Critchley & R. Bernasconi (Eds.), *The Cambridge companion to Levinas* (pp. 188–205). Cambridge: Cambridge University Press.

Chapter 3

Building a Case for Centered Patient-Physician Communication: Standardizing Genuine Interaction in the Medical Context

Jennifer Malkowski

Introduction

Rhetorics of health and medicine—both official and vernacular rhetorics—often enter into dialogue with one another during patient-provider interactions. During the patient intake interview, for example, vernacular rhetorics used by patients to describe personal experiences of health interface with official rhetorics of medicine used by healthcare providers to diagnosis and treat illness. For example, a patient may come in complaining about sensitivity to light, a throbbing headache, and "a sharp pain that's piercing behind one eye," a physician would label this condition a "migraine with aura" and in doing so indicate to other medical professionals that some prescription drugs (like certain types of birth control) exacerbate symptoms that could lead to stroke. The significance of this communication interface is that through these types of interactions larger structures of health and illness are defined by both parties. In the migraine example, by using labels, pain gets linked to a level of severity, a gendered drug option, and a threatening condition. Since these labels can now be accessed by the patient to explain his or her condition to others, this type of interaction suggests ways that the field of medicine actively influences the course of U.S. culture, with respect to health, through individual patient contact (Conrad, 2007; Lupton, 2007; Showalter, 1997).

Serving as both a pedagogical tool and a relational device, engaging in patient intake interviews requires medical students to enact communication skills to elicit patient information, as well as patient trust (Barley, Boyle, & Johnson, 2001). As a communication scholar, I entered the field of medicine convinced that the patient intake interview was an important part of the overall medical process and a place when and where communication theory could better serve the medical curriculum. However, as a rhetorician of health and medicine, I paid particular attention to the ways that standardized patient interviews operate to reify a rhetoric of

Chapter 3 **37**

doctoring that defines the role of communication in the medical context. Through this discourse, I argue, fixed understandings of "effective" patient-physician interaction and ways that communication theory ought to inform the patient-physician relationship emerge. By illuminating how standardized training and evaluation practices might better prepare future physicians for the situationally dependent nature of patient interviewing, this chapter theorizes about ways that the medical curriculum might better conceptualize, incorporate, promote, and assess effective patient-physician communication as an interdependent, interpersonal process.

Following an overview of patient-physician communication as an essential component of the healthcare system, this chapter interrogates the current patient-centered model of medical interviewing to assess how well-standardized patient interviews prepare future physicians for real-time patient communication. Using qualitative data collection and analysis, specific issues of genuineness are questioned to explore the possibility of a more principled approach to health communication. The concept of *centered patient-physician communication* then is introduced as one way to reconceptualize the role of communication in the patient-physician encounter. The chapter concludes by exploring how the concept of efficiency can be leveraged to better orient future medical professionals to the types of interactions they will likely experience during medical practice.

Patient-Centered Communication

Across countries, healthcare has experienced a shift in health messaging from physicians and public health officials on behalf of the public to a venture of pharmaceutical companies targeting individual, private consumers (Donohue, Cevasco, & Rosenthal, 2007; Mackenzie, Jordens, Ankeny, McPhee, & Kerridge, 2007; Saltman, 1994). Of the many social, political, and economic challenges that this shift has caused, a particularly immediate and enduring strain has been placed on the relationship between healthcare providers and receivers and on each of their roles in the overall health decision-making process (Venetis, Robinson, Turkiewicz, & Allen, 2009). This shift has demanded the renegotiation of traditionally paternalistic medicinal practice (Conrad & Leiter, 2008). Therefore, at an institutional level, medical professionals have needed to incorporate a more patient-centered approach to health (see Bates & Ahmed, 2012, this volume, for a review). Patient-centered models of healthcare can be detected across rhetorics of doctoring and tend to dominate discussions about proper medical interviewing protocol.

The Standardized Patient Interview Experience

Over the past year, I have volunteered as a communication coach in a Standardized Patient Interview (SPI) program at a medical school in the southwestern United States. In addition to learning how to better invoke empathy, this particular SPI program encourages physicians to help patients be self-reflective in order to take part in the diagnosis, prevention, and/or treatment process. In theory, the opportunity to engage in the interview process in a controlled environment helps each future provider to understand the significant role communication plays in healthcare. Moreover, the use of standardized patient actors paired with direct, immediate feedback from peers and trained communication coaches helps students recognize their role as a liaison between official and vernacular rhetorics of health and medicine. Through programmatic communication training, students, ideally, become more aware of how their communication influences the patient-provider relationship and, ultimately, how that relationship determines patient compliance. Despite these intentions, however, physicians struggle when trying to reconcile institutional expectations with patient autonomy and performance with genuine human interaction. I offer an overview of what this experience entails:

> Four medical students sit in a sterile room poised in black, ergonomically-correct chairs. They are arranged around a large, rectangular table at the center of the room that draws them into conversation and away from the glass walls that enclose the space. From my vantage point—the hallway looking in—the fishbowl spectacle exemplifies the nature of the qualitative experience. I compromise the glass barrier by pushing open the door and enter the space while introducing myself as their "communication coach for the afternoon." I wiggle around the table, weaving between chairs and bags. Making my way toward a window wall I hear one young male student state simply and unaffectedly, "This is all totally fake. I mean they can't expect us to act *real* when the whole thing is a set-up. "His colleague nods in affirmation, a slow, chin-up-first manner that encourages the other two female students to join the debate over the absurdity of a simulated experience serving any real-world function. As I gain my own ergonomically-sound spot around the table I take note of the business-meets-medicine decorum of our fishbowl: Fluorescent lighting, a muted color palate, sparse furniture, and a hand-sanitizing dispenser.

The temperature is moderate; the sun shines through one wall of windows; the only noise is the efficient hum of the heating and cooling system; and, the space smells clean in an unmemorable way. I look out across the hall through our glass barrier into an adjacent fishbowl where the same distribution of people and artifacts reside. To me, this hall, lined with compartmentalized redundant scenes screams nothing but veneer, and I agree with the cries of falsity. And yet, despite this common sentiment, each team of coaches and students readies themselves for an impromptu medical interview as tasks are assigned, furniture is moved, and the first volunteer rises to greet their "patient" in the hall. As the door opens, the performance of a medical-student-in-training begins: "Hello Ms. Jones. May I call you Betty?" From inside our glass enclosure we hear mumbles before the medical student offers, "Please come on in." A frail, elderly woman with smeared lipstick, one earring, and eyes fixed on the floor shuffles into the room clutching her purse and both performers—medical student and Betty Jones—take seats in the front of the room, knee-to-knee, actively ignoring the peanut gallery that scribbles notes from across the imposing table. While the medical student asks, "So what brings you here today?" the irony of our situation enters the marginalia of my fieldnotes.

As this introductory scene illustrates, during any single interview there exists an actor playing the part of a patient, a student playing the part of a medical professional, three other students playing their parts as critical observers, and a communication coach playing the part of a mentor. The performativity involved with the encounter is revealed in moments when the simulation halts and actors come out of character to offer guidance to the medical student interviewer. During these "time-outs," when role-playing stops, each piece of advice seems informed by the real-life, personal experiences of each individual's time spent in the healthcare system. To better illuminate standardized patients as an interviewing tool used to condition medical students for real-life experiences, this particular study focuses on responses offered by the three types of actors involved in the execution of the standardized intake interview. Each actor is now introduced in detail.

Standardized Patients. Variation across standardized patient medical programs tends to be found in the specific character descriptions. Each character description usually includes: a first and last name, some basic demographic information (e.g., age, profession, etc.), an opening line (e.g., "I haven't been sleeping, Doc"), a specific concern (e.g., "I'm worried it might be cancer. My mom died of cancer"), a specific diagnosis ("Active TB"), and, a mention of things the patient values (e.g., "family and exercise"). These character descriptions are often developed by each SPI program to best reflect the localized population that students will likely encounter during their internships. Each description for each standardized patient helps actors to better understand the character they portray to react to questioning "as the patient would." For example, if a married male patient values family and the student interviewer never mentions his wife and kids, that patient may appear standoffish and uncertain as to whether the interviewer really "gets him." At the particular site I studied, paid actors are hired and trained through a full-service assessment and education center located on campus that specializes in the use of standardized patients, teaching associates, and simulators across disciplines. The center is staffed with experts trained in the intersections of improvisational theater and medicine.

Medical Students. By the end of their second year of medical school, students at the SPI program under observation are required to complete a sequence of communication-based trainings that emphasize the interpersonal nature of the patient-practitioner interview. All student doctors are either first- or second-year medical students. Although they vary in age, ethnicity, race, and nationality, most are U.S. citizens and can be categorized as traditional, matriculated students.

Communication Coaches. At this particular site, all communication coaches volunteer their time and most consistently return, which means that these coaches support an understanding of communication skills as important to the overall medical process. However, the standards for successful coaching remain under formal review. At the time this study was conducted, standardized qualifications, trainings, and evaluation procedures were yet to be developed. During an interview, the director of this SPI program explained, "If I meet someone who I feel like might be a good coach, then I will invite him or her to coach. And usually they know someone else who will also be a good coach." The casual, all-inclusive, snowball method of recruitment has been both praised and critiqued. In praise, the recruitment method brings together professionals who are loosely tied to the medical system and, therefore, offer diverse feedback about the interview process.

Methods: Exploring Mis(sed) Communication in the Medical Interview

In line with a tradition that has recognized both the conceptual and operational elements of human interactions as central challenges to advancing knowledge in the field of medicine, I entered the field ready to observe how interpersonal communication training might be improved. I was able to meet and mingle with medical professionals at all levels of the healthcare process, leading to a nuanced understanding of the challenges that face medical professionals in contemporary U.S.

healthcare. In accordance with recommendations offered by Lindlof and Taylor (2012), I engaged the site guided by the belief that qualitative research should involve collecting more than one type of data.

Over the course of four months, I shadowed and assisted two veterans of the SPI program as they coached half-day sessions, acted as lead coach for four half-day sessions, participated in six coaching lunches, attended six medical student lectures focused on interview skills, helped to review and interpret survey data collected by SPI leaders to assess the status of this particular program's coaching, and conducted five individual interviews with SPI program affiliates. In addition to my "on-the-clock" fieldwork, I engaged in many hours of candid face-to-face and online discussions with fellow communication coaches and visited the medical campus numerous times to become familiar with relevant artifacts, spaces, and persons influencing the standardized patient interview process. In total, I spent approximately 90 hours familiarizing myself and engaging with the SPI program, and thereby, gained an insider's perspective on the nuances of this component of the medical curriculum.

Participant Observation

For this study, I took part, as a participant observer, in three types of informal focus group discussions that took place during coaching lunches, during coaching sessions, and during post-coaching debriefing sessions held with medical students. I became part of my participant pool to actively blur the lines between "us" and "them." Feedback from medical students, standardized patients, and communication coaches over the course of four months yielded a total of 32 opportunities to engage in one-on-one conversations with SPI affiliates. Consistent immersion in the focus group format worked as an embodied reminder of the complex, interdependent, discursive nature of medicine and afforded opportunities to recognize emergent themes in the rhetoric of doctoring before conducting individual interviews.

Individual Interviews

After an initial thematic analysis of my fieldnotes, I interviewed five affiliates of the SPI program: The director of the SPI program, the director of curriculum for the SPI program, the director of the standardized patient training center, a lead communication coach charged with standardizing the training and evaluation of SPI communication coach volunteers, and an active communication coach who had 10 years of experience running a similar program abroad. During each of the five formal interviews, I asked each SPI affiliate to explain, in as much detail as possible, his or her experiences with communication in the healthcare context, his or her history with the SPI program, and his or her evaluation of the medical curriculum. Although the interviews maintained a conversational quality, an interview guide was used to solicit each interviewee's opinion concerning four specific areas of interest: (1) experience with meeting patient needs in the healthcare system (e.g., What is the best part about interacting with patients?); (2) views about the role of the intake interview in the medical process (e.g., "What patient needs do you feel like the standard intake interview usually meets?); (3) understanding of the role of patient-centered communication in disease diagnosis and treatment (e.g., How do you come to understand what a patient "really means" as opposed to what they are saying?); and (4) evaluation of how standardized patient interviews respond to the needs of future medical professionals (e.g., If you could change one thing about current medical curriculum, what would it be and why?). Each personal interview ranged from 1–3 hours and took place in public places, usually over a meal.

Survey Data and Analysis

Through the individual interview process I gained access to data collected online via the "Communication Coach Survey" administered in 2010 by SPI personnel. Only persons with a history of coaching with the SPI program were permitted to respond to the survey, and in total, 27 anonymous coaches completed the questionnaire. In addition to fieldnotes and interview transcripts, I also analyzed these questionnaire responses as a way to complement and clarify patterns that emerged in my original body of research.

During my time spent as a qualitative researcher in the field, I took note of the things that I had been *attracted to* and *convinced by* (Goodall, 2000, p. 87) during conversations with others. I read and re-read my fieldnotes to allow participants' words to interact with each other in ways that revealed patterns about the factors that medical professionals consider to be important with regard to patient-physician interaction. To better interpret what I read as a "meaningful *pattern*" (Goodall, p. 87) found across the responses, I invoked organizational methods embedded in the rhetoric of medicine. This process ensured that although I stayed close to the data to pay homage to the individual, private nature of experiences with healthcare, I also was committed to making sense of these discursive patterns in ways that would prove useful to the medical community. Therefore, to better "balance rhetorical sources of creativity [qualitative modes of inquiry] with the inevitable sources of rhetorical constraint [appealing to a medical audience]" (Goodall, p. 92), what follows is a presentation of my qualitative findings guided by structured, collage sensibilities.

Findings: Locating the Center of Patient-Physician Communication

As a general approach to diagnosis, medical students are taught to distinguish between patients' chief concerns and chief complaints to efficiently and effectively determine a course of action (Schleifer & Vannatta, 2011). Patients' *chief concerns* can include social, political, and professional considerations that weigh on their ability to properly address illness, whereas patients' *chief complaints* tend to home in on the particular, embodied ailments that account for the visit to the physician. In the data presentation that follows, I emulate this process of lending order to the seemingly chaotic, disjointed, bits-and-pieces-type delivery of personal testimony using an organizational scheme that resonates with the ways that medical students are taught to process, organize, and prioritize information. I sought to process information gathered during my interviews using the sense-making model (chief concern versus chief complaint) offered through the medical curriculum, and I present the findings in a manner that appeals to a wider audience of readers—patients,physicians, and scholars, alike.

For this study, the bits and pieces of testimony collected during participant observations, focus group discussions, individual interviews, and through survey research are arranged in atemporal yet scripted ways to capture the everyday realities, complexities, and contradictions shared among the medical community. As Calvo (2004) explained:

> Collage as an art form takes existing images and through a process of selection and combination shifts the terms of their meaning. Collage is not unlike the process of the constitution of the postmodern subject, who must piece together as self, however fragmented and shifting, by sampling bits and pieces from different histories, iconographies, and relationships. (p. 218)

A collage-like organization of data helps to emulate the qualitative process and the polyvocal rhetoric of the SPI curriculum. Despite the postmodern sense-making technique invoked through collage art, each collage is categorized according to chief complaints and chief concerns, in order to emulate medical checklist sensibilities.

The remainder of this chapter illustrates the possibility of a more centered approach to medical interviewing. In capturing the individual, personal, and private nature of interview responses through collage art, I merge patient vernacular with the ordered, hierarchical, and impersonal rhetoric of medicine to demonstrate how a middle ground can be located somewhere between the spheres of patient and physician understandings and experiences of health.

Simultaneously, the voices and life-experiences of patients are preserved, and the diagnostic and treatment paradigms are put to work. Although this commingling illustrates a way that patients' and physicians' vernacular co-constructs the narrative of health, the merger also exposes the limits of effectively blending vernacular and official medical rhetorics needed to fully realize a centered patient-physician approach to health communication.

Chief Concern: Developing a Skills-Based Approach for Patient-Physician Interaction

Throughout my experiences as a communication coach, I witnessed an avid dedication to a model of human interaction based on a series of skills that, if executed properly, could help medical students to "build rapport" with their patients. At the site under review, the SPI curriculum divided these skill sets into three levels of training that built on previous. standardized patient sessions.

The first level of interpersonal training offered through the SPI program familiarized medical students with basic communication verbal and nonverbal skills. Much like techniques used by medical students to learn and memorize medical procedures and disease diagnosis and treatment, the acronym ILS was assigned to this introduction to communication theory to help students remember to *invite* discussion through the use of open-ended questions, *listen* through congruent use of verbal and nonverbal signs, and to *summarize* patient information to ensure accuracy and to communicate engagement in and with the issue at hand (Boyle, Dwinnell, & Platt, 2005).

The second training module, entitled "Communicating Empathy," refined these basic communication skills by moving beyond interpersonal niceties toward an exploration of the relational side of medicine. During this module, medical students were taught to present themselves as a partner in a patient-centered healthcare process, and the motivational aspect of interviewing was emphasized. Finally, the third installment, entitled "Difficult Encounters," began to address patients' pushback via communication intervention. At this level, contentious issues were built into character descriptions (e.g., promiscuous behavior) and standardized patients were encouraged to resist the interview process (e.g., respond with one-word answers). In doing so, medical students became aware of the situatedness of patient interviewing and of patients' experiences of health and illness. Unlike the previous modules, the third installment emphasized the need for adaptability during the medical interview. Through personal reflection and peer feedback during and after the standardized interview experience, students' narratives suggest that not only do they understand the skills-based approach to patient interviewingbut they also embrace the method as a way to conceptualize patient-physician interaction.

The following script illustrates the current skills-based approach to communication promoted by the medical curriculum and, thus, adopted by medical students. Revisiting the introductory scene above, the script below pieces together actual quotes gathered across interviews conducted with characters to compose a simulated patient interview. I have selected quotes that represent sentiments expressed across interviewees and pair them with characters in the scene most likely to voice each opinion. I intentionally present these findings as one coherent script with dialogue that is disjointed, tangentially related, and without contextual cues required to build a holistic understanding of the relational dynamics guiding the encounter. I present data in this manner to illustrate the contradiction and complication that often accompany student attempts to adopt a skill-based approach to medical interviewing. The "screenplay formatting" should leave the reader desiring more contextual information, more character explanation, and an overall slower pacing of conversation—all sentiments commonly expressed across medical student interviews.

FADE IN

INT. FISHBOWL CLASSROOM – EARLY AFTERNOON

The interview with Betty Jones has just ended. The medical student interviewer turns to the table of observers for feedback. Betty stares at the floor until prompted to speak.

INTERVIEWER
(energetically)

It just feels weird to ask, "So what brings you here today?" because I have notes in front of me. What other open-ended question can I ask? I feel like I need to figure out a go-to question.

PEER 1

You used phrases like "Tell me more" or "Can you explain that a little further" to invite the patient to talk. I thought that this was a good way to just sort of open up the conversation. You know, make it feel more like a conversation than like an interview.

PEER 2

I thought it was a good technique when you asked the patient to spell out the name of her children—I could tell that you were buying yourself some time, but it came across as a summary used to check your facts and it came off as really personal.

BETTY
(spacey and aloof)

Your facial expressions really showed you were paying attention. When I mentioned that my husband passed away you had this look of concern on your face that made me feel like it was okay to talk about how much I miss him.

INTERVIEWER

I have things I need to know in order to diagnose properly so how much time should I spend just talking about things that aren't related to diagnosis? Don't I have to steer the conversation back to a checklist even if I'm not going down a checklist?

PEER 3
(emotional)

I have a history with depression and I know that if I were [Betty] I would have been pissed if you started preaching to me about getting help. It felt like you empathized with her situation because you didn't push her into doing anything that she wasn't ready for.

PEER 2

Seriously, with the Internet now so many patients probably come in with a good idea of what's wrong.

INTERVIEWER

If it's left up to the patients most of them just want medication to fix these problems. I told [Betty] that changing [her] diet would help prevent [her] from having a heart attack and [she] said, "So would my meds." I mean [she's] right, but it just doesn't feel right to always be putting people on drugs. There are things they can do to help prevention.

PEER 3
(frustrated)

Betty says she can't afford her diabetes medication. Here's a woman who is willing to comply but can't. How do I help her come up with a plan if what she needs is ultimately money?

FADE OUT

The adoption of ILS as a tool used to inform patient-physician interaction is understood as beneficial for medical professionals new to interviewing. However, common causes for concern among professionals-in-training included the competing requirements across skills and the—sometimes contradictory—nature of particular skills. For example, the need for medical students to listen required that they "remain present" in the interaction. That is, students were often asked to engage in reflective listening and repeat back portions of patient statements to communicate that they were present. However, this skill often competed with students' simultaneous needs to summarize and diagnose. Students felt it was difficult to "remain present" while figuring out the cause of the illness "as quick as they can" and using summaries to guide the conversation in intentional, premeditated ways. In other words, students felt it was difficult to orchestrate a genuine, human connection amid an ulterior, biomedical agenda. With regard to contradiction implicit within single skills, students expressed concern about how invitation skills seemingly required a medical student to "ask open-ended questions, even when I'm really just interested in yes-no answers."

An additional skill that presented a paradox for medical students during interviews was the need to effectively and appropriately communicate about health prevention behaviors. With no clear indication of who operates as an authority over this information area, students felt trapped by the sentiment: "You know what's best for the patient, but so do they." Contradictions, competitions, and complications surrounding the ways that a skills-based approach failed to bridge theory with practice during live interactions led students to articulate the need for an alternative model of medical communication.

Chief Complaint(s): Reconciling Genuineness with Efficiency

Current medical curricula conceptualize communication as a set of skills that can and ought to be proactively learned and invoked according to needs that arise in particular, predictable, communication situations. Indeed, data suggest that students become familiar with the ILS acronym, demonstrate their grasp of the ILS skillset during the interview process, and use ILS to help to retroactively make sense of their interview experience. However, data also suggest that when students refer to ILS sensibilities they are, more often than not, left with more questions than answers. In this way, the ILS "tool-box approach" to communication—encouraging students to assess a situation and then draw a specific skill from a repertoire of operationalized, mnemonic devices pre-intended to meet the challenges of particular situations—leaves physicians at a significant disadvantage when it comes to understanding and honoring the complex and unpredictable nature of personal health. According to participant response, it appears that a "principled approach" to communication might better capture the innovative, situationally dependent reality of patient-physician interaction.

A principled or theory-based approach to communication conceptualizes human interaction as something other than predictable and prescriptive. A principled approach to communication, unlike a skills-based approach to communicating, admits that most human interaction happens spontaneously and reactively and, therefore, is best guided by larger principles as opposed to context-specific, reactive communication skills training. Data gathered through participant observation in this study suggest that official and vernacular rhetorics of health overlap in meaningful ways. When put in conversation with one another, *time* is illuminated as one common principle of communication, intelligible to both patients and physicians alike, that is used to structure and guide patient-physician interactions.

Focusing on the role that time plays in both the rhetoric of doctoring and in the narrative of patient health, the following scene illustrates the need for a more principled approach to communication as expressed across student, professional, and patient discourse. Once again, the jolting, uncontextualized experience of the data demonstrates ways that the current curricular model of communication in medicine detracts from the possibility of genuine patient connection.

FADE IN

INT. FISHBOWL CLASSROOM – LATE AFTERNOON

The final medical student has now completed his interview. Everyone focuses on gathering their things while they provide feedback. The patient remains in the room and interjects opinions when possible.

COACH
(authoritatively)

Right now students spend 0.5 percent of their time working with us on communication although communication will be 50 percent of their difficulties in the practice of medicine. I want to convey that communication can happen quickly and can fit into modern medicine.

PEER 1

My preceptor only allows me a couple of minutes with each patient. I would get in trouble if I started to develop a relationship with a patient. And I don't even mean an unprofessional relationship, just, you know …

PATIENT
(quietly)

You didn't rush me, and I really appreciated that.

INTERVIEWER

Honestly, the whole time I'm talking to the patient I'm just trying to figure out what clues will help me to diagnose their issue. After that I can move onto the next step and actually treat them. So pretty much the shorter time spent diagnosing the more time spent figuring out a plan.

PATIENT
(softly interjecting)

I did not want to come in here. And when I saw you were a man I really did not want to talk about sex. But, I appreciated that you waited to ask me about what was going on until I got a little more comfortable with you.

PEER 2

I haven't even spent time with my preceptor yet and I already feel like I understand the pressure of how little time docs can spend with their patients.

PATIENT

I hate coming to the doctor, so most of the time I want to spend as little time in the office as possible. But, I mean, when you asked about my family, I could have talked for such a long time. You didn't make me want to run out of here.

FADE OUT

Although the broader categories—chief concern and chief complaint—successfully work to make sense of larger narratives used to guide patient-physician interaction, I argue that the underlying tendency for medical students to translate interpersonal interaction back into a checklist format to then attribute sense and value to those experiences ultimately does a disservice to the practice of medicine. It is my hope that the presentation of personal and contextualized participant responses in disjointed, overly organized ways helps readers witness the challenge to interpersonal sensibilities that traditional standards of medicine impose on opportunities intended to foster genuine, human connection. Regardless of when a checklist device is introduced to the patient-physician interaction—before, during, and/or after the intake interview—the mere presence of checklist-logic reifies the impersonality of patient-physician interaction and, ultimately, should work to motivate scholars to explore new options for how to better bridge official and vernacular rhetorics of health and medicine. Both patients and physicians recognized that time contributed to the relational dynamics of medicine, but neither party was able to articulate how to make the best use of time. Complaints arose over the inability to identify and talk openly about time as a problem influencing the patient-physician interaction. Although both patients and medical professionals recognize time as an important factor in health practices, the meaning of time differs across parties; patients feel respected when physicians spend more time as interviewers, physicians feel respected when patients spend less time as interviewees. The ambiguity surrounding how time matters to the patient-physician interaction presents an opportunity to explore principles of communication for medicine.

The need to talk and think about time as a way to read and interact with the health context exposes a principle of interaction that requires medical students to interact with patients on an individual basis and to respond to interaction cues in real time. Whereas a skills-based approach to managing time might emphasize the pace of conversation (e.g., "interview patients as quickly as possible"), a principled approach to medical communication could ask patients to emphasize efficiency as it relates to medical treatment ("based on your read of each patient, adapt your behaviors to provide effective and efficient care in that particular context"). A principle of efficiency would focus on the extent to which time is well used (quality), rather than focus on how much time is used (quantity). This type of principle could advise a student to move quickly through the interview protocol if a patient appears angry, in excruciating pain, or unwilling to talk. Conversely, a student could be expected to spend more time with a patient if it seemed that what might help that patient most is to feel heard. Rather than apply a predetermined "best practice" that emphasizes speed over quality, a principle of efficiency could help students negotiate between biomedical and relational content during an interview to provide the best personalized healthcare for each patient.

Discussion: Defending a Standard of Centered Patient-Physician Communication

The presentations of these findings suggest human interaction requires an element of spontaneity that cannot be captured through checklist protocol and is even more difficult to standardize. The variability in interaction requires the exploration of an alternative means of communication training in medicine. Forcing official and vernacular rhetorics to rub up against one another in organized, productive ways allows audiences to better witness distinctions, similarities, and possibilities concerning modes of communication used to guide patient-physician interaction. Identifying modes of communication intelligible to both patients and physicians enables medical curricula to better articulate principles of interaction to inform best medical interviewing practices.

Centered, Patient-Physician Communication (CPPC)

Studies, theories, and subsequent curricula have yet to work toward an approach to teaching communication skills that recognizes both patients and physicians as capable of and responsible for the relational dynamic of healthcare. Developing an understanding of both patients' and physicians' perspectives about the health experience has been recognized as an essential component of proper disease outcomes (Barley, Boyle, & Johnson, 2001; Cole & Bird, 2000; Haidet et al., 2008). However, most studies target either patients (to help teach them how to better "speak physician") or target physicians (to help them learn to make sense of patient vernacular using medical sense-making tools that emphasize efficient diagnosis over relational needs). Rarely are both patients and physicians offered an interdependent model of communication. Building on findings from a previous work, Kenny et al. (2010) conducted a study that addressed the value of using a dyadic data-analytic approach to the study of physician-patient communication. In defense of their research agenda, Kenny et al. claimed that:

> Conceptualization and operationalization of effective communication as an interpersonal and interdependent process (i.e., when those involved influence each other) between physicians and patients have important consequences. First, it emphasizes the need for concept definitions that are congruent with an interpersonal and interdependent process. ... [And, second] the measurement of effective communication as an interpersonal and interdependent process requires a dyadic measurements and analytic methods. (p. 764)

Although Kenny et al.'s study operationalized dyadic analysis through a methodological design, this chapter addresses the conceptualization of effective communication as an interpersonal and interdependent process. Although few studies have operationalized dyadic analysis, even fewer studies have explored how to better theorize patient-physician communication to inform current and future medical curricula. The conceptualization of patient-physician communication, thus, remains a significant "[challenge] in advancing knowledge in this area" (Kenny et al., 2010, p. 764). I argue that implementing a centered patient-physician communication across medical curriculum can meet this end.

Centered patient-physician communication (CPPC) is derived from a curricular history that has opted to teach either a physician-centered or a patient-centered approach to medical interviewing but that has neglected to operationalize a relational approach to communication (see Kenny et al., 2010). The concept of CPPC suggests that principles of human interaction inform medical pedagogy rather than a skills-based approach. This means that every interaction recognizes both patients and physicians as participants in the construction of a health narrative. The relational element of medicine continues to be acknowledged as both important and central to proper diagnosis and treatment of health conditions and, therefore, needs to be prioritized in the medical curriculum. CPPC presents one way to theorize communication for medical training.

The CPPC agenda requires that each actor become skilled in the art of encoding and decoding health experiences in ways that foster the communication competencies of the other. From an ontological standpoint, this task requires that practicing physicians, future physicians, and those who study medicine reconceptualize patient-physician communication as dyadic and always in flux. I argue that identification of a linguistic middle ground that can be occupied by patients and physicians alike offers an opportunity for partnership in medicine. Specifically, principles of interaction can emerge from issues deemed mutually important to both patient and physician communities. This study acts as a first step in a programmatic line of research dedicated to illuminating meeting points between patient and physician vernaculars that cast each participant as a key stakeholder and influential partner in the medical process.

Principled Approaches to Communication

Data presented in this study suggest that a preoccupation with time characterizes U.S. patient-physician interaction. Although patients and physicians express somewhat irreconcilable orientations toward time, time remains a common measure of relational status for both parties. Participants in this study identified the ambiguity surrounding how time is monitored and structured during an intake interview as one cause for mis(sed)communication between patients and physicians. Because the length of time spent interviewing and the overall pacing of the questions can easily communicate either respect or disrespect for either member of the patient-physician dyad, the need to clarify the rhetoric of time seems apparent. Such a due reverence for time as a contextual factor contributing to the genuineness of patient-interaction can be informed by the communication discipline.

The need to establish a common language shared between physicians and patients has been noted in the literature as one task for future scholars. The findings of this study suggest that time acts as a mode of communication intelligible to both patients and physicians during the interview process. The current ILS model of patient interviewing would suggest that the physician cater to the patient's desire for more time to be spent interacting during the intake interview to successfully establish rapport. However, medical students express the competing need to expedite the interview process to better treat a health condition and to maintain good working relationships with their colleagues. In this way, the current ILS, patient-centered model does not adequately prepare medical students to address time in order to doctor effectively. Without a reconceptualization of time as an opportunity for a patient and physician to establish a middle ground, medical students will likely continue to communicate time as an irreconcilable condition of medical interviewing.

Ultimately, conceiving of time as evidence of how a skillset approach to health communication fails to meet the reality of the medical interview experience and pits doctoring against relationship building. To uphold and defend the place for communication theory in medical education, communication scholars are charged with the task of reconceptualizing and re-presenting patient-physician interaction as an opportunity born from communication. Identifying principles of interaction valuable to both patients and physicians alike reinforces an understanding of interviewing as situationally dependent and reinforces an understanding of successful, genuine human interaction as in need of recognizing and utilizing modes of communication that bridge gaps between communicators. Findings from this study identify time as a common mode of communication that, if standardized, could work to promote a more centered patient-physician interaction and a more realistic expectation of how time is to be spent during the interview process. For example, future medical curriculum might consider helping students to better monitor their time during patient interviews, medical institutions might consider standardizing time devoted to a patient intake interviews across hospitals, or patients might be helped to better recognize how time serves the processes of diagnosis and treatment during the intake interview. When the human interaction is situated in a particular place with a particular reference to time, I argue that genuine communication might better thrive in the medical context. The challenge then becomes identifying and standardizing other modes of centered patient-physician communication.

Conclusions and Implications

This chapter has investigated the status of communicative exchanges between patients and physicians in the contemporary U.S. healthcare context. Data collected via participant observation, personal interviews, and focus group discussions testimonies suggest that the communication paradigm currently informing medical curricula is pragmatically insufficient. This particular dilemma—the divide between theory and practice in medical interviewing—suggests a need to explore an approach to communication that produces an organic, genuine, reactive, and intuitive understanding of interpersonal interaction. Instead of teaching medical students how to recognize the patient interview as a certain type of standardized scenario that invokes a particular type of communicative response, the data suggest that what future physicians desire and, indeed, what patients need is a more thorough grasp of the communication principles that inform successful human interaction. These principles can and should be founded on modes of communication that actively bridge the patient-physician divide.

Findings offered by this study indicate that medical students exhibit a sincere commitment to the tenets of medicine and these data demonstrate that they regard communication theory and practice to be an important component of doctoring. Since our audience is captive, what needs to be improved are curricular efforts aimed at capturing and operationalizing the unpredictable nature of human interaction. Although ILS fills each medical student's toolbox with communication skills, dialogue presented in this study demonstrates that often this awareness further separates vernacular and official experiences of health. For example, if unaddressed, the factor of time will likely continue to separate patients from physicians instead of working toward a more relational model of medical interviewing. An alternative framework that mobilizes points of tension between official and vernacular discourses can capture the nuanced, situationally dependent practice of medical interviewing and promote partnership via language. The framework championed by centered patient-physician communication emphasizes the need to identify and move toward a linguistic middle ground located somewhere between patient and physician understandings of health.

A centered patient-physician model does not promote either the adaptation of a patient vernacular or the adherence to a medical rhetoric. Instead, centered patient-physician communication requires the careful examination of the ways that both official and vernacular rhetorics rub up against one another in productive ways. It becomes the work of a rhetorician of medicine to explore the ways that principles of patient-physician communicating—modes of communication intelligible to both parties—might lead to a more centered rhetoric of medicine.

Through a centered approach to patient-physician interaction, principles of communicating can be used as opportunities to signify the interdependent nature of the patient-physician dyad, as opposed to evidence of the irreconcilable foundations of doctoring. If scholarship continues to juxtapose and enmesh patient and physician vernacular in productive ways, curricula might then better represent a centered approach to patient-physician interaction. By identifying and then standardizing certain contextual boundaries of communicating in the medical context, medical students, standardized patients, communication coaches, and professional organizations might better work to foster genuine human interaction needed to establish the relational dimension of medicine. Both patient and physician are central actors in the performance of medicine and, therefore, the art of medicine will be better served when the gap between patient vernacular and official rhetoric of health and medicine can be bridged. CPPC offers one platform to further this agenda.

References

Barley, G., Boyle, D., Johnston, M. A. (2001). Rowing downstream and the rhythm of medical interviewing. *Medical Encounter, 16*, 6–8.

Bates, B. R., & Ahmed, R. Introduction to medical communication in clinical contexts. In B. R. Bates & R. Ahmed (Eds.), *Medical communication in clinical contexts* (pp. 1–16). Dubuque, IA: Kendall Hunt.

Boyle, D., Dwinnell, B., & Platt, F. (2005). Invite, listen, and summarize: A patient-centered communication technique. *Academic Medicine, 80*, 29–32.

Calvo, L. (2004). Art for the Archbishop: The semiotics of contemporary Chicana feminism and the work of Alma Lopez. *Meridians: Feminism, Race, Transnationalism, 5*, 201–224.

Cole, S. A., & Bird, J. (2000). *The medical interview: The three function approach*. St. Louis: Mosby.

Conrad, P. (2007). *The medicalization of society: On the transformation of human conditions into treatable disorders*. Baltimore: Johns Hopkins University Press.

Conrad, P., & Leiter, V. (2008). From Lydia Pinkham to Queen Levitra: Direct-to-consumer advertising and medicalization. *Sociology of Health and Illness, 30*, 825–838.

Donohue, J. M., Cevasco, M., & Rosenthal, M. B. (2007). A decade of direct-to-consumer advertising of prescription drugs. *New England Journal of Medicine, 357*, 673.

Goodall, H. L., Jr. (2000). *Writing the new ethnography*. Walnut Creek, CA: Altamira Press.

Haidet, P., O'Malley, K. J., Sharf, B. F., Gladney, A. P., Greisinger, A. J., & Street, R. L. (2008). Characterizing explanatory models of illness in healthcare: Development and validation of the CONNECT instrument. *Patient Education and Counseling, 73*, 232–239.

Kenny, D. A., Veldhuijzen, W., Weijden, T. V., Leblanc, A., Lockyer, F., Legare, F. et al. (2010). Interpersonal perception in the context of physician-patient relationships: A dyadic analysis of physician-patient communication. *Social Science and Medicine, 70*, 763–768.

Lindlof, T. R., & Taylor, B. C. (2010). *Qualitative communication research methods* (3rd ed.). Thousand Oaks, CA: SAGE Publications.

Lupton, D. (2007). *Medicine as culture*. New York: SAGE Publications.

Mackenzie, F. J., Jordens, C. F. C., Ankeny, R. A., McPhee, J., & Kerridge, I. H. (2007). Direct-to-consumer advertising under the radar: The need for realistic drugs policy in Australia. *Internal Medicine Journal, 37*, 224–228.

Saltman, R. B. (1994). Patient choice and patient empowerment in northern European health systems: A conceptual framework. *International Journal of Health Services, 24*, 201–229.

Schleifer, R., & Vannatta, J. (2011). The chief concern of medicine: Narrative, *phronesis*, and the history of present illness. *Genre, 44*, 335–347.

Showalter, E. (1997). *Hystories: Hysterical epidemics and modern media*. New York: Columbia.

Venetis, M., Robinson, J., Turkiewicz, K., & Allen, M. (2009). An evidence base for patient-centered cancer care: A meta-analysis of studies of observed communication between cancer specialists and their patients. *Patient Education & Counseling, 77*, 379–383.

Chapter 4

Hassan, Ami, and Dalia's Mom: Narrative Medicine in Pediatrics

Eva Berger and Isaac Berger

Introduction

Communication among human beings has become increasingly mediated by technology in many areas, including medicine, where the mediation has moved doctors and patients apart. Physician-patient communication has been studied from various perspectives, including Narrative Medicine, which deals with clinical narratives—stories of therapeutic activities created by physicians for and with patients over time. But, despite the fact that the field of Narrative Medicine is by now quite rich, relatively little can be found in the literature that deals with the specific area of Narrative Medicine in the management of illness in children—a challenge characterized by the need for communication among three parties (the physician, the child, and the parents). Through the stories of three child-patients, this chapter addresses this gap and attempts to characterize what constitutes an effective, life-saving, and enhancing pediatric narrative, and to make a contribution toward an integrated and coherent theory of Pediatric Narrative Medicine.

Ilana has been experiencing excruciating pain in her elbow for about six months. She has gotten a few shots and is taking part in an experimental study, yet nothing seems to work. During our daily walk together the other day, she told the story of her latest visit to the doctor. He never examined her. He just wanted to talk to her. So she sat across the desk from him telling him of how it is getting harder and harder to do even basic daily chores. He never took his eyes off the computer screen and, still typing, he said: "You are simply hitting your backhand wrong." It *is* tennis elbow, you see. But had he taken a moment to talk to her and hear her story, he would have found out that Ilana was a professional tennis player for about 20 years, Israel's champion five years in a row, and famous for her killer backhand. He would have also found out that she is a coach now, and that the pain is interfering with her livelihood, with her income. And that she is worried about the future.

The obvious and quite banal point of this story is that communication between physician and patient is important. And that without it, not only the physical pain we experience is at stake, but our psychological well-being as well.

The computer screen at which doctors look while talking to us these days is only the most recent in a series of technologies that have mediated between doctors and patients throughout history. Each new medical technology, each new screen in the clinic or the hospital, has brought us closer to an apparently accurate representation of our bodies, in sickness and in health, or at least to the illusion thereof. As Reiser (1978) explains:

> [The invention of the stethoscope] helped to create the objective physician, who could move away from involvement with the patient's experiences and sensations, to a more detached relation, less with the patient but more with the sounds from within the body. Undistracted by the motives and beliefs of the patient, the auscultator could make a diagnosis from sounds that he alone heard emanating from body organs, sounds that he believed to be objective, bias-free representations of the disease process. (p. 38)

This detachment and illusion of objectivity became even truer with visual medical imaging technologies that enable the physician to further disregard the patient's motives and feelings, or worse, regard them as "wrong" and the picture as "true." With these technologies the detachment from patients increased and the art of listening began to falter. Instead of performing as aids in the process of diagnosis, the stethoscope, X-rays, the electrocardiograph, ultrasound, MRIs, and other technologies have almost entirely replaced conversation.

Patients, too, have come to rely completely on tests. They demand them; they feel cheated when not referred to have them done; and, they sue for malpractice when doctors fail to accurately interpret them. And this, in turn, creates an atmosphere in which medical competence is defined by the quantity and variety of technologies brought to bear on the disease.

In a mediated reality reminiscent of Jerzy Kosinski's *Being There*—where pathologists and radiologists interpret the meaning of technical information and have no connection whatsoever with the patient, only with tissue and photographs—the message, as Postman (1992) put it, is that "medicine is about disease, not the patient. And what the patient knows is untrustworthy; what the machine knows is reliable" (p. 100).

This mediation moved doctors and patients apart, the need for direct communication became clear, and the field of health communication developed.

Scholars in the field study physician-patient communication from a variety of perspectives and approaches. But as Cegala and Street (2009) explain, much remains to be done with respect to providing meaningful, theoretical accounts of processes affecting communication and outcomes as well as creating measures that integrate behavioral and perceptual features of communication.

Attempting to fill this gap in theory, one of the relatively newer branches within doctor-patient communication is the idea of Narrative Medicine. But before one can discuss Narrative Medicine, an understanding of the concept of Narrative and of Narrative Inquiry and its method is necessary.

The Concept of Narrative

The concept of narrative has played a central role in various fields during the past two decades or so. Clandinin and Caine (2008) for example, explain that narrative inquiry is first and foremost a way to understand experience. But it is also a research methodology. In other words, it is both a view of the phenomena of people's experiences and a methodology for inquiring into experience and, thus, allows for the intimate study of individuals' experiences over time and in context. Beginning with a narrative view of experience, researchers attend to place, temporality, and sociality, allowing for inquiry into both researchers' and participants' storied life experiences. Within this space, each story told and lived is situated and understood within larger cultural, social, and institutional narratives. Narrative inquiry is marked by its emphasis on relational engagement between researcher and research participants (and as will be seen later, in the context of medicine, between doctor and patient).

Narrative Inquiry, across various disciplines and multiple professional fields, aims at understanding and making meaning of experience through conversations, dialogue, and participation in the lives of the participants. Each discipline and field of study brings slightly different ways of understanding and different contexts to the narrative study of experience.

Pollio, Graves, and Arfken (2006) explain that narrative analysis is based on the belief that one of the best ways to learn something about a person, group, or culture is to get acquainted with the stories they tell. Narrative analysis addresses how stories define meanings and it views life as a text that can be analyzed like literary critics analyze their texts.

The story, narrative, or text, as Riessman (as cited in Pollio, Graves, & Arfken, 2006) explains, provides a reconfigured version of human experience using structures available in language. The narrative is defined by its temporal structure and depends on shared cultural understandings of order and causality. Although our immediate experience of the world does not unfold as a narrative, when we reflect on it and tell it to others, it usually does take on this form.

The development of the narrative happens in two stages. The first stage takes place when personal experience is reconstructed. This reconstruction focuses on certain aspects of the world and leaves others to act as background or context. Language allows us to do this: to direct our attention to certain things and ignore others. And, at the second stage, an account or story is formulated to tell to others.

As can be seen from the discussion thus far, another central concept within narrative inquiry is "storytelling." Peterson (2009) discusses the idea of "making storytelling." He admits that this is an awkward expression; but he explains that it has the advantage of emphasizing the twofold sense of "making" that occurs in storytelling: the making of a story and the making of an event of telling. Scholars from various fields—such as anthropology, literature, linguistics, history, education, psychology, sociology, and communication—explore both these senses of "making storytelling" in studies in, among others, speech play, verbal art, narrative performance, folktales, and oral literature and traditions. They all deal with both the appreciation of the story and the evaluation of the ways in which the storyteller turns the story into an experience. A storyteller is not valued by an audience only for the information or message that the performance conveys. It is the storyteller's skill in making a report of events into something interesting and memorable that draws the audience's attention and response. In storytelling, communication is productive; in other words, storytelling turns the mundane into something special or poetic. And as will be seen later, in the context of narrative medicine, it is the role of the physician to help the patient become a good storyteller not for the purposes of being appreciated by an audience, but to help the doctor make the act of communication productive.

Storytelling or Narrative Inquiry has by now become a popular and heuristic method in many cultures and various academic fields. But more recently, it has become an accepted method in new areas such as nursing, health studies, gerontology, and of course, medicine.

Narrative in Medicine

We all have a story that we tell ourselves about our healthy lives. But illness requires us to reorganize our story. Pollio and colleagues (2006) discuss stories of illness as an example of narrative research and they believe that narratives of illness are a good way to understand how people—as individuals and as part of a culture—deal with chronic conditions.

The general structure (or script) of culturally shared stories frames individual and cultural meanings of specific human experiences. Sontag (1988), for example, traced the development of a social narrative of tuberculosis in the 19th century and paralleled it with a 20th century narrative of cancer. Both diseases have a clear medical origin and, as Sontag points out, share metaphoric meanings that make attributions about their sufferers that may lead to additional problems. Tuberculosis was initially viewed as a disease of the artist—primarily afflicting a person of sensitive and sad temperament—and later as a product of urban moral decay and sexual excess. Cancer is still sometimes viewed as a disease of suppressed or concealed emotions that must be fought, defeated, and removed. Both social narratives affected the experiences of those unfortunate enough to have contracted these diseases and sometimes even led to treatment regimens not al together helpful to the healing process (Sontag expanded her discussion in a later book in 1989 to include AIDS).

In Sontag's footsteps, Charmaz (2000) also claims that experiencing chronic illness means more than feeling physical distress, acknowledging symptoms, and needing care. It includes metaphor and meaning, moral judgments and ethical dilemmas, identity questions and reconstruction of self, daily struggles and persistent troubles. Experiencing serious illness challenges prior meanings, ways of living that have been taken for granted, and ways of knowing the self. For the ill person life is suddenly uncertain. The self becomes vulnerable, and its vulnerability derives, in part, from potential disapproval and devaluation. In short, chronically ill people lose their previously taken-for-granted continuity of life. And they need empowering metaphors and narratives.

Misunderstandings between practitioners and patients can arise from unstated assumptions such as conflicting guiding metaphors. Patients have their own metaphors, values, and feelings. Their stories mediate between their bodies and emotions because their stories make sense of the changes they are going through in their lives, and of the new limitations of their bodies. But stories alone do not cover the experience. Not everyone can find words to express new and unclear feelings. It is the doctor's job—through interviews and conversations—to find, with the patient, useful words, empowering metaphors, and illness narratives.

Kleinman and Seeman (2000) discuss the concept of "illness narratives" developed by medical anthropologists, and they explain that the illness narrative approach is an open-ended approach to the stories that always surround episodes of illness and healing. It is, in fact, so open-ended, that it extends to whatever the teller of the narrative considers to be at stake for him or her. The hopes, fears, personal history, and cultural tradition of the ill person are all brought to bear, and it is up to the listener to adopt an analytic position that is broad enough to accommodate them.

Narrative strategies and poetic conventions, such as voice, genre, metaphors, and rhetorical strategies, need to be taken into account, as they are essential to the way in which illness narratives are constructed. Illness narratives do not simply recount a series of disconnected events; they tell a story that is, typically, a moral one. Illness is located within the autobiography of the person in question. It often includes ideologies and morals (whether implicit or explicit) that may not fit medical conventions. And so, prerequisites to this approach are a developed literary sensitivity and personal empathy from the doctor.

Another issue that needs to be taken into consideration and be understood by physicians is that their own stories about illness and healing (as they tell them to themselves, to each other, and to patients or their families) are also characterized in crucial ways. For example, the idea that patients should always be hopeful, that physicians should always be heroic, or that families of the terminally ill need to be stoic, are all narrative strategies that influence the ways in which care is organized, resources distributed, and meanings applied to the clinical encounter.

In short, as Delvecchio Good and Good (2000) succinctly put it, clinical narratives—stories of therapeutic activities created by physicians for and with patients over time—lie at the heart of doctor-patient communication. Through clinical narrative, physicians create and shape patient experience over time. And they add:

> Physicians in conversation with patients, "emplot" disease and its treatment, constructing meaningful stories, linking the past and the present to potential futures and plotting courses of action … Although clinical narratives are given directionality by physicians … patients are also critical "readers" and "interpreters" of treatment plots, directing—often in collaboration with their clinicians—how the shifts in therapeutic course will affect their lives. (p. 246)

As can be seen to this point, the field of narrative medicine is a rich one. However, it is striking how little can be found in the literature that deals with the specific area of narrative medicine in the management of children's illnesses. Lately, some journals have included sections on narrative medicine—describing the clinical history of child patients or sharing doctors' experiences—some of them in the area of pediatrics. But there is a clear understanding of the need for the integrated and coherent study of the role and potential benefits of the use of narrative in the medical care of children.

The Need for a Theory of Narrative Medicine in Pediatrics A child's illness requires the reorganization not only of the parent's life-story but also of the child's life-story in the minds of parents. The loss of the previously taken-for-granted continuity of life in chronically ill people is regarded as especially tragic in the case of children. Pediatrics presents a special challenge and can be regarded as a specialty narrative. As Kleinman and Seeman (2000) explain, "the experience of illness is not bounded by the bodies or consciousness of those who are ill; it reaches out to encompass a household, a family, or a social network" (p. 232). And this is especially true when the patient is a child.

Streisand and Tercyak (2004) explain that all parents are challenged with the task of promoting normal, healthy development in their children. This task includes promoting not only physical growth and maturation, but also social, emotional, and intellectual development. For parents of children with a chronic illness, these challenges are intensified, because the child's medical condition sets the limits within which the developmental milestones can occur. Sometimes, childhood illness interrupts or delays normal development, which widens the gap among the resources, skills, and achievements of ill children relative to their healthy peers. And this, in turn, further increases the worries and stresses experienced by their parents. In short, chronic illness in children creates unique circumstances for the children themselves, for their parents, and for the relationship between them. In other words, the impact that the illness has on the parent plays a role in how the child adapts to the medical adversity. For example, anxiety on the part of the parent can affect the child's recovery process.

There is a longstanding tradition of health professionals who from the early 20th century wrote about this topic. Arnold Gesell (1940), who was both a psychologist and physician, wrote and lectured about psychological principles in pediatric medicine. And by the middle of the 20th century, pediatrician Benjamin Spock's (1946/2004) famous book was published for the first time. Spock's message of patience, tolerance, and love for children influenced the attitudes and practices of generations of parents throughout the world. However, these and other popular resources concentrated mostly on healthy children, and much less on parenting a sick child.

In the early 1960s, Green and Solnit (1964) wrote about "vulnerable child syndrome." At its basis, this syndrome was about the altered relationship between parent and child when the child experienced an acute illness. The authors explained, for example, that ill children would often be viewed by their parents as fragile, and that this view could lead to child maladjustment over time. And in the later part of the 20th century, theoretical models began to emerge (e.g.,

Wallander, Varni, Babani, Banis, & Wilcox, 1989) that focused on factors affecting adjustment among children with chronic conditions, and on the importance of parental adjustment in promoting positive child functioning under hard medical circumstances.

There are various important themes to assess the social, behavioral, and psychological implications of illness in children. One of the most important ones is what is known as "pediatric parenting stress." The sources of the stress include handling and negotiating complicated and sometimes unfriendly healthcare systems, as well as learning to communicate with service providers using the jargon of the child's illness, among others.

Parents are children's most important health resource. They are the main managers of the child's illness, as it is they who need to continuously bring the child's medical needs to the attention of healthcare providers. Parents are also key players in the identification of behavioral problems, and the quality of their communication with professionals about such problems often determines the quality of the intervention services offered (Garrison et al., 1992; Horwitz, Leaf, & Leventhal, 1998).

The child's developmental phase also affects the impact of the illness and, of course, the level of direct dialogue and building of narrative that the physician may have directly with the child. As Streisand and Tercyak (2004) explain, physical illness during infancy significantly impacts both the infant and the parent. While parents of children of all ages have a natural desire to protect their children, parents of infants may also feel guilty for "causing" the infant's difficulties (in the case of inherited diseases, for instance). Some may even come to question their competency in parenting generally.

Similar to infants, toddlers and preschoolers (ages 18 months to 5 years) are completely dependent on their parents, too. But the challenges to parenting here have to do with helping children understand their illness and cooperate with treatment. Also, development of self-control (so important at these ages) can also be affected by illness as parents feel sorry for their children and they are reluctant to set limits on their behavior.

For school children (6–11 years), their development is affected by interactions with peers, and by comparisons to peers to help in judging their own competencies. Disruption of routine due to illness limits children's opportunities for social interactions, and this, in turn, hampers the personal growth gained from such interaction.

As for adolescents (ages 12–18 years), many challenges happen at this phase, such as identity formation, body image issues, and the move toward independence.

These tasks are especially challenging for ill adolescents, as well as for their parents, as the parents stay involved in every aspect of the teen's lives due to the illness, at a stage when they should be relinquishing responsibilities. This is, of course, the source of difficulties for the parent-adolescent relationship.

It is clear from all of the above that in pediatrics, communication is shaped by three parties (the physician, the child, and the parents), with varying degrees and characteristics of parent involvement, depending on the age of the child.

> DasGupta (2007) explains:
>
> Much of the pediatric story emerges from nonverbal communication on the part of the child. Very young children are developmentally unable to access and to use language in the same manner as adults, but even older children are often unable to articulate their experiences, because of their social voicelessness. (p. e1386)
>
> And he continues:
>
> Despite efforts on the part of pediatricians to elicit and to hear the voices of their patients, stronger still are the nonverbal messages transmitted to children through their parents' expectations of docility and obedience as integral to good public behavior. (p. e1386)

To this, Tates and Meeuwesen (2001) add that studies on doctor-patient communication focus predominantly on dyadic interactions between adults, and even when the patient is a child, the focus is usually on the doctor-parent interaction (instead of on the doctor-parent-child). This leads to an almost complete disregard of the implications of a child's presence in the medical encounter.

It is clear that the medical treatment of children is a challenge to the communication process, and it is widely evident that there is a specific need for the development of a theory of narrative pediatric medicine.

The larger, ongoing project, of which this chapter is part, is an attempt to contribute to the development of such a theory. Using the method of "participatory ethnography or observation," and inspired by William Carlos Williams' *The Doctor Stories* (1984), the study provides an analysis of 20 real cases (anonymous, of course) encountered by one of the authors—Dr. Isaac Berger—over a 50-year pediatric career. The conclusion so far is that the creation of a common narrative among doctor, child, and parents contributes significantly to coping and even to healing. The characterization of what constitutes an effective, life-saving and life-enhancing pediatric narrative is the project's ultimate goal. But, based on three out of the 20 stories selected for inclusion here, it seems possible, already, to at least generally outline what comprises a pediatric narrative and what this requires of the physician. First and foremost, it is a narrative co-authored by three or more participants (doctor-child-parent[s]). In other words, it is the result not of a dyadic but a triadic interaction. This narrative requires of the physician true acknowledgment of the child's presence in the medical encounter, not only—obviously—during the physical exam, but also during the conversation with the parents. And it requires an awareness of the parents' body and verbal language throughout. And along this process, the doctor must "map out" his or her own "role" in relation to the roles of the child and parents in each of their own stories. In other words, it seems like the doctor must act as "editor" rather than the "author" or "co-author" that he is when practicing adult narrative medicine.

Before moving on to retell the three stories selected for presentation in this chapter, a note is in order: Similar to Rawlins (2005), who offers stories about his father as "trusted co-author of his patients' life stories" (p. 208), the stories here were told by Isaac to Eva, and in the process, both had an opportunity to reflect on Isaac's self-positioning in the presentation of the narratives as an "intervener" to better the outcomes of the stories of others, and Eva's position as "re-teller" of these stories, both of which are part and parcel of the three lessons offered here. This reflection leads to our decision to formulate the stories together—referring to the doctor in the third person—rather than in the form of either a first-hand rendition or an interview, for clarity's sake.

Three Stories

Dalia's Mom

Children who suffer from chronic diseases, and who need to visit their physicians regularly and frequently, almost invariably establish a generally friendly relationship with their doctors.

Dalia suffered from rheumatoid arthritis, required close attention, and came to visit Isaac frequently, especially in the early stages of the illness, always accompanied by her mother.

On one occasion, after Isaac finished Dalia's examination, and talking to the mother (as he always did) about the development of the disease and providing instructions about the treatment, Isaac asked: "And how are *you*?" The tears that filled the mother's eyes at the question were touching, and Isaac did not have to say much more for the remainder of the conversation. The first question had been enough for the mother to open up and go into a long narrative describing the difficulties she had been experiencing lately as a result of the attention she needs to give to Dalia. She also described at great length and detail how the jealousy of the younger siblings at home was making everything even harder and more complex, and how her husband—Dalia's father—could not be counted on to cooperate and help.

Should it surprise anyone that starting that day, Dalia began to respond better to the treatment? We think not. Not a lot was said by Isaac in that conversation, but hidden behind the doctor's question of "How are you?" was a test of his assumption that part of the problem was that Dalia's mom had not made her "side of the story" heard. She had kept her own, personal narrative out of view and to herself, and regarded it as illegitimate. The question released the narrative, allowed the mother her own voice, thus alleviating some of the tension that was interfering with life at home and with Dalia's treatment.

Hassan: The Power of TLC

In 1977, the policy of the chief of pediatrics at the hospital where Isaac began to work that year was one of extreme limitations on the time that the parents were allowed to "visit"—to be with their children in the ward. They could be there only one hour a day. This stemmed from a conception or narrative (that translated into this policy) that parents don't know how to cope and they interfere with treatment. Having just arrived in Israel and new to the hospital, Isaac went for his first visit to the baby ward. There—among all the other babies—he saw Hassan, a 9-month-old baby, who was suffering from profound malnutrition.

The treatment and nutrition being given to Hassan were not working, and so Isaac decided to "adopt" the baby. A great believer in the well-known narrative of "Tender Loving Care" from doctors, too, and not only families, Isaac picked Hassan up, held him in his arms, and went for long walks back and forth along the ward corridors every opportunity he got, a few times every day. Hassan began to gain weight, then he started to smile, and six weeks later he was strong and healthy enough to be released from the hospital. Isaac continued to see him periodically and to follow Hassan's development as an outpatient for the following year.

In 1997, Isaac fell ill and was hospitalized. One morning, while being rolled in his wheelchair to have a test done, a middle-aged man approached him. He greeted Isaac and wished him good health. That afternoon, a young man of 21 appeared at Isaac's room, a box of chocolates in his hand and said: "My name is Hassan. Do you remember me? My father told me you were sick. I just came to wish you a fast recovery and lots of health."

This story is not about the patient's narrative, as a 9-month-old baby cannot express himself in words. But it is definitely a story about conflicting narratives among doctors (and specifically pediatricians). One of the narratives was expressed through policy and the other through behavior—not even medical but humane. And they illustrate, together, the profound implications that narratives have for the successful medical care of children. In Hassan's case, it seems safe to assume that the story of how Dr. Berger treated him, as told by his father, was incorporated into his life-narrative generally or he wouldn't have gone to the trouble of coming to visit and "return the favor." It's hard to claim that Hassan's visit made Isaac healthy, but the event left him deeply touched and elated, and it was a confirmation of his narrative.

Ami: 39 Pounds of Love

This last story—Ami's story—is an especially representative example, as the relationship among doctor, patient, and parent lasted 32 years, and bore, throughout those years, a narrative that can be said to have been at least partly responsible for the chronically ill patient's unusually long life expectancy and, more importantly, the quality of his life in his own eyes.

Isaac first met Ami at the age of 10, more than 30 years ago. He was born with spinal muscular atrophy and was confined to a wheelchair since the age of 4. Isaac became his pediatrician and followed him closely until Ami's death at age 41.

Because of his physical impairment and his mother's inability to move him around, he became the only patient in Isaac's practice for whom he made house calls.

Isaac estimates that about half his visits (which were innumerable) were initiated due to the psychological needs of both Ami and his mother. Isaac spoke to Ami and tried to answer his every question. He never lied. He told him of his prospects and explained each element of his condition, but always tried to not let his own personal and professional narratives, values, and metaphors override Ami's. Through their conversations, Isaac tried to help Ami use his own metaphors and create his own empowering illness narrative. As Kleinman and Seeman (2000) put it, Isaac tried to maintain the open-ended narrative approach to the interpersonal context and effects of Ami's illness. He tried to always stay in tune with whatever Ami—the maker and teller of the narrative—considered to be at stake. And he tried to listen carefully to Ami's hopes, fears, and personal history, and to accommodate them.

After examining Ami and talking to him for a while as he lay on his waterbed, Isaac was routinely invited by Ami's mother to join her in the kitchen for a cup of coffee and for what Isaac eventually realized was the weaving of Ami's story through the years in her mind.

In 2001, at the age of about 30 and weighing 39 pounds, Ami decided to visit the United States in search of the neurologist who told his mother when he was 3 that Ami would probably not survive past the age of 6. The trip, and really the story of his life, were captured in a film called *39 Pounds of Love*, produced by one of Ami's best friends. The film includes whole sections of Ami's own animation, and it was purchased and broadcast by HBO. A National Geographic documentary about his life was also produced.[1]

One may ask why Ami's story constitutes such good material for a film. In addition to being inspiring, it is because the narrative at the center of Ami's life, and thus the film's, was created by Ami himself as he tried to make meaning of his existence. The title of the film—*39 Pounds of Love*—is a fitting title for Ami's narrative that was all about his love for his caretaker, his mother, his friends, and mostly for life. And this is what kept him going and happy, against all odds.

During one of Isaac's last visits with Ami, Ami told Isaac he was losing the ability to breathe, and wanted to know what would happen. Isaac explained that were he to stop breathing, he would have to be intubated by tracheotomy and helped to breathe mechanically. Ami immediately said: "I want it!" To Isaac's reply that he didn't need it yet he said: "Not now—when it happens." Ami wanted Isaac to know. Completely dependent on the people around him, at the weight of a child of 5, his words barely uttered, and discerned with great difficulty, he wanted to live. His narrative was one of passion for life.

Conclusions and Implications

The characterization of what constitutes an effective and enhancing pediatric narrative is hoped to be the end result of our project in progress. The three narratives presented here are part of our attempt at this characterization. Although early still, the findings so far point in the direction of the need for a new view of the process that takes place in the three-way encounters among doctors, children, and their parents. This new view includes the conceptualization of various stages in the process, different from the classic ones (such as the taking of the patient's clinical history). These new stages can be called prompting passivity, internalization, and cooperative activity.

The word "passivity" has mostly negative connotations. But a new, operational definition of the word may help us focus on what is required of the doctor to help the child and the parents open up and truly listen. Dalia's story is a good example

---

[1] For a clip from the movie, go to http://www.youtube.com/watch?v=lf29ce3u0jk

of what is meant by this first stage—prompting passivity—as a simple question asked of the mother stands at the beginning of the process, followed by a step back, an openness to listen. Another way of putting this is, as Rita Charon (2005) expressed it: "The state of being required of doctors in order to engage in Narrative Medicine is 'an emptying of self so as to become an instrument for receiving the meaning of another'" (p. 132). Or, as DasGupta (2007) puts it: "This sort of listening demands a radical shift in stance, in grammatical voice, such that physicians not only act but also allow themselves to be acted on" (p. e1385).

Once the prompting has worked and the patient and/or the child have opened up, the doctor may move into the second stage—internalization—and take in and organize in his or her own mind what is being said (or otherwise communicated, through body language, for example). Baby Hassan did not mean to communicate a thing. But a doctor intent on internalizing his patients, acquires an enhanced awareness to cues, unspoken quiet suffering, and the potential stories or narratives waiting to be prompted, internalized, and woven with the child and her or his parents on the way to arriving at a diagnosis, finding solutions and cures, and aiding coping.

This weaving is the last of the three stages—cooperative activity—and its essence lies in the creation of a true creative partnership among physician, child, and parents. Delvecchio Good and Good's (2000) idea that "clinical narratives—stories of therapeutic activities [are] created by physicians for and with patients" should be rephrased to include "with" patients, but not "for" them. In other words, patients should be seen not as "readers" or "interpreters" (as the authors also point out), but as active co-writers of an empowering story. And in the case of pediatrics, as already mentioned, the doctor should be seen as "editor."

Further analysis of the 20 stories of the study will tell whether this is, indeed, a viable theory. Meanwhile, it is clear even from the three stories presented here, that as DasGupta (2007) puts it, "the experiences of children and their families, in the form of pediatric illness narratives, hold unique insights for physicians in how to engage in an ethical, empathetic, and self-reflective practice" (p. e1384). The pediatric context is clearly different from the adult context. We have established the unique challenges for very young children to narrate their experiences as well as the stress involving parenting an ill child. Thus, even though the three lessons—prompting passivity, internalization, and cooperative activity—might have the potential to enhance adult narrative medicine, they seem especially well suited for the triadic communication process required in pediatric narrative medicine. They are some of the tools available to "the pediatrician as editor."

In the introduction to *The Doctor Stories*, Robert Coles (1984)—who compiled the stories—quotes Dr. Williams as having once told a medical student:

> There's nothing like a difficult patient to show us ourselves …
> I would learn so much on my rounds, or making home visits …
> I heard words, lines, saw people and places … There was something else going on, though—the force of all those encounters.
> I was put off guard again and again, and the result was—well, a descent into myself. (p. xiii)

Ami died in late 2009. Hassan must be in his 30s now and perhaps he is a father himself. And who knows what path Dalia's life took, and that of her mother. But for Dr. Berger they are lively memories of the children they were when they crossed paths, and in his heart he hopes and wishes that they are happily weaving their life stories—without illness. He is thankful for his encounters with them, as it is the chapters of their stories that they shared with him that allowed him to "descend into himself" and perhaps to become a better pediatrician.

References

Cegala, D. J., & Street, R. L., Jr. (2009). Interpersonal dimensions of health communication. In C. R. Berger, M. E. Roloff, & D. Roskos-Ewolsen (Eds.), *Handbook of communication science* (2nd ed., pp. 401–417). Thousand Oaks, CA: SAGE Publications.

Charmaz, K. (2000). Experiencing chronic illness. In G. Albrecht, R. Fitzpatrick, & S. C. Scrimshaw (Eds.), *Handbook of social studies and health and medicine* (pp. 277–292). London: SAGE Publications.

Charon, R. (2005). *Narrative medicine: Honoring the stories of illness.* New York: Oxford University Press.

Clandinin, D. J., & Caine, V. (2008). Narrative inquiry. In L. M. Given (Ed.), *The Sage encyclopedia of qualitative research methods* (pp. 541–544). Thousand Oaks, CA: SAGE Publications.

DasGupta, S. (2007). Between stillness and story: Lessons of children's illness narratives. *Pediatrics, 119(6),* e1384-e1391. doi:10.1542/peds.2006-2619

Delvecchio Good, M. J., & Good, B. (2000). Clinical narratives and the study of contemporary doctor-patient relationships. In G. L. Albrecht, R. Fitzpatrick, & S. Scrimshaw (Eds.), *Handbook of social studies in health and medicine* (pp. 243–258). London: SAGE Publications.

Emanuel, E. J., & Emanuel, L. L. (1992). Four models of the physician-patient relationship. *JAMA, 267*(16), 2221–2226.

Garrison, W. T., Bailey, E. N., Garb, J., Ecker, B., Spencer, P., & Sigelman D. (1992). Interactions between parents and pediatric primary care physicians about children's mental health. *Hospital and Community Psychiatry, 43*(5), 489–493.

Gesell, A. (1940). *The first five years of life: A guide to the study of the preschool child, from the Yale Clinic of Child Development.* New York: Harper and Brothers.

Green, M., & Solnit, A. J. (1964). Reactions to the threatened loss of a child: A vulnerable child syndrome. *Pediatrics, 34*(1), 58–66.

Horwitz, S. M., Leaf, P. J., & Leventhal, J. M. (1998). Identification of psychosocial problems in pediatric primary care: Do family attitudes make a difference? *Archives of Pediatric and Adolescent Medicine, 152*(4), 367–371.

Kleinman, A., & Seeman, D. (2000). Personal experience of illness. In G. L. Albrecht, R. Fitzpatrick, & S. Scrimshaw (Eds.), *Handbook of social studies in health and medicine* (pp. 230–242). London: SAGE Publications.

Peterson, E. E. (2009). Performance and storytelling. In W. F. Eadie (Ed.), *21st century communication: A reference handbook* (pp. 147–155). Thousand Oaks, CA: SAGE Publications.

Pollio, H., Graves, T. R., & Arfken, M. (2006). Qualitative methods. In F. T. L. Leong & J. T. Austin (Eds.), *The psychology research handbook* (2nd ed., pp. 254–274). Thousand Oaks, CA: SAGE Publications.

Postman, N. (1992). *Technopoly: The surrender of culture to technology.* New York: Alfred Knopf.

Rawlins, W. K. (2005). Our family's physician. In L. M. Harter, P. M. Japp, & C. S. Beck (Eds.), *Narratives, health and healing: Communication theory, research and practice* (pp. 197–216). Mahwah, NJ: Lawrence Erlbaum Associates.

Reiser, S. J. (1978). *Medicine and the reign of technology*. Cambridge, MA: Cambridge University Press.

Sontag, S. (1988). *Illness as metaphor*. New York: Farrar, Straus, Giroux.

Sontag, S. (1989). *AIDS and its metaphors*. New York: Farrar, Straus & Giroux.

Spock, B. (1946/2004). *Dr. Spock's baby and child care* (8th ed.). New York: Gallery Books.

Streisand, R., & Tercyak, K. (2004). Parenting chronically ill children: The scope and impact of Pediatric Parenting Stress. In M. Hoghughi & N. Long (Eds.), *Handbook of parenting: Theory and research for practice* (pp. 181–197). London: SAGE Publications.

Tates, K., & Meeuwesen, L. (2001). Doctor-parent-child communication: A (re)view of the literature. *Social Science & Medicine, 52*(6), 839–851.

Wallander, J. L., Varni, J. W., Babani, L., Banis, H. T., & Wilcox, K. T. (1989). Family resources as resistance factors for psychological maladjustment in chronically ill and handicapped children. *Journal of Pediatric Psychology, 14*(2), 157–173. doi:10.1093/jpepsy/14.2.157

Williams, W. C. (1984). *The doctor stories*. New York: New Directions.

Chapter 5

Breaking Bad News in the Provider-Recipient Context: Understanding the Hesitation to Share Bad News from the Sender's Perspective

Jayson L. Dibble

Introduction

Arguably, information represents the most critical commodity in healthcare settings. Providers and recipients both require timely and accurate information to make the best decisions regarding the recipient's care. Unfortunately, health outcomes are not always positive. Healthcare providers often find themselves in the position of having to share negative information with their recipients and their recipients' families. Sharing negative information is commonly referred to as breaking bad news. And because bad news typically contains information directly relevant to the recipient, it is important that providers are able to break bad news optimally.

Breaking bad news is not straightforward. It is an inherently complicated process involving several interrelated communication events, each influenced by myriad variables. For example, at a minimum, providers must initially recognize the information (i.e., the "news") as unfavorable, make ongoing assessments of how negative the bad news is (i.e., its severity), consider the outcome(s) signaled by the bad news, and determine the way(s) in which to relay this information to the recipient. Moreover, those who deliver bad news accomplish these tasks with considerable variability (Dibble, 2008; Dibble & Levine, 2010).

Of course, all the events of the previous paragraph occur amid a tangle of actual emotional reactions and anticipated future emotional reactions. Thus, it is not surprising that providers who claim confidence at breaking bad news are rare (e.g., Rider, Volkan, & Hafler, 2008). Complicating matters further, providers face a great deal of resistance to share bad news in the form of physical and cognitive reluctance. At times this reluctance hampers the communication goal(s) of the provider-recipient encounter. Namely, the recipient does not get the information he or she needs. For example, physicians who suspected dementia diagnoses in their patients have delayed sharing these suspicions with the patient or the patient's family for up to two years (Paterson & Pond, 2009). Other physicians, seeking to soften the impact of the bad news, have (in)appropriately resorted to the use of implicit language (Del Vento, Bavelas, Healing, MacLean, & Kirk, 2009). In these situations, it is not difficult to imagine certain recipients taking offense at their physician's "failure" to level with them. Other evidence points to sizable stress-related and emotion-related personal costs incurred by providers (Buckman, 1984; Harrison & Walling, 2010; Ptacek, Ptacek, & Ellison, 2001). To further exacerbate the issue, many providers report receiving inadequate training in breaking bad news, if they received any training at all. A recent national survey of psychologists found that only 2.7 percent of the sample (N = 329) claimed familiarity with existing guidelines (Merker, Hanson, & Poston, 2010). In sum, the situation of breaking bad news carefully is a critical one, but it is fraught with costs, drawbacks, hesitancies, inadequacies, and opportunities for miscommunication.

This chapter addresses the situation of breaking bad news interpersonally from healthcare providers to their care recipients. Specifically, we focus on the bad news delivery process from the perspective of the one giving the bad news. As we show, this perspective is not well understood and is only recently being taken up by researchers. Guided by these goals, this chapter is organized as follows. First, we define and explicate the concept of bad news. Next, we present a brief history of bad news scholarship as it has been treated by both the medical and the social scientific fields. Then, we more fully articulate the bad news delivery process from the perspective of the sender. A brief discussion of candidate theories capable of enlightening the bad news delivery process follows. The chapter concludes with practical suggestions for those faced with breaking bad news.

What Is Bad News?

Most definitions of bad news come from the medical domain. For example, Fallowfield and Jenkins (2004) consider bad news to be "any information that produces a negative alteration to a person's expectations about their present and future" (p. 312). Similarly, Buckman (1984) labels information as bad news if it drastically alters the recipient's views of his or her future. Other authors consider news to be bad if it results in persistent cognitive, behavioral, or emotional deficits in the receiver (Ptacek & Eberhardt, 1996). Objectively defining bad news is problematic because what counts as bad news for one person might not be perceived as bad news by another (Eberhardt-McKee & Ptacek, 2001; Eggly et al., 2006; Fallowfield & Jenkins, 2004; Ptacek & Eberhardt, 1996). The Fallowfield and Jenkins definition seems to capture the lay understanding of bad news in the sense that people do tend to continue labeling a piece of information "news" even when that information is technically no longer novel (e.g., "I received some bad news earlier this week"). However, this definition might be overly inclusive in the sense that intrapersonally derived information (e.g., a frightening dream resulting in a negative memory) becomes indistinguishable   from news received from an outside source. Ptacek and Eberhardt's (1996) and Buckman's (1984) definitions come closer to reserving the label bad news only for the negative information as it is being conveyed for the first time. Also, this definition reflects the view that the news must be transmitted socially (Eberhardt-McKee & Ptacek, 2001).

In the strictest sense, bad news is receiver defined. Nevertheless, extant definitions of bad news minimally imply that providers perceiving themselves as faced with delivering bad news think, feel, and act in accordance with what they anticipate will constitute bad news for the recipient. Thus, bad news is defined here as *a message communicating information that is assumed to be previously unknown to the receiver, anticipated to be personally relevant to the receiver, and is perceived by the messenger to be negatively valenced by the receiver* (Dibble & Levine, 2010).

Bad news messages can be characterized as varying according to their values on an array of underlying dimensions having to do with the nature of the bad news itself. For example, all bad news messages convey negative information (i.e., the *valence* is negative by definition), but the *extremity* of the message refers to how negative the news is (Sweeny & Shepperd, 2007). That is, there are gradations of bad news (Dibble & Levine, 2010; Fallowfield & Jenkins, 2004). The *involvement* of a message refers to how personally relevant the negative consequences are for the receiver (Rosen & Tesser, 1972). Sweeny and Shepperd (2007) also identify the *controllability* of the negative consequences (from either the sender's or the receiver's perspective), as well as the *likelihood* of the negative consequences actually befalling the recipient, assuming the recipient does not act (or cannot act) to prevent them. Finally, some senders relay bad news for which they are directly responsible, whereas other senders bear negative tidings on behalf of some other responsible party. The party or root stimulus responsible for initiating the negative consequences implied by the bad news message might be fruitfully labeled the *agent* of the consequences of the bad news. Note the agent does not have to be human. In the provider-recipient context, the provider typically relays bad news that he or she did not cause. Thus, the provider is not also the agent. In other situations, however, the sender and the agent will be one in the same (e.g., a provider admitting to a recipient that the provider has made a mistake). When the provider is also the agent, the bad news arrives through self-disclosure. In this way, bad news and self-disclosure do share some conceptual overlap, but not all self-disclosure is bad news, just as not all bad news is self-disclosure.

It is generally assumed that these dimensions influence the specific experience of providers who are faced with delivering bad news (Sweeny & Shepperd, 2007). To provide an example, consider the situation of a physician who prepares to reveal a terminal cancer diagnosis to a patient. This situation will no doubt be fairly extreme for the patient. Involvement is also high in that this particular diagnosis gets assigned to this particular patient. Further, there is nothing the patient can do to avoid the terminal cancer. Thus, controllability may be low. Finally, in this particular example, the agent of the negative consequences may actually be ambiguous. The cancer might have developed due to any number of causes (e.g., poor diet, smoking, lack of exercise, genetics). To the extent that these causes are known, the agent of the negative consequences brought by the diagnosis can be identified. Regardless, to the extent that the physician anticipates the situation characterized by a given pattern of values on these dimensions, his or her communication with the patient will be markedly different than if he or she anticipated a different configuration of dimension values (e.g., relaying news of a cancer that is relatively easy to treat).

History of Bad News Scholarship

Scholarship on the bad news delivery process is typically carried out within two broad domains. First, the medical domain is probably the largest producer of scholarly writing on bad news delivery. This makes sense given the frequency with which medical caregivers have to reveal bad news. The second domain where bad news research is conducted is the social sciences, particularly the fields of communication and social psychology. This section discusses the work of each domain in turn.

Medical Scholarship on Bad News Delivery

Physicians and other healthcare providers routinely find themselves in the position of having to deliver bad news to patients and care recipients. Thus, it is not surprising to find much writing on the topic of breaking bad news in the medical literature. Articles addressing bad news abound in many types of medical and health-oriented journals, ranging from general practice guidelines (Baile et al., 2000) to more localized specialties such as oncology (Back et al., 2008; Cherney, 2010; Spiegel et al., 2009; Walling et al., 2008; Yun et al., 2010), breast imaging screening (Adler, Riba, & Eggly, 2009; van Vliet et al., 2011), children's hearing loss (Gilbey, 2010), and genetic counseling (e.g., Adelsward & Sachs, 2003; McAllister, Dunn, & Todd, 2010; McAllister et al., 2007), to name a few.

Traditional writing on bad news delivery emerging from the medical fields is offered as instruction to healthcare providers about how to "best" break bad news to their recipients in ways that maximize the recipient's benefit (Ptacek & Eberhardt, 1996). As others have noted (Eggly et al., 2006; Harrison & Walling, 2010), healthcare provider guidelines tacitly assume that the bad news delivery process is linear, and that providers should expect the process to unfold in three broad phases. First, providers should prepare for the bad news encounter by securing an appropriate location, earmarking adequate time for the interaction, and so forth. Second, providers should disclose the news using simple language, monitor the pace of delivery, and verify that the recipient has understood. Third, once the bad news has been delivered, providers should allow for and then respond to the recipient's reactions, answer questions, and point out the future course(s) of action. For example, the SPIKES protocol (Baile et al., 2000; see also Amason, Horvath, & Smith, this volume) continues to be highly cited and regarded as a straightforward method of disclosing unfavorable information. SPIKES is an acronym describing the bad news delivery process as comprising six stages: [S]etting up the interview, assessing the patient's [P]erception, obtaining the patient's [I]nvitation, giving [K]nowledge and information to the patient, addressing the patient's [E]motions with empathic responses, and [S]trategy and summary. Other similar mnemonics have been developed (e.g., ABCDE, Vandekieft, 2001).

Some articles are beginning to report tests of the effectiveness of such recommendations. For example, Bruera and colleagues (2007) used videorecorded sequences of physicians delivering cancer diagnoses to determine whether patients preferred a sitting or standing physician. They found that sitting was preferred, but that posture was less important than other communication behaviors. Other articles report tests of communication skills training workshops for residents (e.g., Back et al., 2007; Brown & Bylund, 2008; Lienard et al., 2010; Schildmann, Kupfer, Burchardi, & Vollmann, 2011), and the use of simulated interviews to teach medical students how to reveal cancer diagnoses (Supiot & Bonnaud-Antignac, 2008).

Not surprisingly, the overwhelming focus of these articles is to instruct providers on the best ways to break bad news for *the recipient's benefit*. Interestingly, although the authors of SPIKES acknowledged the costs incurred by the bearers of the bad news, the protocol only indirectly addresses these costs vis-à-vis the use of a standard protocol for the patient's satisfaction. In a sense, the implication of this and similar approaches is that satisfied recipients equal satisfied providers. Put differently, delivering bad news would otherwise be a simple matter if the recipient's emotions could somehow be managed. As is shown later, however, the recipient's emotionality is not the only motivator of the hesitation to share bad news.

It is the notion that other motivations drive providers' uneasiness with break-ing bad news that is only recently beginning to reach providers. Thus, articles about bad news between providers and recipients are now emerging that attempt to revise the view that breaking bad news can even be considered a straightforward duty (Eggly et al., 2006; Villagran, Goldsmith, Wittenberg-Lyles, & Baldwin, 2010; Whitney, McCullough, Fruge, McGuire, & Volk, 2008). More is discussed on this issue later. Now, our attention turns to the other domain where bad news research is conducted.

Social Scientific Scholarship on Bad News Delivery

Compared to the work from the medical domains, social scientific research ap-pears to be following a different trajectory. Here, researchers concern themselves with the variables that influence the sender's hesitation to share bad news. Since Rosen and Tesser's (1972) early work more than four decades ago, social scientists have documented the hesitation to share bad news in a variety of settings, and they have conducted scores of experiments to identify the factors that influence this reluctance to break bad news. Because social science has uncovered much about this process since the 1970s, we devote the entire next section to discussing these findings.

The most common finding in social scientific bad news research is that people are hesitant to share bad news. This hesitancy reflects a systematic bias in interper-sonal communication that Rosen and Tesser (1972) referred to as the MUM effect (MUM being an acronym for keeping [M]um about [U]ndesirable [M]essages). The MUM effect reveals itself in various forms and across diverse settings. For exam-ple, senders have been found to delay the negative information (Bond & Anderson, 1987; Dibble & Levine, 2010; Tesser, Rosen, & Tesser, 1971; Yariv, 2006), distort or downplay the negativity of the message or its consequences (Fisher, 1979), or opt for less immediate channels of bad news delivery (e.g., e-mail, Sussman & Sproull, 1999). The example given at the beginning of the chapter when physicians delayed dementia diagnoses for up to two years (Paterson & Pond, 2009) might represent one manifestation of the MUM effect. Other settings in which the MUM effects have been documented include supervisor-subordinate communication (e.g., Wagoner & Waldron, 1999; Yariv, 2006), between coworkers (Bisel, Kelley, Ploeger, & Messersmith, 2011), and between college student peers (Dibble & Levine, 2010; Weenig, Wilke, & ter Mors, 2011).

Tesser and Rosen (1975) considered the MUM effect to be multicausal, and they detailed three categories of possible causes. The first collection of explana-tions argues that MUM effects result because of sender *self-concerns*. For example, senders might prefer to avoid feeling guilty (especially if they do not share the receiver's fate), senders might fear being evaluated negatively by the receiver, or senders might wish to avoid adopting a mood congruent with the tone of the tidings they bear. The second group of explanations proposes situations where senders are reluctant to share bad news out of a concern for the *receiver*. For example, senders may wish to avoid upsetting the receiver, or they may believe receivers do not wish to hear bad news (as opposed to good news). Most medical bad news research seems grounded within these concern-for-receiver explanations. The third category of explanations concerns the *social norms* surrounding bad news transmission. For example, MUM effects might emerge because senders prefer to adhere to some norm that forbids sharing bad news, or because the norms regarding bad news delivery are themselves ambiguous.

Subsequent experimentation has revealed varying support for the hypotheses grouped under each class of concerns, and studies continue to explore the tenability of several of these explanations. The latest research appears to focus on those explanations having to do with concerns about self and concerns about the other. For example, Bond and Anderson (1987) found that the MUM effect they observed was driven less by actual *private* discomfort on the part of the sender and instead reflected a *public* display of contrition. This research suggests that the bulk of the sender's concern was self-directed. Dibble (2008) hypothesized that having to share bad news with a close friend (as opposed to a stranger) might trigger a situation in which concerns for the other outweigh self-concerns. The data were more consistent with Bond and Anderson's (1987) findings regarding self-directed concerns.

The latest social scientific research on bad news delivery appears to be following two lines. First, the nature of the temporal delay before senders begin the onset of their bad news messages is being explored (e.g., Dibble & Levine, 2010; Dibble et al., 2011). A series of experiments is under way to determine whether the delay is but an incidental artifact of having to plan a negative message or if instead the delay might contain communicative value. If this delay serves as a communication stimulus (effected consciously or otherwise), it might be a nonverbal cue meant for the receiver. In this way, the delay might function as a sort of "warning shot," foreshadowing the valence of the forthcoming news. Determining the nature of this delay holds implications for providers who seek alternate ways to soften the blow of bad news.

The second line of inquiry takes a more global approach. Weenig, Wilke, and ter Mors (2011) are integrating the bad news literature with the literature on rumors in the service of developing a general theory of news sharing. They noted that not *all* bad news is shared with the expected reluctance. In some situations, they posited, people might share bad news even more rapidly than comparable good news. Weenig, Wilke, and ter Mors found the relationship between news valence and reluctance to be moderated by three variables: the extent to which the negative consequences are uncertain, the extent to which the sender shares the receiver's fate, and the closeness of the relationship between the sender and receiver. Contrary to typical MUM findings, they argued that what they call "black rumors" might represent a kind of bad news where the combination of fate uncertainty, fate similarity, and relationship closeness is such that senders might not hesitate to spread the news.

Considering the individual hypotheses already generated to explain the MUM effect (e.g., self-presentation concerns, concern for receiver's feelings), a link to face concerns is plain. Indeed, casting the hesitation to share bad news as a public self-presentation display (Bond & Anderson, 1987; Uysal & Oner-Ozkan, 2007) automatically calls to mind concerns about face. What follows next is a discussion of the need for theory with regard to the bad news delivery process, as well as relevant communication-based approaches that may facilitate an investigation of the face threats associated with delivering bad news.

Candidate Theories to Illuminate Bad News Delivery

The time has come for bad news research to move beyond experimental MUM effect demonstrations toward theoretical development. Fortunately, work has begun in this area. This section discusses three theories that hold potential to inform the bad news delivery process between providers and recipients. As will be seen, none of these theories capture the bad news delivery process in its entirety. Thus, this chapter advocates an eclectic approach that relies on any combination of these (or other) theories based on the portion of the bad news delivery encounter of primary interest. We examine the bad news response model (BNRM), identity implications theory (IIT), and communicative responsibility theory (CRT).

Bad News Response Model

The Bad News Response Model (BNRM) (Sweeny & Shepperd, 2007) emerged to standardize what it means to give bad news successfully, and to assist givers of bad news in guiding recipients toward so-called desired responses. This perspective holds that senders of bad news have as their goal to evoke a desired response in the recipient. According to the BNRM, senders encourage news recipients to respond using watchful waiting (e.g., "wait and see"), active change (e.g., vigorous, engaged information-seeking), acceptance (e.g., revising one's life to cope with the negative consequences), and/or nonresponse (e.g., denial, disbelief, dismissal). Situational factors, including the controllability, likelihood, and severity of the news, are proposed to influence the sender's choice of which response should be the "desired" response.

As useful as the BNRM (Sweeny & Shepperd, 2007) should be, this model is mute on face threat processes that could mediate the relationship between situational factors and the choice of the desired response. The nature of the face threats involved may explain additional variability in good and bad news sharing not accounted for by bad news message dimensions alone. In other words, it may not necessarily be the characteristics inherent to the bad news that bring about the sender's response, but that these characteristics portend certain face threats that, in turn, influence the sender's goals, affective responses, and communicative actions. Moreover, communication literature reveals that, during any given interaction, individuals often pursue multiple goals (O'Keefe, 1988). Thus, there could be salient goals in addition to the one posed by the BNRM. A communication analysis of the anticipated threats to face and the specific goals pursued benefits investigations of the mechanism through which the types of bad news impact the sender's cognitive, affective, and message production experiences.

Further, the BNRM (Sweeny & Shepperd, 2007) appears to conceptualize face threats too coarsely. The BNRM seemingly takes face threats for granted, as an implicit and monolithic background factor associated with delivering bad news. As Wilson, Aleman, and Leatham (1998) noted, however, threats to the receiver's face are not the only salient face concerns in any given interaction. Thus, the BNRM fails to address the more nuanced view of face threats that has emerged from communication research of late. It is this chapter's position that attending to the finer-grained attributes of face threats is important to understanding the bad news delivery process. We next discuss a theory that holds the potential to augment the BNRM by further articulating the nature of face threats associated with delivering bad news.

Identity Implications Theory

Identity Implications Theory (IIT) (Wilson, Aleman, & Leathem, 1998; Wilson & Feng, 2007) emerged as a revision of politeness theory (Brown & Levinson, 1987). Like politeness theory, IIT also assumes that individuals in interaction with others manage two face desires. First, people prefer to be approved of by others (positive face). Second, people desire to remain free from imposition (negative face). Further, IIT assumes that people typically prefer to consider each other's faces in interaction (Goffman, 1967). The aim of IIT is to predict a communicator's recognition of face threats based on the communicator's implicit knowledge of (a) the defining conditions for speech acts (Searle, 1969), and (b) the primary goals for interaction. IIT revises the analysis of politeness theory to account for the possibility that several types of face concerns can be simultaneously salient in a given interaction. Unlike politeness theory, IIT assumes that, depending on the situation, both interactants' positive and negative faces can be concurrently and differentially threatened.

As one might expect, the IIT analysis begins by identifying a specific illocutionary speech act of interest (e.g., requests, refusals, criticisms, promises) (Searle, 1969) and then identifying its relevant face concerns. IIT might be fruitfully extended to the context of bad news delivery for at least two related reasons. First, a seemingly indefinite range of speech acts can be regarded as bad news. Because bad news is largely receiver defined, any of a request, denial, assertion, or promise could be construed as bad news. To illustrate, a dentist *requesting* a patient to schedule a dental examination can signal "bad news" for the patient who anticipates that cavities will be discovered. A provider's *denial* of pain medication will no doubt mean "bad news" for the patient in pain. Thus, applying IIT to a larger communication situation might enhance the theory's explanatory reach. Increased analytical efficiency is a companion benefit because IIT would be applied to a collection of speech acts related through their proclivity to count as bad news, instead of single speech acts that have been dissociated from context. Researchers interested less in zero-order speech acts and more in the higher level and context-bound bad news these speech acts convey may appreciate such versatility in a theory.

Second, many communication situations cannot be easily reduced to a tidy and organized collection of individually identifiable speech acts. Human conversation is messy. Thus, successful application of IIT to the situation of delivering bad news would broaden the theory's scope and demonstrate its utility beyond analyses of isolated speech acts.

When leveraged in the case of bad news delivery, the IIT analytical procedures serve to identify the defining conditions for bad news delivery as well as the primary goals of the provider. Individuals often manage multiple and sometimes conflicting goals when interacting with others (O'Keefe, 1988). With respect to goals, the situation of delivering bad news is interesting because a provider can pursue a variety of goals, each involving an information valence that is negative (at least from the receiver's perspective). Thus, the provider who informs a recipient of the decision against issuing a new prescription for pain medication might pursue the primary goal of compliance with regulations. A physician delivering a cancer diagnosis might be pursuing the primary goal of providing medically necessary information. In both cases, the senders would likely anticipate themselves to be breaking bad news even though their goals were qualitatively different. The negativity of the message and its implied consequences are believed to shade the planning and achievement of the provider's goal(s).

Communicative Responsibility Theory

Communicative Responsibility Theory (CRT) (Aune, Levine, Park, Asada, & Banas, 2005) is a theory of message processing. Essentially, CRT invokes the level of responsibility one perceives for establishing shared meaning to explain the extent to which interlocutors engage in redundancies, conversational implicatures, and inference making during the communication encounter. The provider-recipient bad news encounter is rife with opportunities for implied and indirect communication (e.g., van Vliet et al., 2011). Thus, in the context of delivering bad news there is likely a disproportional distribution of communicative responsibility between the communicators. Consequently, as a provider relays bad news to a recipient, inference making and conversational implicature might be expected to vary in ways specific to that communication situation. Moreover, it is theoretically interesting to document the role of the valence of the news (i.e., its "goodness" or "badness") in the way(s) bad news messages are processed and communicated. The relationship between the bad news context and CRT is therefore one of reciprocal benefit: The bad news delivery context enables a test of CRT, and the application of CRT facilitates a deeper understanding of the communicative mechanisms that underpin the delivery of bad news messages.

Conclusions and Implications

Thus far we have defined bad news, discussed the typical ways bad news delivery has been studied, and presented three theories with the potential to enlighten our understanding of the bad news delivery process. What follows are some practical suggestions for providers based on the research findings to date.

Eggly et al. (2006) summarize nicely several assumptions often associated with breaking bad news in the provider-recipient context. These assumptions are presented here to justify the practical recommendations they inspired. First, as evidenced by the various protocols that abound for bad news sharing, providers should not assume that bad news interactions can be perfectly predicted and, therefore, planned. Recall that bad news is largely receiver defined, and that bad news sharing interactions are intensely variable. For example, Eggly et al. observed that some patients react to information about participating in a clinical trial with relief, despair, or without any visible cues that would suggest to a provider how the recipient is taking the news. Eggly et al. suggested that instead of attempting to systematize bad news interactions, providers equip themselves for any interaction in which information will be shared, no matter how grave or trivial that information may appear. In this sense, providers do not prepare for a "bad news encounter," per se, but a potentially stressful encounter that may or may not reveal itself to be a bad news interaction. Thus, competent providers assume a more macro approach—one that recognizes the potential for any information to be received as "bad" and, thus, calls for behaviors appropriate to that sensitivity.

The Eggly et al. (2006) data point to a second assumption: Provider-recipient bad news interactions tend to focus on only one central piece of information (e.g., the death of a loved one, the Alzheimer disease diagnosis). To the contrary, provider-recipient encounters often involve multiple pieces of important information (e.g., necessity of further testing, treatment options, risks and consequences associated with various courses of action, clinical trials). An initial diagnosis is no doubt critical, but it is only one piece of a universe of important information that recipients must receive. Thus, focusing one's preparation only on some central piece of information can leave the other important pieces of information laid out with less care. It is incumbent on providers to ensure that recipients comprehend these other details. This is consistent with the call of Duggan and Bradshaw (2008) to boost providers' responsiveness to their recipients. In response, Eggly et al. recommended that providers discuss all pieces of information with the same due diligence as the "central" piece. Thus, just as a physician would relay a cancer diagnosis using lay language, speaking in small chunks, and so forth, he or she should practice the same care with any piece of information, hastening to add repetition of critical material, clear transitions between pieces of information, and clear explanations of how the pieces of information are related. This sentiment is underscored by other researchers (e.g., Gillotti, Thompson, and McNeilis, 2002; McNeilis, 2001), whose data suggest that providers consider the amount of time necessary for the bad news encounter. Depending on the situation, providers might wish to deliver the information over multiple appointments. In this way, the recipient's comprehension and understanding can be checked.

Third and finally, extant bad news sharing protocol appears to operate under the mistaken assumption that bad news encounters are dyadic in nature. In contrast, companions and family members often accompany receivers/patients during these interactions. More to the point, Eggly et al. (2006) found that more information seeking and questions originated from the companions than the patients themselves! Providers will no doubt already recognize that recipients are often not alone during bad news sharing episodes (Villagran et al., 2010). Unfortunately, little attention is paid to this issue by the current bad news sharing guidelines. Eggly et al. called for more strategies that equip providers to handle encounters with multiple participants. More specifically, when providers ask about prior knowledge, desire for information, understanding, and the like, they should attempt to do so from every participant in the interaction.

The social scientific research conducted thus far inspires practical recommendations that also attend to the well-being of the provider. Dibble and Levine (2010) found that the sender's cognitive and behavioral responses vary concomitantly with the valence of the news (i.e., its "goodness" or "badness"). Specifically, strongly negative news prompted the most reluctance and longest delays, mid-range valences prompted moderate levels of reluctance and moderate delays, and strongly positive news prompted little to no reluctance and little to no delay. This finding stresses the importance of the provider's accurate appraisal of the negativity of the bad news. To combine this notion with the assumptions already described by Eggly et al. (2006) reveals a practical suggestion. Providers who wish to avoid unnecessary stress and worry should work to remain acutely sensitive to the recipient's judgments of the news. Errors in appraising the negativity of the news could lead to unnecessary worry, reluctance, and/or—much worse—a miscommunication of information. The work of Weenig et al. (2011) also suggests providers compensate for the relative lack of a close relationship between themselves and the recipient by reducing the cost(s) associated with transmitting the bad news. This might be accomplished through training that teaches providers how to cope with emotional and/or angry reactions from the recipient. Such training serves the additional purpose of helping the provider manage his or her face concerns in that he or she brings the news in a way that will be respected by the recipient.

Any of these suggestions can be admittedly difficult to execute given limited time resources. In choosing to tailor these strategies, however, providers must carefully weigh the costs and benefits of such decisions. What initially appears to be a time saver could instead be a missed opportunity to elicit or provide critical information that might have influenced a subsequent course of action. Competent providers must exercise a great deal of flexibility in their approach(es) to disclosing potentially negative information.

Flexibility is perhaps the competent provider's greatest asset. As we have seen, bad news transactions are anything but a one-size-fits-all process. Bad news encounters are as idiosyncratic as the recipients for whom the providers care. Future guidelines would do well to acknowledge the requirement of flexibility and build in strategies for teaching providers how to increase their flexibility (Cegala, 2006; Sparks, Villagran, Parker-Raley, & Cunningham, 2007; Villagran et al., 2010). In so doing, providers will be equipped with a much broader and deeper skillset with which to attend to the sensitive situation of breaking bad news.

Adelsward, V., & Sachs, L. (2003). The messenger's dilemmas: Giving and getting information in genealogical mapping for hereditary cancer. *Health, Risk, & Society, 5*, 125–138. doi:10.1080/1369857031000123911

Adler, D. D., Riba, M. B., & Eggly, S. (2009). Breaking bad news in the breast imaging setting. *Academic Radiology, 16*, 130–135. doi:10.1016/j.acra.2008.08.006

Amason, P., Smith, C., Romanin, S., & Hovath, M. (2012). Physicians' views of interpersonal communication training, the importance of communication in their medical practices and the delivery of bad news. In B. R. Bates & R. Ahmed (Eds.), *Medical communication in clinical contexts* 169–188. Dubuque, IA: Kendall Hunt.

Aune, R. K., Levine, T. R., Park, H. S., Asada, K. J., & Banas, J. A. (2005). Tests of a theory of communicative responsibility. *Journal of Language and Social Psychology, 24*, 358–381. doi:10.1177/0261927X05281425

Back, A. L., Anderson, W. G., Bunch, L., Marr, L. A., Wallace, J. A., Yang, H. B. et al. (2008). Communication about cancer near the end of life. *Cancer, 113*, 1897–1910. doi:10.1002/cncr.23653

Back, A. L., Arnold, R. M., Baile, W. F., Fryer-Edwards, K. A., Alexander, S. C., Barley, G. E. et al. (2007). Efficacy of communication skills training for giving bad news and discussing transitions to palliative care. *Archives of Internal Medicine, 167*, 453–460.

Baile, W. F., Buckman, R., Lenzi, R., Glober, G., Beale, E. A., & Kudelka, A. P. (2000). SPIKES—a six-step protocol for delivering bad news: Application to the patient with cancer. *The Oncologist, 5*, 302–311. doi:10.1634/theoncologist.5-4-302

Bisel, R. S., Kelley, K. M., Ploeger, N. A., & Messersmith, J. (2011). Workers moral mum effect: On facework and unethical behavior in the workplace. *Communication Studies, 62*, 153–170. doi:10.1080/10510974.2010.551314

Bond, C. F. Jr., & Anderson, E. L. (1987). The reluctance to transmit bad news: Private discomfort or public display? *Journal of Experimental Social Psychology, 23*, 176–187.

Brown, P., & Levinson, S. C. (1987). *Politeness: Some universals in language usage.* Cambridge: Cambridge University Press.

Brown, R. F., & Bylund, C. L. (2008). Communication skills training: Describing a new conceptual model. *Academic Medicine, 83*, 37–44.

Bruera, E., Palmer, J. L., Pace, E., Zhang, K., Willey, J., Strasser, F. et al. (2007). A randomized, controlled trial of physician postures when breaking bad news to cancer patients. *Palliative Medicine, 21*, 501–505. doi:10.1177/0269216307081184

Buckman, R. (1984). Breaking bad news: Why is it still so difficult? *British Medical Journal, 288*, 1597–1599.

Cegala, D. J. (2006). Emerging trends and future directions in patient communication skills training. *Health Communication, 20*, 123–129. doi:10.1207/s15327027hc2002_3

Cherney, N. I., & Palliative Care Working Group of the European Society for Medical Oncology. (2010). Factors influencing the attitudes and behaviors of oncologists regarding the truthful disclosure of information to patients with advanced and incurable cancer. *Psycho-Oncology.* Advance online publication. doi:10.1002/pon.1853

Del Vento, A., Bavelas, J., Healing, S., MacLean, G., & Kirk, P. (2009). An experimental investigation of the dilemma of delivering bad news. *Patient Education and Counseling, 77*, 443–449.

Dibble, J. L. (2008). *On the hesitation to share bad news: Three empirical studies* (Doctoral dissertation). Available from ProQuest Dissertations and Theses database, UMI No. 3331893.

Dibble, J. L., & Levine, T. R. (2010). Breaking good and bad news: Direction of the MUM effect and senders' cognitive representations of news valence. *Communication Research, 37*, 703–722. doi:10.1177/0093650209356440

Dibble, J. L., Wisner, A. M., Fujimoto, J., Koo, M., Higashi, A., Mendoza, S. et al. (2011). Reluctance to share bad news: Communication stimulus or byproduct of planning a negative message. *Paper presented at the annual meeting of the Western States Communication Association,* Monterey, CA.

Duggan, A. P., & Bradshaw, Y. S. (2008). Mutual influence processes in physician-patient communication: An interaction adaptation perspective. *Communication Research Reports, 25*, 211–226. doi:10.1080/08824090802237618

Eberhardt-McKee, T., & Ptacek, J. T. (2001). I'm afraid I have something bad to tell you: Breaking bad news from the perspective of the giver. *Journal of Applied Social Psychology, 31*, 246–273.

Eggly, S., Penner, L., Albrecht, T. L., Cline, R. J. W., Foster, F., Naughton, M., et al. (2006). Discussing bad news in the outpatient clinic: Rethinking current communication guidelines. *Journal of Clinical Oncology, 24*, 716–719.

Fallowfield, L., & Jenkins, V. (2004). Communicating sad, bad, and difficult news in medicine. *Lancet, 363*, 312–319.

Fisher, C. D. (1979). Transmission of positive and negative feedback to subordinates: A laboratory investigation. *Journal of Applied Psychology, 64*, 533–540.

Gilbey, P. (2010). Qualitative analysis of parents' experience with receiving the news of the detection of their child's hearing loss. *International Journal of Pediatric Otorhinolaryngology, 74*, 265–270. doi:10.1016/j.ijporl.2009.11.017

Gillotti, C., Thompson, T., & McNeilis, K. (2002). Communicative competence in the delivery of bad news. *Social Science & Medicine, 54*, 1011–1023.

Goffman, E. (1967). *Interaction ritual.* New York: Pantheon Books.

Harrison, M. E., & Walling, A. (2010). What do we know about giving bad news? A review. *Clinical Pediatrics, 49*, 619–626. doi:10.1177/0009922810361380

Lienard, A., Merckaert, I., Libert, Y., Bragard, I., Delvaux, N., Etienne, A.-M. et al. (2010). Is it possible to improve residents breaking bad news skills? A randomized study assessing the efficacy of a communication skills training program. *British Journal of Cancer, 103*, 171–177. doi:10.1038/sj.bjc.6605749

McAllister, M., Dunn, G., & Todd, C. (2010). Empowerment: Qualitative underpinning of a new clinical genetics-specific patient-reported outcome. *European Journal of Human Genetics, 19*, 125–130. doi:10.1038/ejhg.2010.160

McAllister, M., Payne, K., Nicholls, S., MacLeod, R., Donnai, D., & Davies, L. M. (2007). Improving service evaluation in clinical genetics: Identifying effects of genetic diseases on individuals and families. *Journal of Genetic Counseling, 16*, 71–83. doi:10.1007/s10897-006-9046-3

McNeilis, K. S. (2001). Analyzing communication competence in medical consultations. *Health Communication, 13*, 5–18.

Merker, B. M., Hanson, W. E., & Poston, J. M. (2010). National survey of psychologists' training and practice in breaking bad news: A mixed methods study of the MUM effect. *Journal of Clinical Psychology in Medical Settings, 17*, 211–219. doi:10.1007/s10880-010-9197-0

O'Keefe, B. J. (1988). The logic of message design: Individual differences in reasoning about communication. *Communication Monographs, 55*, 80–104.

Paterson, N. E., & Pond, D. (2009). Early diagnosis of dementia and diagnostic disclosure in primary care in Australia: A qualitative study into the barriers and enablers. *Alzheimer's & Dementia, 5*(5), e15.

Ptacek, J. T., & Eberhardt, T. L. (1996). Breaking bad news: A review of the literature. *JAMA, 276*, 496–502.

Ptacek, J. T., Ptacek, J. J., & Ellison, N. M. (2001). 'I'm sorry to tell you …' Physician's reports of breaking bad news. *Journal of Behavioral Medicine, 24*, 205–217.

Rider, E. A., Volkan, K., & Hafler, J. P. (2008). Pediatric residents' perceptions of communication competencies: Implications for teaching. *Medical Teacher, 30*, e208–e217. doi:10.1080/01421590802208842

Rosen, S., & Tesser, A. (1972). Fear of negative evaluation and the reluctance to transmit bad news. *Journal of Communication, 22*, 124–141.

Schildmann, J., Kupfer, S., Burchardi, N., & Vollmann, J. (2011). Teaching and evaluating breaking bad news: A pre-post evaluation study of a teaching intervention for medical students and a comparative analysis of different measurement instruments and raters. *Patient Education and Counseling.* Advance online publication. doi:10.1016/j.pec.2011.04.022

Searle, J. R. (1969). *Speech acts: An essay in the philosophy of language.* Cambridge: Cambridge University Press.

Sparks, L., Villagran, M. M., Parker-Raley, J., & Cunningham, C. B. (2007). A patient-centered approach to breaking bad news: Communication guidelines for healthcare providers. *Journal of Applied Communication Research, 35*, 177–196. doi:10.1080/00909880701262997

Spiegel, W., Zidek, T., Maier, M., Vutuc, C., Isak, K., Karlic, H. et al. (2009). Breaking bad news to cancer patients: Survey and analysis. *Psycho-Oncology, 18*, 179–186. doi:10.1002/pon.1383

Supiot, S., & Bonnaud-Antignac, A. (2008). Using simulated interviews to teach junior medical students to disclose the diagnosis of cancer. *Journal of Cancer Education, 23*, 102–107. doi:10.1080/08858190701849437

Sussman, S. W., & Sproull, L. (1999). Straight talk: Delivering bad news through electronic communication. *Information Systems Research, 10*, 150–166.

Sweeny, K., & Shepperd, J. A. (2007). Being the best bearer of bad tidings. *Review of General Psychology, 11*, 235–257.

Tesser, A., & Rosen, S. (1975). The reluctance to transmit bad news. In L. Berkowitz (Ed.), *Advances in experimental social psychology* (Vol. 8, pp. 193–232). New York: Academic Press.

Tesser, A., Rosen, S., & Tesser, M. (1971). On the reluctance to communicate undesirable messages (the MUM effect): A field study. *Psychological Reports, 29*, 651–654.

Uysal, A., & Oner-Ozkan, B. (2007). A self-presentational approach to transmission of good and bad news. *Social Behavior and Personality, 35*, 63–78.

Vandekieft, G. K. (2001). Breaking bad news. *American Family Physician, 64*, 1975–1978.

van Vliet, L., Francke, A., Tomson, S., Plum, N., van der Wall, E., & Bensing, J. (2011). When cure is no option: How explicit and hopeful can information be given? A qualitative study in breast cancer. *Patient Education and Counseling.* Advance online publication. doi:10.1016/j.pec.2011.03.021

Villagran, M., Goldsmith, J., Wittenberg-Lyles, E., & Baldwin, P. (2010). Creating COMFORT: A communication-based model for breaking bad news. *Communication Education, 59,* 220–234. doi:10.1080/03634521003624031

Wagoner, R., & Waldron, V. R. (1999). How supervisors convey routine bad news: Facework at UPS. *Southern Communication Journal, 64,* 193–210.

Walling, A., Lorenz, K. A., Dy, S. M., Naeim, A., Sanati, H., Asch, S. M. et al. (2008). Evidence-based recommendations for information and care planning in cancer care. *Journal of Clinical Oncology, 26,* 3896–3902. doi:10.1200/JCO.2007.15.9509

Weenig, M. W. H., Wilke, H. A. M., & ter Mors, E. (2011). Personal outcomes and moral responsibility as motives for news transmission: The impact of fate similarity, fate uncertainty, and relationship closeness. *Communication Research.* Advance online publication. doi:10.1177/009365021140219

Whitney, S. N., McCullough, L. B., Fruge, E., McGuire, A. L., & Volk, R. J. (2008). Beyond breaking bad news: The roles of hope and hopefulness. *Cancer, 113,* 442–445. doi:10.1002/cncr.23588

Wilson, S. R., Aleman, C. G., & Leatham, G. B. (1998). Identity implications of influence goals: A revised analysis of face-threatening acts and application to seeking compliance with same-sex friends. *Human Communication Research, 25,* 64–96.

Wilson, S. R., & Feng, H. (2007). Interaction goals and message production: Conceptual and methodological developments. In D. Roskos-Ewoldsen & J. Monahan (Eds.), *Communication and social cognition* (pp. 71–95). Mahwah, NJ: Lawrence Erlbaum Associates.

Yariv, E. (2006). 'Mum effect': Principals' reluctance to submit negative feedback. Journal of Managerial *Psychology, 21,* 533–546.

Yun, Y. H., Kwon, Y. C., Lee, M. K., Lee, W. J., Jung, K. H., Do, Y. R. et al. (2010). Experiences and attitudes of patients with terminal cancer and their family caregivers toward the disclosure of terminal illness. *Journal of Clinical Oncology, 28,* 1950–1957. doi:10.1200/JCO.2009.22.9658

Chapter 6

Side Effects Talk in General Practice Consultations

Kevin Dew, Maria Stubbe, Anthony Dowell, and Lindsay Macdonald

Introduction

Adverse drug reactions (ADRs), or side effects to prescribed medications, are a frequent reason for doctor-patient contact (Miller, Britt, Valenti, & Knox, 2006) and fatal ADRs may be as high as the fourth leading cause of death (Lazarou, Pomeranz, & Corey, 1998). They are regarded as one of the most costly and common sources of preventable harm (Pham et al., 2012). ADRs therefore constitute an important public health problem in terms of mortality, morbidity, and cost (Lopez-Gonzalez, Herdeiro, & Figueiras, 2009). It is also known that patients evaluate medications in part on the basis of perceived adverse reactions and that this may lead to noncompliance or the institution of their own strategies to reduce side effects (Pound et al., 2005). This possible response by patients can have a number of consequences. It may lead to the nonreporting of adverse drug reactions, but patients may also alter the way they use medication due to their perception of its effects. There are major consequences for health in this regard. Yet little research has looked at doctor-patient interactions specifically in relation to side effects talk.

Reporting, monitoring, and responding to ADRs is a public health priority (Gibbons et al., 2010). However, research in this field suggests that significant underreporting of ADRs occurs. One systematic review suggests underreporting rates for ADRs could be as high as 94 percent (Hazell & Shakir, 2006). As a result of increasing concern over the detection of adverse drug events pharmacovigilance systems have become more common in nation-states since the 1990s (Lopez-Gonzalez, Herdeiro, & Figueiras, 2009). The World Health Organization (WHO) Uppsala Monitoring Centre, which collects and assesses information from the pharmacovigilance systems of WHO member countries, contains over 3 million reports of suspected ADRs (WHO, 2006).

The way in which clinical trials are conducted suggests that a great deal more attention should be paid to the issue of ADRs. Petryna's (2007) extensive research on clinical trials uncovered concerns about the nature of some trials. There were claims by scientific officers who oversee the conduct of clinical trials for contract research organizations that companies would select specific populations to improve the chances of identifying drug benefits and avoid the identification of adverse reactions (Petryna, 2007). Trial recruitment strategies could be employed using subject inclusion criteria to "engineer out" the possibility of detecting ADRs (Petryna, 2007, p. 27). Petryna (2007) argues that companies conducting clinical trials of medications operate within a "paradigm of expected failure" (p. 32). That is, there is limited focus on the prevention of problems with medications before they go to market, particularly in identifying any long-term issues. As such, failure in terms of the safety of medications is expected. Petryna argues that we lack the means to evaluate the safety of drugs once they are on the market. From this perspective ADRs are something to be expected, yet, as already noted, they are extensively underreported. Hence, processes central to the reporting of ADRs are an important health concern worthy of investigation. An important element in the reporting process is the assessment of ADRs at the level of primary care, as general practitioners are primarily responsible for the prescribing of medications and responding to patients' reported reactions to medications.

In this chapter an overview is provided of the little research that has been undertaken on communication issues related to ADRs in the consultation. This is followed by an outline of research on primary care consultations in which the topic of ADRs was explored and a summary of the findings from this research. The chapter concludes by detailing the interactional difficulties that the topic of ADRs may give rise to in primary care consultations, and suggests some ways for health professionals to respond to these difficulties.

Literature Review

A number of studies have attempted to identify why health professionals underreport ADRs. In a systematic review of questionnaire-based research with health professionals, Lopez-Gonzalez and colleagues (2009) found that health professionals were not always aware of the kinds of reactions that need reporting, and they were concerned about reporting only suspected ADRs, with some holding the view that only safe drugs are released to the market. Similar factors were identified in research undertaken in Sweden with general practitioners and hospital physicians. Reasons for reluctance to report ADRs included whether the reaction was considered well-known or not, the severity of the reaction, hesitation to report only on suspicion, lack of knowledge of existing rules, giving priority to other matters, and lack of time (Backstrom, Mjorndal, Dahlqvist, & Nordkvist-Olsson, 2000).

Medawar and colleagues (2002) examined emails from users of a particular antidepressant, paroxetine, that were sent in response to a BBC-TV program on the medication. They note that users reported that doctors either denied their reports of symptoms (in this case from withdrawal of the medication) or attributed their symptoms to some other cause (Medawar, Herxheimer, Bell, & Jofre, 2002, p. 168).

Another area of research is the exploration of side effects talk in the consultation using qualitative data. In one such study, a qualitative interview-based study of patients' decisions in relation to antihypertensive drugs, Benson and Britten (2002) discuss patients' reservations about medicines, which include adverse perceptions due to previous use of prescribed drugs. In another general study on misunderstandings in prescribing decisions, which included analysis of interactions between doctors and patients, Britten and colleagues (Britten, Stevenson, Barry, Barber, & Bradley, 2000) note cases where the patient and the doctor disagreed about the causes of side effects. They specifically note one consultation where the doctor played down an association between a treatment and possible side effects, but the patient appeared to misunderstand and assumed the doctor agreed with the patient's view that the two were connected. Another interview-based study (Britten, Stevenson, Gafaranga, Barry, & Bradley, 2004) found that most patients attending general practice consultations expressed an aversion to medications. Those interviewed also had consultations with their GP recorded, and it was found that there were no cases where there was a "genuine discussion" of the patients' views, and that patients tended to express their aversion to medicines in the consultation in a muted fashion (Britten et al., 2004). In a Swedish study of 51 doctor-patient consultations about antihypertensive medication, 21 patients talked in the consultation about the effects of medication, mainly unwanted reactions or side-effects (Kjellgren, Svensson, Ahlner, & Saljo, 1998). In interviews, 20 out of 33 patients reported side-effects from their current antihypertensive medication (Kjellgren et al., 1998). However, the authors note that side effects as a term was seldom used by either patients or physicians.

Seale and colleagues (2007) note that, in consultations related to antipsychotic medication, patient concerns are routinely underestimated. When presented with such concerns by patients, the psychiatrist would commonly offer no response, change the subject, or disagree with the patient's interpretation (Seale, Chaplin, Lelliot, & Quirk, 2007). Such avoidance of discussions of side effects may be due to the need of both participants in the consultation to save face and avoid potentially awkward or difficult exchanges; such discussions may be face-threatening acts for either party (Goffman, 2006), or they may be designed to resist patient noncompliance to medication regimes considered by the psychiatrist to be in the best interests of the patient.

Looking at the detail of interactions between patients and doctors can give us clues as to why patients do not tell doctors about their resistance to medication (Pound et al., 2005), and to why doctors might not attend to such talk when it is presented. Research using interactional data has tended to focus on the content of interactions rather than how the interactions unfolded (Britten et al., 2000; Kjellgren et al., 1998), although Britten and colleagues' (2004) study of the expression of aversion to medications did look at the unfolding of interactions. This chapter complements that work by focusing on the ways in which GPs and patients talk about side effects in the consultation, and it also considers the consequences of these interactions for the doctor-patient relationship, use of prescribed medicines, and patient safety. It argues that the outcomes can in part be understood as a consequence of the interactional dilemmas that doctors and patients face in relation to the medical consultation (Gill & Maynard, 2006).

Methods

The data analyzed here were collected as part of two related projects, one exploring clinical decision making and the other tracking the interactions of individual patients with health professionals as they move through the primary and secondary care systems in New Zealand. The data set analyzed here comprises video recordings of 105 consultations involving 104 patients and nine GPs. The GPs were recruited from a mix of central city and suburban practices. GPs were sampled on a purposive basis, with attempts made to obtain a range of practice types and socioeconomic populations. Once a GP had agreed to participate, patients attending the clinic session would be approached if they fulfilled the criteria. (Those under 18 and acute cases were excluded.) The transcription conventions used in this chapter are a simplified version of those developed by Gail Jefferson (ten Have, 1999) and are appended.

Findings

There were 88 sequences of talk where side effects issues were raised and they occurred in 54 of 105 consultations in the data set (i.e., some consultations had more than one sequence of talk). A broad definition of side effects was used to include any association of a medication with an unanticipated consequence; this definition covered talk of allergic reactions and unwanted symptoms. Table 6.1 outlines the main categories of side effects talk identified. The most common category, with 39 instances, was GP-initiated talk where GPs mention possible side effects when prescribing a new or adjusted medication. This was not the only form of GP talk—there were also five instances where GPs associated a patient's symptoms with side effects even though the patient did not, and two where the GP inquired about side effects of a current medication and the patient or the GP represented these side effects in a positive light, for example, having less energy as a side effect to sleeping pills that was seen as a good thing for an overactive patient. There were 31 instances where patients associated adverse symptoms with a prescribed medication, and other categories with smaller numbers that included inquiries being made about side effects and patient resistance to medication as a result of generic concerns about side effects.

Table 6.1

Instances	Category
39	GP initiated talk
31	Patient association
5	GP association only
2	Positive side effects talk
2	Patient resistance to medication
4	Patient inquiry (possible side effects—new medication)
2	Patient concern (possible side effects—current medication)
2	Patient unsolicited comment on being side effect free
1	Side effect elicited during history taking

Some of the categories noted in Table 6.1 could potentially be merged if other information were available, for example, a patient's unsolicited comments on being side effect free are likely to relate to an earlier consultation where new medication was being tried.

The most common occurrences of side effects talk were when GPs discussed possible future side effects from a new or adjusted medication (39 instances) and where the patient suggested an association between a medication and a side effect (31 instances). The focus in the rest of this chapter is on these two aspects of side effects talk in the consultation.

GP-Initiated Side Effects Talk

GP-initiated side effects talk in relation to a new or changing prescription ranged from minimum talk of a possible effect to more extensive discussions. However, a lack of specificity about possible side effects was common in the data set, even when the term itself was mentioned or alluded to. Extracts 1, 2, and 3 exhibit this lack of specificity.

In this first extract the patient is taking a drug to treat gout:

Extract 1:

GP02-03

```
1 GP: yeah I- if that (2) turned out for any reason not to
2    be (.) suiting you in terms [of] =
3 PT: [mm]
4 GP: =prevention either not effective enough or giving you
5      side effects then er um there are other things that
6      ( )we can try as well
```

In lines 1–2 of this extract we see a commonly used euphemism for an adverse outcome of the medication—"not to be suiting you"—but in this instance the GP outlines more explicitly in what ways a medication might not suit, namely by either failing to work or causing side effects. The GP does not, however, elaborate on what the likely side effects are, so that the patient may not clearly understand what symptoms could be associated with the medication (although it is possible that side effects symptoms were covered in earlier consultations). We see a similar scenario in the following extract where the GP is increasing the dose of the patient's blood pressure medication.

Extract 2:

GP05-02

```
1 GP: now I (.) would like to see you next (.) in around six
2      weeks time [because I've]
3 PT: [oh I see ]
4 GP: changed the medication [a bit ] (2) so it's this one
5 PT: [yeah yeah]
6 GP: enalapril (.) it's gone to twenty (.) it was ten [and now]
7 PT: [mm hm ]
8 GP: it's twenty ((inhales))
  ((lines omitted))
9 GP: but I'd just like to see you sort of half way in between
10 [to check that this ] is suiting you all right
11 PT:[yeah yeah yeah yeah yeah yeah]
12 PT: yeah okay
13 GP: okay
```

In this extract the GP is concerned to "check that this is suiting you" (line 10), which suggests a concern for possible side effects—but again this is implied and no specific side effects are mentioned. The phrase "suiting you" in extracts 1 and 2 also contains an implicit presupposition that side effects are unlikely, and thus arguably sounds more benign than the term "side effects." We can consider what reasons there might be for the lexical choice and the lack of specificity in these examples; one possibility is that the GP is avoiding "priming" the patient to look for certain side effects. GPs may be concerned that to do so would encourage a negative placebo or nocebo effect—the untoward effects of an inert treatment. If this is the case, then GPs face a dilemma when raising the issue of side effects: To talk candidly about side effects informs the patient and enhances a genuine process of shared decision making, but it also increases the risk of the prescribed medication having a negative effect on the patient. Another possible reason is that, as part of their professional working life, it is important for GPs to maintain a particular perspective on medications so that they do not have to continually question their value each time they prescribe, as to do so brings into question the main therapeutic focus of their work.

Prescribing antibiotics was one context where the issue of side effects was common. Extract 3 provides an example of this where the patient has an infected foot.

Extract 3:

GP04-03

```
1 PT: I think that's about the only reason I come to the doctor
2    is (.) infections or (.)broken bones or something
3 GP: you did- did you have any problems with the antibiotic we
4    put you on [in ]march=
5 PT: [nah]
6 PT: =nah
7 GP: same one again
8 PT: yep that's what I figured
```

The simple inquiry (line 3) "did you have any problems with" appears to be mutually understood as referring to unwanted side effects, and possibly effectiveness, but again this is implied rather than overtly stated. Other statements of this nature from elsewhere in the data set include "and that works fine for you" (GP04-04) and "you're not allergic to any antibiotics I should know about are you" (GP06-03).

Similarly, general inquiries about allergies were sometimes made, as in the following consultation where an older man is having a review of all his medications. The wide-ranging nature of the doctor's inquiry here is highlighted by the patient's humorous response (lines 5 and 7) and the GP's ironic retort.

Extract 4:

GP06-06

```
1 GP: just out of interest there's nothing that you can't take
2  you're very good (.) so (.) I - nothing that I've got
3  you down [for] that you're allergic to
4 PT: [mm ]
5 PT: redheads (.) used to be
6 GP: what
7 PT: redheads I [used to be]
8 GP: [redheads ] oh no I won't prescribe redheads
```

Extracts 5, 6, and 7 all provide examples where side effects are more explicitly stated. Extract 5 takes place nearly 13 minutes into a consultation, when the patient requests a repeat prescription for a blood pressure medication.

Extract 5:

GP08-06

```
1 PT: could I get um a repeat for the spironolactone while [you]
2 GP: [yes]
3 PT: are there (.)
4 GP: and (.) how is everything going on that (.) are you still
5  on one hundred once a day
6 PT: mmhm
7 GP: you are quite happy with it
8 PT: yep its fine
9 GP: (.) no side effects at all
10 PT: eerrh what side effects are you expecting ha ha I haven't
11 noticed anything ha ha
12 GP: but you don't get any major diuretic side effects [()]
13 PT: [no] no
```

After the patient's initial denial of any problems (line 8), the doctor probes further with "no side effects at all," at which point the patient contests the doctor's inference that side effects might have been expected by explicitly drawing attention to her lack of specificity (line 10) and continuing to deny the occurrence of symptoms, thereby prompting the GP to respond with more detail. The brief half-laughs the patient interpolates into this utterance indicate that this is perceived as a "delicate activity" (Haakana, 2001, 2002).

The following example illustrates another typical situation where specific side effects are often mentioned. Extract 6 occurs towards the end of a consultation in which the GP prescribed antibiotics.

Extract 6:

GP02-05

```
1 GP: there shouldn't be a problem for the antibiotics but
2      occasionally they cause sort of slightly loose bowel
3      motions so er take it with food.
```

Here the GP's caution about possible side effects is minimized in that "sort of slightly" loose motions are presented as an "occasional" effect, and it is implied that the side effects can be prevented or tempered by the precaution of taking them with food. In extract 7 we see a situation where the GP is more obviously concerned about potential harm from the medication (and extract 12 discussed later in this section illustrates a more explicit elaboration on harm concerns). This example again hints at the medical dilemma GPs face when they are prescribing a medication for the patient's benefit but have to warn of potential harm or discomfort. To overstress the warning may put patients off taking the medication and, from the GP's viewpoint, may exaggerate the likelihood of harm. The medical dilemma leads to an interactional tension between the need to clearly convey information about a potential problem and the need to avoid creating undue concern for the patient.

```
Extract 7:

GP02-10

1  GP: yeah well that's not ah not a good scenario ((inhales))
2      well (.) there are some tablets which will improve it
3      but they- they do have some side effects which may
4      trouble you a wee bit the worst one is that it causes
5      a dry mouth um
6  PT: mm
7  GP: ah and so what I'll do is start you off on a very small
8      dose of it (.) ah so that that (.) doesn't cause you too
9      much trouble and then we'll (.) sort of increase it (.)
10     um if ah um (.) if it suits you and if it looks like
11     it's going to have some ah some benefit ((inhales))
12     so we'd probably give it a try on the very lowest dose
13     for (.)perhaps a month and then maybe (.) increase it
14     slightly after that
```

In this instance the GP is more cautious in his presentation, presenting the potential side effects as something to be concerned about, while at the same, time mitigating this concern considerably with his statement, "they do have some side effects which may trouble you a wee bit." Use of the indefinite determiner "some," the modal auxiliary "may," and the minimizer "a wee bit" all function to downgrade the potential scale and seriousness of the side effects, while the term "trouble" suggests something that is not a condition but more of an irritant. Moreover the doctor is suggesting a small dose to begin with which will at worst cause some discomfort but not "too much trouble." In this way the GP is delicately negotiating the issue of prescribing a drug that will hopefully do some good but also warning the patient that it may not, and that it might have some side effects.

In the following example, the GP places the patient on a new medication. In this extract the GP strongly suggests that this drug is one that few people have to worry about as "most people tolerate this really well," therefore, side effects are unlikely. In what could be seen as a compromise position, the GP draws the patient's attention to the insert in the packet listing potential side effects, which would then make the description of side effects explicit at the level agreed between the manufacturer and regulatory authority for patient information.

> **Extract 8:**
>
> **GP08-21**
>
> ```
> 1 GP: and I am going to put you on a medication called
> 2  Omeprazole or Losec which     you take one a day
> 3 PT: yeah
> 4 GP: and (.) most people (.) tolerate this really well and
> 5  don't have any side effects
> 6 PT: yep
> 7 GP: there will be a list of side effects inside the packet so
> 8 PT: yep
> 9 GP: have a look at them but most people are absolutely fine on
> 10  this
> 11 PT: yes
> ```

The extracts presented so far illustrate a number of strategies that GPs use to deal with the medical and interactional dilemmas inherent in side effects talk. GPs can be nonspecific in their reference to side effects, and where specific side effects are mentioned, they can mitigate, downplay or suggest preventative action, or they can refer to other information, such as the packet inserts, so as to avoid mentioning any specific side effect.

The following excerpt illustrates yet another strategy: ignoring the issues raised by a patient. Here the GP initiates talk about side effects but then does not explicitly respond to the issues raised by the patient at all.

```
Extract 9:

GP05-08

1  GP: and you- do you feel you're having any troubles with
2     medications
3  PT: (2) no I mean I still have the cold feet but (.) it's not
4     bad [um] (2) and=
5  GP: [mm]
6  PT: =sometimes (.) er (.) I get that real er sort of I don't
7     know (3) I was (.) I don't know whether it's to do with
8     medication or the blood pressure but (.) for a while I'm-
9     I've come right again now but it was like in the afternoon
10    having that (.) [absolute] weariness
11 GP: [mm ]
12 GP: mm
13 PT: um but [that-] this last (oh I suppose I've wound up a
14 GP: [mm ]
15 PT: bit) but this last week things [haven't] been so bad (.)
16 GP: [mm ]
17 PT: but apart from that nothing really
```

Although the GP has made an inquiry about adverse drug reactions or "troubles" (line1), when troubles are then mentioned by the patient (lines 3–10), the GP does not attend to them explicitly: The patient's troubles apparently do not align with the troubles the GP was looking for. The patient's answer to the GP's inquiry comes after a two-second interval suggesting upcoming resistance. She opens with "no," the preferred response (Heritage, 1989), but immediately qualifies this with a contrast statement, "I mean I still have the cold feet," and an extended description of other symptoms, which the patient suggests may be linked to her medication. The patient presents the troubles in a vague and hesitant way. Her references to "still" having "the cold feet" (line 3) and "I've come right again now" (line 9) position her symptoms as not newsworthy, and her subsequent qualifications–"but (.) it's not bad" (line 4), "I don't know whether it's to do with the medication" (lines 7–8), and "but this last week things haven't been so bad" (line 15)—further downplay their significance. The GP listens, but provides only minimal response tokens throughout this presentation, and then turns to the paperwork before handing the patient forms for renewed scripts and terminating the consultation. The patient's ambiguous presentation of possible side effects does not attain uptake from the GP.

From the above examples it can be seen that GP-initiated discussions of side effects in our data tended to downgrade or minimize side effects issues. However, the presentation could sometimes be more forceful, as in the following example.

Extract 10:

GP06-04

```
1 GP: well what I could do I can give you some old fashioned ear
2     drops that dissolve wax and you could try that for about
3     three or four days
4 PT: mm
5 GP: I warn you though it might make you a bit deaf you put it
6     in first thing in the morning [(.)] and last thing at
7 PT: [mm ]
8 GP: night and you might want to do one ear at a time you know
9     [one ear for three or four days and then the other ear]=
10 PT: [yeah yeah mm ]
11 GP: =for three or four days
```

In line 5 the GP uses the performative utterance "I warn you though" as an emphatic strategy (Searle, 1976) to explicitly caution the patient about a possible side effect of the proposed ear drops—but even in this case the warning of deafness is downgraded with the modal "might" and qualifier "a bit," and the GP offers a strategy to minimize its impact: "do one ear at a time." The strong warning here is perhaps more allowable because the deafness is a temporary phenomenon, although this is not explicitly stated.

These examples suggest that GPs may be more likely to make concerns about side effects explicit in particular situations—for instance when they are of a transient nature—and inquiries can also readily be made about past side effects when deciding on what medication to prescribe. But in all instances where discussion of possible future side effects is initiated by the GP we see the use of mitigators to downgrade the concerns.

Only rarely in the dataset do GPs use the issue of side effects as a reason not to prescribe, as in the following example, where an older man is having his complex set of medications reviewed.

Extract 12 is part of the most extensive discussion of side effects in the data set. Prior to this sequence, there has already been discussion initiated by the GP about the need for caution with pain killers for this particular patient who is on a number of other medications. The specific issue relates to a painful shoulder. This long sequence of side effects talk is most probably a result of the complex medication regime that the patient is on where there are multiple opportunities for adverse interactions among medications.

Extract 12

GP07-06

```
1  GP: your choices for pain killers are (.) you should certainly
2   be taking panadols (.) two four times a day (.) because
3   it's (.) it's safe and it (.) will work (.) for at least
4   part of the pain (.)
5  PT: m[hm]
6  GP: [um] have you got plenty of panadols at home
7  PT: no no I haven't
8  GP: right we'll give you a prescription for some cos it's
9   cheaper if you're using a lot to get it on prescription um
10  (.) the next- you ne- other (.) two other possibilities
11  are codeine which is in the tramadol family but doesn't
12  cost (.) the same amount that tramadol [does ] (.)
13 PT: [((laughs)) hm]
14 GP: bungs you up a bit (.) um but um (.)otherwise it's a- it's
15  a good pain killer [((inhales))] (.) voltaren (.) um (.)
16 PT. [okay ]
17 GP: tut I can give you um a- a- it's kind of a member of that
18  family that's not quite as hard on the stomach the trouble
19  is with the (.) with the warfarin (.) if you rough up
20  [your] stomach with er an anti inflammatory and it (.) for
21 PT: [yeah]
22 GP: example if you get a stomach ulcer (.) you'll bleed and
23  bleed and bleed and bleed and and it's a bit of a disaster
24  so have to be (.) pretty careful with (.) with voltaren
25  (.) cos all the (.) kind of list of other pills (.)
26  [um so ] we can either we can either (.) go (.) er
27 PT: [yeah it's ( )]
28 GP: in my- and my feeling is we should probably try and go
29  safely with the one we- that we know is not going to cause
30  any bleeding problems and then if that one doesn't work we
31  can give you the lowest possible dose (.) anti
32  inflammatory that will work I don't mean that you should
33  (.) have horrible pain all the time but we'd try and get a
34  pain killer that (.) kills your pain but (.) doesn't
35 PT: mm hm
36 GP: interact with all the rest of the medicines ((inhales))
37  what do you think
38 PT: (.) ((exhales)) well god (.) I'll try- try anything
39  [to get] (.) er get rid of this
40 GP: [mm ]
```

In this example the doctor outlines a number of choices of painkillers the patient could potentially use and that are commonly prescribed. The Voltaren is potentially dangerous since the patient is on the anticoagulant Warfarin. The GP is explicitly outlining safety concerns in relation to pain relief that works: "panadol … because it's (.) it's safe and it (.) will work" (lines 2–3), "we should probably try and go safely with the one we—that we know is not going to cause any bleeding problems" (lines 28–30). There is also a degree of minimization and downgrading—"codeine … bungs you up a bit" (line 14), bleeding due to Voltaren may be "a bit of a disaster" (lines 22–23), another anti-inflammatory may be "not quite as hard on your stomach" (line 18). We also see extensive upgrading or boosting of both the possible risks and the doctor's preferred course of action realized by a clustering of linguistic and pragmatic devices. There is an explicit imperative—"you should certainly be taking panadols" (lines 1–2); a number of other unqualified assertions—"it's safe" and "it will work" (line 3), "it's a good pain killer" (lines 14–15), dramatic word choice—"disaster" (line 23), "rough up your stomach" (lines 19–20), "horrible pain all the time" (line 33), and linguistic devices like multiple repetition—"you'll bleed and bleed and bleed and bleed" (lines 22–23), which individually and collectively creates an emphatic effect. The patient's reaction when the doctor asks, "what do you think" in line 37 suggests he is overwhelmed. He exhales and exclaims, "well god" before going on to say he will try anything to get rid of the pain. This example supports our earlier point about why doctors might often avoid such explicit talk about side effects, saying it explicitly may overwhelm the patient with too much information.

The final example illustrates a situation where the GP is considering prescribed medications as a reason for the patient's symptoms of swelling in the legs, and in this instance the patient provides a counterrationale to the GP's suspicions about the medication. The GP asks the patient what medications she is on, and the patient names a number of medications immediately before the following:

Extract 13:

TSGP08-10

```
1 PT: and I mean I'm stabilised on all those medications
2 GP: yeah
3 PT: for yonks
4 GP: yeah
5 PT: nothing Selena just introduced the bendrofluazide
6 GP: yeah
7  ((GP then establishes more detail - lines omitted))
8 GP: I'm just going to quickly
9 PT: yeah
10GP: look up and see if any of these that's a common side
11 effect
12PT: ohhh okay but surely the fact that I've been on all of
13PT: [them this time]
14GP: [well not ] necessarily you would think
15PT: yeah
16GP: Lorna that you would [( )and ] usually side effects to
17PT: [yeah ]
18PT: do kick in immediately yeah
19GP: occur but not always and you can get things
20PT: yeah
21GP: and we don't really understand why
22PT: its just that [pain ]
23GP: [certainly] the um (.) the nardil can which
24 is a common side effect of [that]
25PT: [yeah] but you see I've been on
26 nardil
27GP: yeah
28PT: for (.) years
```

The patient here invokes a time dimension to dispute the association of her regular medications with unwanted symptoms (lines 12–13). This is countered by the GP stating that side effects do not always occur immediately, and "we don't really understand why" (lines 14–21), and that the information he has just looked up (line10) suggests that pain is a common side effect of Nardil (lines 23–24). The patient then re-invokes the time dimension, "yeah but you see I've been on Nardil for years" (lines 25–26) to cast doubt on the GP's explanation. This is the only instance of such a qualified statement about the state of medical knowledge in relation to side effects talk in this data set (although there are other instances that relate to diagnosis).

The data presented so far demonstrate a common pattern of GPs downplaying or mitigating the issue of side effects when it is the GP who initiates the side effects talk, although in particular circumstances, as in Extract 13, we see some variation from the norm. The following section examines what occurs when the patient raises the topic of side effects in the consultation.

Patient Associations of Side Effects and Symptoms

This section focuses on side effects talk initiated by patients in situations where they associate signs and symptoms with a doctor-prescribed medication. Table 6.2 summarizes the GP responses in the 31 instances where there was a patient association of side effects with symptoms. Patients in this data set typically made such associations indirectly and/or in a highly mitigated fashion. In 13 cases the GP provided an acknowledgment (positive in 12 cases, neutral in one), while in the remaining 18 cases, there was either a negative response or a minimal response with no further uptake. Of the eight negative responses, the GP initially downplayed the association in two cases but then acknowledged the possibility of side effects. There were three occasions where the GP downplayed the association, and three where the GP gave a no association response.

Table 6.2		
GP Response	Transcript examples	Numbers
Positive acknowledgment	Patient reports the medication sort of "screws you up." GP responds by saying, "yeah, [the locum] made the comment that your leg was shaking so much the computer was rocking."	13
Negative response	Patient reports recent weight gain and says, "I was just wondering if it was the medication." GP responds by saying, "no it shouldn't."	8
No (or minimal) response	Patient reports, "I had no problems with those pills I was taking (except I sort of) the um sexual prowess or whatever you call it seems to be diminishing." GP responds minimally by saying, "right" and does not discuss the issue.	10
Total		31

Two of the 10 instances where the GP did not respond at all could be explained by the fact that the problem was old, in one the statement made was general, and in another the patient normally saw another GP who would deal with the issue. That still left six cases where there was no substantive response by the GP to the association being made by the patient. Given the frequency with which the GP provided a negative response or no substantive response to a patient's reporting of side effects, a number of these instances are analyzed in detail below, focusing on the way in which the patient presents the association and the GP's response.

The following examples from the data set illustrate the indirect discourse strategies typically deployed by patients when suggesting an association of symptoms with side effects and GPs' responses to patient claims.

The patient in the next example has presented with a chronic rash for which he has sought advice on previous occasions, receiving conflicting advice from other doctors and ineffective treatment. After recounting this history, he implies that the rash may have been a reaction to a course of Terbinafine (Lamisil) prescribed by this GP about a year ago.

Extract 14:

GP02-08

```
1 PT: I've got a rash (.) which um (2) is getting worse
2 GP: ok yep
3    ((lines omitted))
4 PT: it's in it's (.) big phase at the moment it's active phase
5    but) its spreading round inside my leg so (.) it's time to
6    (.) do something about that
7 GP: its been there over a year hasn't it
8 PT: yep
9 GP: yep
10 PT: it- it actually started after um (.) I think you (.) I
11   came- the first time I saw you I had that problem with the
12   um (.) rash on my toes and stuff and you gave me a
13   prescription for er (2) the er foot stuff (.) couple of
14   big horse pills
15 GP: yep lamisil
16 PT: lamisil that's [right ] so (.) I finished that=
17 GP:               [yep yep]
18 PT: =and it started up round about the same sort of time
19 GP: was june oh three that's interesting (.) if it was a (.)
20   reaction to the (.) tablets which I mean you can get a
21   reaction to any of them it- it- you wouldn't expect it to
22   carry on [( ) um]
23 PT: [no so it's] it seems to be a permanent feature
24   now
```

Two features of the delivery of the claimed association are noteworthy. First, the patient does not make an explicit claim that the medication (Lamisil) is the cause of the problem. Rather, he states that the GP gave him a prescription and the problem "started up around about the same sort of time" (line 18). The upshot is not explicitly stated, but it is implicated as a "non-attributive tacit linkage proposal"(Gill & Maynard, 2006). That is, the patient has not made a definitive claim and so it is possible to act later as though no such claim was made. These tacit explanations do not have a "because" statement (e.g., I have got the rash because of Lamisil), rather they use "and" or "but" constructions and this "invites the doctor to analyze the report's relationship to the complaint, while stopping short of overtly proposing that those circumstances or experiences are causal factors"(Gill & Maynard, 2006). This is a common strategy when patients are offering their own problem explanations in the face of the expertise of the practitioner (Gill & Maynard, 2006). The conclusion is drawn but not explicitly stated.

Secondly, both the patient and the GP invoke a time dimension to sanction their conclusions. For the patient the problem "started up around the same sort of time." The patient's hedges—"around about" and "sort of"—can on one reading be seen as vague and imprecise. Alternatively, they can also be read as doing a particular form of interactional work, functioning as a "face saving" device for both participants. The patient is providing the GP with options to contest the timing and, at the same time, providing himself with an escape if his implicit claim is rejected by the GP.

The GP displays immediate recognition of the upshot and his response is "cautious, in ways that 'dispreferred' responses are canonically performed" (Gill & Maynard, 2006, p. 129). That is, the GP confirms the theoretical possibility, "I mean you can get a reaction to any of them" (lines 20–21), while at the same time implying there is unlikely to be a causal relationship. The statement that reactions *can* occur saves face for the patient before the GP delivers his rationale for minimizing any association: "you wouldn't expect it to carry on" (lines 21–22), and at this point the patient affiliates with the GP by stating that it is now a "permanent feature" (line 23), and does not offer a challenge to the GPs interpretation. Neither the patient nor the doctor pursues the side effects explanation from this point.

Overall, then, the GP assesses the possibility of the medication causing the problem as low. Extract 15 shows how later in the consultation he proffers a diagnosis that could be summarized as "exacerbated by stress," and in lines 7–9, both GP and patient explicitly demonstrate their alignment to this as a shared explanation.

```
1 GP: in terms of the (.) um stress relation thing er er very
2  common association with skin rashes and
3  [(.) and stress type]=
4 PT: [oh okay yep ]
5 GP: =things yep so (.) er (.) uncommon for it to be the cause
6  but often a (.) um a- a- a- an exacerbating thing
7 PT: oh okay yep (.) much the same as lack of sleep (.)
8 GP: that would do it yes [((laughs))]
9 PT: [yeah ] okay
```

Extract 16 provides a contrasting example where a GP positively acknowledges the patient's association of a complaint with a medication, despite in the first instance proffering a contrast proposal. The patient presents with a symptom that could, from a clinical perspective, be explained by a number of causes with side effects to the drug coming toward the bottom of the list.

Extract 16

GP04-02

```
1  PT: I just- woke up and my head was just going round and round
2      and round...I just had (.) an incredible vertigo (.) that
3      made me feel quite ill (.) um (.) and then it sort of went
4      away although I am still a little bit (.) you know I don't
5      sort of rush to (.) throw my head around
6  GP: mm hm
7  PT: um (.) I wondered if it was something to do with that m-
8      ah anti malaria drug that (.) that the specialist has put
9      me on
10     ((lines omitted))
11 GP: and do you feel nauseous with [it ] yeah
12 PT: [yeah]
13     ((This is followed by further detail on the symptoms and
14     the GP pronounces that the condition is vertigo))
15 GP: well there are a number of different causes one of the
       commonest is a virus
16 PT: all right
17 GP: mm
18 PT: so it could of been the start of this virus
19 GP: yeah though that would (.) yeah that's possible but it (.)
20     you know it's not sort of   typical for what's going round
21  at the moment
22 PT: oh okay
23 GP: so when y- when you (.) (but) we'll come- maybe come back
24  to that (.) when the cold started what did it- what
25  symptoms did you start off with
```

The patient presents her suggestion of a link between the drug and her symptoms in a tentative way, "I wondered if it was something to do with that m- ah anti malaria drug" (lines 7–9), and provides an implicit contrast proposal as well by stating, "I should get my ears checked and things like that" (not shown), thus providing another possible explanation for her symptoms. The GP is typing while the patient is talking about this and makes no response to the suggestion of a drug reaction. (Note that in this case the drug was not prescribed by the GP but by a specialist). After a further elaboration on the symptoms by the patient (lines omitted) the GP inquires about the symptoms: "and do you feel nauseous with it." The GP then names it as "vertigo" and suggests a virus but then states he might come back to it. In this instance, and this is the only occasion that this occurs in the data set, the GP does come back to it.

Extract 17

GP04-02

```
1 GP: now you asked a question (that) haven't yet answered which
2    is (.) whether     hydroxychloroquine can cause um vertigo
3    which I confess I don't know so I'm just going to look it
4    up ((long inhalation)) (2) however I suspect (.) oh (.) hy-
5    drox- y (.) I suspect it's um (.) related to the virus
6    rather [than it's-] jus- it's [( ) ] timing
7 PT: [okay ] [but it's-]
8 PT: so it's not likely to be like (.) the kids used to get
9    glue ear and that sort of thing that doesn't make you c-
10   have vertigo does it
11 GP: no n- well in fact it can cause vertigo (.) it's uncommon
12   according to the (.) information sheet but it certainly
13   can
14 PT: mm
15 GP: well there you go (.) you learn something every day
```

At line 6 the GP invokes the time dimension to suggest that the apparent connection between taking the drug and the unwanted symptom of vertigo is a coincidence. However, on looking at the drug sheet, he discovers that it is, in fact, a possibility, and responds fulsomely to the threat to face with "well there you go (.) you learn something every day" (line 15). From his other consultations, it is clear that this GP uses approaches to diagnosis and treatment that are labeled as complementary and alternative medicine, and as such, he may be more likely to question medications that are prescribed.

The next example involves a patient on a complicated regime of medications who, earlier in the consultation, has already expressed a dislike of taking so many pills. After some talk about a possible mix-up in the timing and dosage of the drugs she is taking, the following occurs.

Extract 18

GP04-06

```
1 PT: well I hope that's one that's making me feel bad (.)
2  it's for[blood pressure (isn't it)]
3 GP: [so (.) when you say ] feel bad
4 PT: oh I just feel sick all the time
5 GP: as in nauseous or tired
6 PT: both
7 GP: both
8 PT: mm
```

The GP reaffirms that the patient is getting "both" symptoms (nausea and tired-ness), but makes no comment on the patient's association of these symptoms with the medication "for blood pressure" that is "making me feel bad." At this point the GP attends to the printer for 30 seconds. Later in the same consultation the follow-ing interaction takes place:

Extract 19

GP04-06

```
1 PT: and I looked at this cartia and it had tuesday was the
2  last tablet to take and I thought ah good (.) I haven't
3  taken it because I was keeping them in order
4  (6)
5 PT: yeah that part of my memory's not functioning very well (.)
6  that sort of recall of simple things
7  (2)
8 GP: yeah
9  (2)
10 PT: it's the drugs isn't it that's doing it
11 GP: (.) p::ossibly
12  (2)
13 PT: ((laughing)) you're supposed to say yes ((laughs))
14  (2)
15 GP: mm (3)
```

The GP's lack of uptake of the patient's concerns about the possible effect of her medications on her memory is marked by the long pauses she leaves unfilled (lines

4, 7, 9, 12), and her minimal response tokens in lines 8 and 14. In Line 11 she offers a strongly hedged response with the patient's yes-preferring suggestion that "it's the drugs isn't it that's doing it" (line 10), and then fails to respond to the patient's humorous attempt in line 13 to challenge this lack of agreement. An additional complication in this extract is that the consultation follows a recent hospital visit with the treatment regime initiated by other doctors. In this case, the GP's hedging and face saving is on behalf of third parties.

The following is a simple dismissal of a patient's suggestions about an association between medications and weight gain.

Extract 20

GP06-04

```
1 PT: and now that you're talking about medication would any of
2    that caused me to put on weight because I diet and- I mean
3    I'm careful what I eat [and] I exercise and don't seem to
4 GP: [mm ]
5 PT: be able lose weight and I was just wondering if the
6    medication- any of the medication I'm [taking] would tend
7 GP: [um ]
8 PT: to make me put on weight
9 GP: well no there's the [lipex] you're on the lipex at night
10 PT: [yeah ]
11 GP: your indapamide[shouldn't] and d- no it shouldn't
12 PT: [no ]
13 PT: we'll why is that I'm you [know ]
14 GP: [it depends] (.) on what you eat
15    and if you're doing enough exercise for what you eat selena
16 PT: <yeah yeah>
```

In this instance, the GP uses the strategy of invoking her expert status by simply naming the drugs the patient is on and saying "well no ... ... no it shouldn't" (lines 9–11), then suggesting a cause that the patient has explicitly rejected in her opening (lines 14–15). The interactional work in this instance is placed on the health promotion aspects of weight reduction after having discounted the Lipex as a possible cause for weight gain.

This same GP uses a similar strategy in the following example where a patient who has English as a second language pulls out her medications to show the GP and suggests that one of them may be affecting her memory.

```
Extract 21

GP06-09

1 PT: ah this one
2  (2)
3 GP: yep
4  (2)
5 PT: that's have somebody told me (.) er er can't remember
6  good and she say might be this one
7 GP: (.) oh that your memory's not so good
8 PT: mm
9 GP: (.) I don't think so this here is for blood pressure (.)
10  it usually doesn't do anything to your memory (.) no
11 [(.) no no (.) yeah]
12 PT: [that's why ]I bring it here to show you
```

The GP does not resolve the memory issue for the patient even though the patient is on many medications. The GP does mitigate the claim by saying, "I don't think so" (line 9) and "it usually doesn't do anything to your memory" (line 10), which would suggest that it could and so saves face for the patient, but then strongly resiles from such a possibility by saying "no (.) no no" in line 11.

While there are certainly a number of instances where GPs do acknowledge and consider options to deal with possible side effects to medication as suggested by patients, in our current data set at least, the more common response is for doctors to contest, downplay, or ignore patient-initiated side effects talk.

Conclusions and Implications

A focus on the unfolding of the interaction in side effects talk in the general practice consultation provides insight into the relationship between the rules of ordinary talk and the rules of therapeutic talk (Skelton, 2002). In summarizing the patterns in this data, three levels of analysis have been considered: the discourse function or action performed by the talk, the interactional strategies at play, and the particular linguistic forms and structures by which those strategies are realized (Holmes, Stubbe, & Vine, 1999). In general, GPs act to persuade patients to accept and take prescribed medications while making them aware of possible side effects. In dealing with the sociomedical dilemma that this raises (Heritage & Maynard, 2006), GPs tend to use a number of specific discourse strategies that include avoidance, unspecified reference to side effects, and specified references that are downgraded or otherwise qualified. The forms that the latter strategy takes include use of mitigators and euphemisms. GP presentation of side effects is therefore often vague and general, giving little indication to patients of what they should be looking for.

In addition, GPs may be concerned about the nocebo effect of explicit and specific side effects talk. The extracts above have illustrated situations where GPs have provided some, if minimal, information about side effects. There are many other consultations where medications are prescribed and side effects are not mentioned at all. This is less surprising when we consider that to initiate a discussion about possible side effects opens up a potential Pandora's Box—where would the GP stop? Given that potentially any drug could cause a range of side effects, addressing all potential concerns could paralyze many consultations. This issue is exemplified in the statement in extract 13 where the GP concedes that side effects can occur but "we don't really understand why."

In negotiating this situation GPs run the risk of providing the patient with too little information, and therefore, not adequately facilitating an environment of shared decision making and not making the patient aware of symptoms that the patient should look out for to determine if the medication was "unsuitable."

For the patient, to make a claim that a prescribed medication is causing a side effect runs the risk of threatening the therapeutic relationship between doctor and patient. The claim may threaten the face of the GP, as the GP prescribed the medication that is seen to have a negative effect, and further, threatens the therapeutic approach of the GP in a situation where prescription medications are the prime source of therapy. The patient's delivery of a claimed association between symptoms and a medication can thus be likened to bad news delivery. Maynard and Frankel (2006) argue that there are particular identifiable features that are associated with the delivery of bad news by a physician to a patient. Disfavored news may contain hesitations, hedges, minimizers, and mitigators. The upshot of the news delivery may not be stated outright, but is cautious and circumspect. A possible explanation for the delivery by the patient being similar to a bad news delivery is that by making a claim that the symptoms are an outcome of a drug prescribed by the doctor, there is the danger of implying some wrong on the part of the doctor. The hedges and qualifiers can be seen as face-saving work, a way of distancing the patient from any direct criticism of the doctor's prescribing, and so minimizing the impact of these "face threatening acts" (Brown & Levinson, 1987) on both the patient and the doctor. The doctor uses similar face-saving hedges and qualifiers when required to refute the presumption on the part of the patient of symptoms due to an adverse event.

In short, GPs have to persuade patients to take and adhere to medications that may have adverse effects, and they use rhetorical strategies, such as downplaying, mitigating, being nonspecific about side effects, and using euphemisms, to achieve this goal. Patients engage in a face-threatening act when claiming a prescribed medication is causing symptoms, and manage this by using rhetorical strategies such as tacit linkage proposals, hedges, and qualifications to mitigate these threats to face.

These co-constructed interactions around side effects talk may have a number of outcomes. First, due to the GP's downplaying of side effects patients may not attend to them, and so may miss the relationship between a prescribed medication and symptoms. The GP response may be partly explained by the doctor's knowledge or presumption that many patient assertions of possible side effects are unlikely to have a strong evidence base for a well-founded causal link. In only one case in our data set did the GP come back to a possible link that he had already stated as being unlikely but then, on looking up possible side effects of the implicated drug, he did leave it as a possible explanation. Second, due to patients' indirect presentation of side effects talk and the tendency seen in the data for GPs to downplay patients' associations of prescribed medication with symptoms, GPs may therefore fail to appropriately examine the possibility of side effects that their patients are raising. In this case, one consequence would be an undercounting of side effects from prescribed medications. In addition, the common response of GPs to ignore or provide a negative response to patients' claims may lead to noncompliance issues for patients.

It is difficult to see how this complex issue can be resolved, as both parties to the interaction are involved in delicately balanced negotiations. There is no evidence to suggest that the current compromise between open presentation of all available information and complete nondisclosure of information in relation to side effects is not, in fact, an appropriate one. However, given the high suspected prevalence of iatrogenic problems caused by medications and the underreporting of ADR incidents (Pound et al., 2005), it is important to consider ways in which consultations can be facilitated to better support appropriate side effects talk. There are examples in the dataset (such as Extract 17) where GPs do explore the possibility of side effects when patients raise concerns and do not seek ways to dismiss the claims before more evidence is sought. This approach may provide a useful model for other GPs. Britten and colleagues (2004) argue that there is a need for a "culture shift" so that patients can express their aversion to medicines. GPs may be able to foster such a shift by taking patients' claims at face value as being worthy of investigation.

An important implication of this research is that health professionals should reflect on how they respond to patients' concerns about side effects. Health professionals are unlikely to be aware of the common pattern of downplaying side effects concerns, but with this knowledge they are in a better position to be aware of what they do in their own consultations and to look out for evidence that they are themselves following the common pattern. This in turn has implications for patient safety and for the level of reporting of ADRs at primary care level. The common pattern of downplaying patient concerns may leave patients taking medications that they are anxious about, and for some patients this may lead them to experiment with their medications, either reducing the dose or stopping altogether. The common pattern could also mean a greater likelihood of actual side effects being missed and not being reported.

There is no attempt here to make claims about the actual validity of patient queries or claims about side effects. What the research does show is the existence of distinct patterns in how side effects issues are raised and responded to in consultations. The analysis of this data set has indicated that we can understand this patterned behavior as a consequence of interactional dilemmas, in this case dilemmas faced by both the patient and the GP. By examining *how* side-effects issues are raised, not only the fact *that* they are raised, we can see particular features like hesitations and vagueness that may be interpreted as conveying uncertainty. We can see how GPs tend to respond by immediately downplaying any association. The evidence from this data set of a pattern of negative responses and no response by the GP provides a possible explanation for other documented cases where patients have not reported their concerns about medication to doctors (Pound et al., 2005). This chapter demonstrates the complexity and "face saving" that is contained in consultations concerned with adverse drug events, and given the potentially serious consequences of adverse reactions indicates a need for further research in this area.

Acknowledgments

This research was funded by the New Zealand Health Research Council and the Marsden Fund. The research team would like to thank the participants and Dr. Deborah McLeod and Dr. Libby Plumridge for their input.

Transcription Conventions

(.)	denotes a micro-pause
(2)	denotes a pause of the specified number of seconds
(and)	words in single parentheses denote candidate hearings
( )	parentheses without words denote indecipherable talk
((laughs))	double parentheses denote descriptions of action
[ ]	denotes overlapping talk
<>	denotes marked rising in intonation
=	denotes latching or no gap between talk
<u>Surely</u>	underlined word denotes increased emphasis
< >	denotes slowing down of talk

Backstrom, M., Mjorndal, T., Dahlqvist, R., & Nordkvist-Olsson, T. (2000). Attitudes to reporting adverse drug reactions in northern Sweden. *European Journal of Clinical Pharmacology, 56*(9–10), 729–732.

Benson, J., & Britten, N. (2002). Patients' decisions about whether or not to take antihypertensive drugs: Qualitative study. *BMJ, 325*(7369), 873–877. 10.1136/bmj.325.7369.873

Britten, N., Stevenson, F. A., Barry, C. A., Barber, N., & Bradley, C. T. (2000). Misunderstandings in prescribing decisions in general practice: Qualitative study. *British Medical Journal, 320,* 484–488.

Britten, N., Stevenson, F., Gafaranga, J., Barry, C., & Bradley, C. (2004). The expression of aversion to medicines in general practice consultations. *Social Science & Medicine, 59,* 1495–1503.

Brown, P., & Levinson, S. (1987). *Politeness: Some universals in language usage.* Cambridge: Cambridge University Press.

Gibbons, R. D., Amatya, A. K., Brown, C. H., Hur, K., Marcus, S. M., Bhaumik, D. K. et al. (2010). Post-approval drug safety surveillance. *Annual Review of Public Health, 31,* 419–437.

Gill, V., & Maynard, D. W. (2006). Explaining illness: Patients' proposals and physician' responses. In J. Heritage & D. W. Maynard (Eds.), *Communication in medical care: Interaction between primary care physicians and patients* (pp. 115–150). Cambridge: Cambridge University Press.

Goffman, E. (2006). On face-work. In G. Massey (Ed.), *Readings for sociology* (pp. 105–114). New York: W. W. Norton and Company.

Haakana, M. (2001). Laughter as a patient's resource: Dealing with delicate aspects of medical interaction. *Text, 21,* 187–219.

Haakana, M. (2002). Laughter in medical interaction: From quantification to analysis. *Journal of Sociolinguistics, 6,* 207–235.

Hazell, L., & Shakir, S. A. W. (2006). Under-reporting of adverse drug reactions—A systematic review. *Drug Safety, 29*(5), 385–396.

Heritage, J. (1989). Current developments in conversation analysis. In D. Roger & P. Bull (Eds.), *Conversation: An interdisciplinary perspective* (pp. 21–47). Clevedon, UK: Multilingual Matters.

Heritage, J., & Maynard, D. W. (2006). Introduction. In J. Heritage & D. W. Maynard (Eds.), *Communication in medical care: Interaction between primary care physicians and patients* (pp. 1–21). Cambridge: Cambridge University Press.

Holmes, J., Stubbe, M., & Vine, B. (1999). Constructing professional identity: Doing power in policy units. In S. Sarangi & C. Roberts (Eds.), *Talk, work and institutional order: Discourse in medical, mediation and management settings* (pp. 351–388). Berlin: Mouton de Gruyter.

Kjellgren, K. I., Svensson, S., Ahlner, J., & Saljo, R. (1998). Antihypertensive medication in clinical encounters. *International Journal of Cardiology, 64*(2), 161–169.

Lazarou, J., Pomeranz, B. H., & Corey, P. N. (1998). Incidence of adverse drug reactions in hospitalized patients: A meta-analysis of prospective studies. *Journal of the American Medical Association, 279*(15), 1200–1205.

Lopez-Gonzalez, E., Herdeiro, M. T., & Figueiras, A. (2009). Determinants of under-reporting of adverse drug reactions: A systematic review. *Drug Safety, 32*(1), 19–31.

Maynard, D. W., & Frankel, R. (2006). On diagnostic rationality: Bad news, good news, and the symptom residue. In J. Heritage & D. W. Maynard (Eds.), *Communication in medical care: Interaction between primary care physicians and patients* (pp. 248–278). Cambridge: Cambridge University Press.

Medawar, C., Herxheimer, A., Bell, A., & Jofre, S. (2002). Paroxetine, Panorama and user reporting of ADRs: Consumer intelligence matters in clinical practice and post-marketing drug surveillance. *International Journal of Risk & Safety in Medicine, 15*, 161–169.

Miller, G. C., Britt, H. C., Valenti, L., & Knox, S. (2006). Comment: Adverse drug events: Counting is not enough, action is needed. *Medical Journal of Australia, 184*(12), 19.

Petryna, A. (2007). Clinical trials offshored: On private sector science and public health. *BioSocieties, 2*, 21–40.

Pham, J. C., Aswani, M., Rosen, M., Lee, H. W., Huddle, M., Weeks, K. et al. (2012). Reducing medical errors and adverse events. *Annual Review of Medicine, 63*, 447–463.

Pound, P., Britten, N., Morgan, M., Yardley, L., Pope, C., Daker-White, G. et al. (2005). Resisting medicine: A synthesis of qualitative studies of medicine taking. *Social Science & Medicine, 61*, 133–155.

Seale, C., Chaplin, R., Lelliot, P., & Quirk, A. (2007). Antipsychotic medication, sedation and mental clouding: An observational study of psychiatric consultations. *Social Science & Medicine, 65*(4), 698–711.

Searle, J. R. (1976). A classification of illocutionary acts. *Language in Society, 5*, 1–23.

Skelton, J. (2002). Commentary: Understanding conversation. *British Medical Journal, 325*, 1151.

ten Have, P. (1999). *Doing conversation analysis: A practical guide.* Thousand Oaks, CA: SAGE Publications.

World Health Organization (WHO). (2006). *Adverse drug reactions monitoring* (Vol. 2006). Geneva: World Health Organization.

Chapter 7

Hearing That Doesn't Help: An Evaluation of Appraisal Support During High-Risk Pregnancies

Jennifer Hall

Introduction

Health situations are stressful for a variety of reasons, including the many unknowns. Patients are often unsure of how they should be progressing, how they should be feeling, and how they should be coping. One strategy patients use is to compare themselves to others in similar situations. In making comparisons, patients can consider if others are doing better or worse than they and they can also learn possible strategies for improving their situation. Social Comparison Theory attempts to understand the impacts of such comparisons in terms of the support they give people.

The purpose of this chapter is to explore the practice of encouraging upward and downward comparison when offering social support in medical situations. According to the person-centered model of comforting communication, the supportive messages that are most effective and evaluated most highly are those that "recognize and legitimate others' feelings, by helping the other to articulate those feelings, elaborating reasons the other might feel those feelings, and assisting the other to see how those feelings might fit into the broader context" (Burleson & MacGeorge, 2002, p. 395). One strategy for helping individuals think about how their feelings fit into the broader context so they can potentially reframe how they think about their situations is to offer appraisal support in which one assists an individual in reappraising his or her situation (Burleson & Goldsmith, 1998; Jones & Wirtz, 2006).

This qualitative study investigated how women who experienced high-risk pregnancies and/or premature birth responded when they were offered appraisal support in the form of prompted social comparisons. These women were an important group to study as so many women in the United States experience high-risk pregnancies and premature birth. This problem is a growing one. In 2007, the March of Dimes reported that the rate of preterm births has been steadily rising, with a 20 percent increase in preterm births since 1990 (March of Dimes, 2007). In 2005, the most recent year for which statistics are available, 12.7 percent of infants, or just over a half-million, were born prematurely. The reasons for the increase in preterm births remain largely unknown. One reason that is known, however, is the increased number of multiple births due to the more frequent use of fertility treatments and in-vitro fertilization. The number of twin births has risen 67 percent since 1980 and triplet births have experienced a drastic increase (Ventura, Martin, Curtin, Menacker, & Hamilton, 2001). Many women also are delaying childbearing, which has led to more women becoming pregnant after 35 years of age, which is a risk factor for preterm birth (Tough et al., 2002; Ventura et al., 2001).

Literature Review

Premature infants are at an increased risk for anemia, jaundice, and infection due to an immature immune system. They also have a greater risk for long-term health problems, including mental retardation, learning disabilities, cerebral palsy, and vision and hearing problems. Infants born at less than 32 weeks are at an increased risk for more severe problems, including respiratory distress syndrome, brain bleeds that can lead to brain damage, heart conditions, necrotizing enterocolitis (a life-threatening intestinal problem), retinopathy of prematurity (which, if untreated, can lead to vision loss), and apnea (the cessation of breathing for 20 or more seconds). The majority of premature infants require a stay in the neonatal intensive care unit (NICU) where they can be closely monitored as they grow. Generally, these infants are discharged near their original due date (McDermott-Perez, 2007).

One way to support women experiencing pregnancy complications or women who have given birth prematurely is to assist them in reframing their situations by encouraging downward or upward comparisons. Prompted social comparisons can spark the appraisal process as individuals gain perspective on their own situations by comparing themselves to others. Social comparison is a natural process as individuals often look to those around them to evaluate their own situations (Festinger, 1954). According to Social Comparison Theory, individuals make assessments about their own opinions and desires by comparing themselves to others. Through comparison to others, individuals learn about themselves. Social comparisons are frequently prompted by uncertainty when we lack objective standards to assess ourselves. A new mother might be unsure of what she should be feeling and doing, and therefore, will look to other new mothers as a way to gauge herself. Initially, Festinger proposed that individuals will typically compare themselves to those who are superior. Subsequent work, however, has argued that individuals will compare themselves to both superiors in the process of upward comparison, and to inferiors in the process of downward comparison (Buunk, Zurriaga, Paira, Nauta, & Gosalvez, 2005; Petersen & Ritz, 2010; Wills, 1981).

In upward comparisons, individuals compare themselves to a superior who is perceived as doing better in a given situation. This upward comparison can be a positive experience as the superior individual can serve as a role model or provide inspiration. Upward comparison also can produce negative affect if an individual feels they are inferior or will not be able to match the progress of the superior individual. Downward comparisons have generally been considered to serve a self-enhancing function, as comparisons are made to inferior others, which make individuals feel better about themselves. Research has demonstrated, though, that downward comparisons also can create negative affect in situations where individuals feel empathetic to the inferior person (Michinov, 2007).

During times of illness or stress, individuals may be motivated to engage in social comparison as a means of evaluating how they are doing in the situation. One's self-esteem can also influence the direction of comparison as well as one's reaction to it. Those with higher self-esteem tend to have more positive reactions to social comparison, whether upward or downward, due to their propensity to view themselves in a positive light. Those with lower self-esteem not only tend to make more social comparisons, but they tend to feel more negative after those comparisons. Another factor that influences social comparison is an individual's sense of control. If an individual feels as if they can control situations, then they are more likely to make upward comparisons as they seek out information that will assist in self-improvement or provide inspiration (Taylor & Lobel, 1989).

A few studies have specifically examined the social comparison activities of medically high-risk women. Dias and Lobel (1997) argued that pregnancy can be highly conducive to social comparisons as it is time of great uncertainty and as there is such a wide variation in what is considered normal. Women's pregnancies vary widely, and the experience of a high-risk pregnancy can make a pregnancy seem even more confusing and different from a woman's other experiences with pregnancy or the experiences of those she knows. Dias and Lobel found the social comparison activity of medically high-risk pregnant women was similar to that of groups facing other health threats, such as cancer or AIDS. The researchers also discovered that women who were pregnant for the first time made the most social comparisons and those with higher self-esteem made more upward comparisons.

Barlow, Hainsworth, and Thornton (2008) studied the experiences of pregnant women who were hospitalized due to hypertension. Since this was a new experience for many of the women, they engaged in frequent comparisons, both upward and downward, finding themselves doing better than some women and feeling worse than those they saw or heard delivering healthy infants. Padden and Glen (1997) found that mothers of infants in the NICU frequently used downward comparisons to make assessments about their child's situation, comparing their child born at 34 weeks to an infant born at 29 weeks or comparing an infant who could breathe on their own to an infant on a ventilator. Many referred to themselves as lucky to have a healthy infant as compared to other infants they observed in the NICU. Women would also engage in upward comparison which often led to negative affect. One woman commented on how seeing a set of triplets bigger than her single infant made her feel worse about her situation as her one infant was so small. Rather than giving her hope or something to aspire to, the larger infants made her feel bad because her own infant was not as big or doing as well.

Upward comparison can offer motivation and hope, while downward comparison can increase esteem. For example, a nurse treating a breast cancer patient may share the story of a former patient whose chemotherapy was successful in putting that patient into remission in order to provide a sense of hope to the current patient. Alternatively, a physician who is informing a patient that he has a heart condition could share the story of another patient whose heart condition is much worse in an attempt to make the current patient feel better about his situation. The research project described here indicates, however, that offering targets for social comparison may not always be the best technique for providing social support and getting patients to reappraise their situations. In some cases, both upward and downward social comparisons can be harmful to individuals' emotional and psychological well-being. To examine this potential, I examined the upward and downward social comparisons as understood and narrated by women who experienced a high-risk pregnancy.

Methods

Participants

Participants for this study were women who experienced a high-risk pregnancy with the threat of preterm labor or birth as labeled by their physician, women who experienced preterm labor, and/or women who gave birth prematurely (i.e., a gestation of less than 37 weeks). This included any woman with diabetes or gestational diabetes, women diagnosed with an incompetent cervix, and women pregnant with two or more infants. Participants were recruited using a purposive sampling technique, which is most appropriate for this uniquely personal topic and merits attention to these women's demanding schedules (Boyatzis, 1998; Lindlof & Taylor, 2002). This sampling strategy enabled the recruitment of women with a rich variety of pregnancy and birth experiences. Women were recruited by sending announcements to moms of multiples clubs and posting on message boards for mothers of premature infants and multiples. Women who participated were also asked to refer anyone they knew who might be interested in participating.

Demographics

Of the 47 women, nine had singletons, 20 had twins, 17 had triplets, and one had quadruplets. One mother started her pregnancy with quintuplets, but reduced the pregnancy to triplets, and one started with quadruplets and reduced to twins. Twenty-five of the pregnancies were spontaneous, and 22 of the women had some kind of fertility assistance (ranging from the use of the ovulation-inducing drug chlomid to in-vitro fertilization). The women's ages ranged from 24 to 43. The time that had passed from the end of the women's high-risk pregnancies ranged from three months to 12 years. The gestation at which the women's child(ren) were born ranged from 23 to 40 weeks. Three of the women had experienced more than one high-risk pregnancy.

Data Collection

For this study, 47 women who experienced high-risk pregnancies and/or premature birth participated in in-depth interviews in which they described the types of stories they encountered and observed during their pregnancies and while their infants were in the NICU. Interview questions explored the participants' pregnancy and birth experiences, the narratives they encountered and observed during their pregnancy, how they encountered or observed the narratives, how they used those narratives, and whether there were any narratives they avoided. The interviews were based on a series of guiding questions, but took the form of a conversational interview (Mattson & Stage, 2003). A contextualized conversational approach is a way to move away from the traditional researcher-dominated interview that consists of a researcher asking questions and gathering responses. Conversations are "based on a common understanding and are marked by a lack of explicit purpose, avoidance of repetition, balanced turn taking, use of abbreviation, occurrence of pauses, expressed interest, and curious ignorance by both parties" (Mattson & Stage, 2003, p. 99). When conversational techniques are applied to interview situations, the participants are able to contribute to a dialogue and become a partner in knowledge production.

Conversational interviewing techniques have been used in a variety of qualitative and ethnographic research to investigate issues such as airline safety (Armentraut-Brazee & Mattson, 2004; Mattson, Petrin, & Young, 2001), recovery from childbirth (O'Reilly, Peters, Beale, & Jackson, 2009), pain (Finnstrom & Soderhamn, 2006), and international business (Stage, 1999).

Results

For most of the women in the study, the opportunities for social comparisons were abundant. One way women would hear or read success stories was through interpersonal communication. Women met other mothers with high-risk pregnancies either in person or through the Internet and exchanged stories. Many women described reading stories on others' blogs and being amazed at how far they carried their infants despite extreme circumstances. When seeing or hearing these stories, women inevitably made a comparison to see how they measured up and felt lacking when they did not feel they were as successful in keeping their pregnancies going.

Throughout the interviews women described how they would consider and reconsider their situation as a result of comparing themselves to others. Women compared themselves to others they considered as having better outcomes than they as well as others who they considered had worse than outcomes than they. In addition to making comparisons on their own, women also described situations when others would share stories with them about others who had experienced high-risk pregnancies or premature birth in attempts to provide social support.

Upward Comparison

Most of the women recalled situations when they were asked to make an upward comparison to a woman who was able to carry the pregnancy longer or who had a premature infant who thrived. There were situations where these upward comparisons gave women a sense of hope and encouragement. Women described feeling relieved that there were women who were able to deliver healthy babies. Some of the women described hearing about another woman who stayed on complete bed rest for 20 weeks and feeling encouraged to take bed rest even more seriously or gaining comfort from hearing the story of child who was born at 28 weeks and at age 10 was living a completely normal life comfort.

For example, Ambrosia, mother of triplet sons, described how hearing the stories of other healthy triplets helped ease some of her anxiety:

J: Was it helpful to hear other stories about triplets when you were pregnant?

A: Yeah, I actually had a student whose mom had triplets and they were 19 at the time and they were spontaneous, but they were all normal. You know and I think that was one of my other fears. I think I had read too much about how preterm babies are more likely to have cerebral palsy, so I was always worried.

Knowing there were triplets who had been born and suffered from no long-term complications allowed Ambrosia to see the possibility of her sons growing up and leading normal lives. She realized that it was not definite that her sons would be disabled and she was able to consider a positive life and future for her sons.

Other mothers also used others' stories to find hope and possibility. Kiera's triplets were born at 25 weeks and one of her daughters, Zoe, suffered from extensive complications, including hearing loss, and needed continued oxygen support. Kiera often worried about her daughter's health and how she would relate to her two sisters with fewer medical issues. Through friends, Kiera was connected to another woman in her town with 8-year-old triplets who had been born at 25 weeks as well. One of this woman's triplets had cerebral palsy, yet continued to make strides and overcome limitations. Hearing that this triplet was able to play golf and keep up with her siblings brought peace and hope to Kiera as she was able to imagine a future for Zoe where she would thrive alongside her sisters.

Frequently though, women described their feelings of guilt, failure, and sadness over the outcomes of their pregnancies that arose as a result of the upward comparisons they made. Rather than inspiring women and being a source of encouragement, upward comparisons made women judge themselves negatively and were a source of further stress rather than a source of social support. When women would begin to experience complications, such as increased contractions or a shortening cervix, they found that upward comparisons became more upsetting than helpful.

Women also encountered these stories when they heard them from other people. For example, many women heard stories from the medical staff of other women with high-risk pregnancies who had had positive outcomes. Women reported that the physicians and other medical personnel frequently told them stories of other patients who experienced similar pregnancy complications. Often they were told stories of women who had successful outcomes to their pregnancies such as women who carried triplets to 35 weeks' gestation or women who managed their high blood pressure from home and were never hospitalized prior to the birth. Women also recalled hearing stories about premature infants who survived and thrived despite being born at less than 28 weeks and weighing less than two pounds. Women felt that they were told these stories to give them hope and to encourage them to hang on when things got difficult. However, for some of the women, the upward comparisons these stories prompted led to increased feelings of anxiety and distress as they saw themselves as failing compared to their social comparison targets and felt increased anxiety about their abilities to achieve similar outcomes. Many of the women felt they lacked control over their situations, which increased their feelings of anxiety. They knew they wanted to have a successful outcome and would do anything it took, but even with extreme medical interventions some women went into labor anyway. Women described wanting to shut out all the stories around them so they could focus on their own situations and outcomes.

Often women felt envious when they heard or read the stories of women who had experienced positive outcomes and these stories led them to question why some women had better outcomes than others. Catt, mother of surviving twins born at 34 weeks, described meeting a woman pregnant with twins and its effect on her,

> Last night we had our last meeting for the year of the twin club and we have a mom who is expecting. Her 38th week will be tomorrow. And I just sat there and was like, "How did you?" And, you know, that's horrible. It's like two and a half years later and I am like, "That is so not fair."

Although she was happy for her fellow club member, she could not help but question why her own outcome, which included the loss of one of her triplets, was so different.

Another common emotional response was guilt or questioning one's abilities as a woman and a mother. Laurie, mother of identical twin boys, described her guilt over her difficulties with breastfeeding her sons and her lack of desire for doing it,

> I think I feel guilty about the breastfeeding thing. There are plenty of people out there who breastfeed their twins with no problems, so I wondered what was wrong with me. I just never really wanted to do that. I was really happy to stop pumping at three months … It never seemed natural for me. So, you know, I felt guilty about that.

Hearing or reading of other women who were easily able to breastfeed twins and enjoyed the process made Laurie feel guilty because she thought she was not being a good enough mother to her sons. Her story became one of regret because she felt she should have been able to do better and she should have had more a maternal instinct about breastfeeding.

Encountering these positive stories sometimes evoked guilt in women about what they had or had not done during their pregnancy that could have contributed to the early birth of their children. Christine's daughter was born at 33 weeks after Christine's water broke unexpectedly. As she talked with other women who carried infants to term, she began to question the events leading up to her water breaking. Although her daughter is doing well now, she did have a four-week stay in the NICU. Specifically, Christine expressed guilt over possibly not recognizing the signs of premature labor. She often thinks back to the time shortly before her water broke and replays the events in her mind, trying to determine when she should have said something to her physician, and wondering if she would have been able to change the outcome.

The process of upward comparison shaped women's stories about their pregnancies as they used the stories they heard or read to make sense of their own experiences. In situations where upward comparison resulted in negative emotions, women came to understand their situations through the new stories they created. Women incorporated their guilt and disappointment in themselves into their stories as they described how their pregnancy had failed and the role they played in that failure. Helene, a mother of triplets born at 28 weeks, included in her story, "I totally felt like a failure after my kids were born at 28 weeks. I thought, 'I have failed them miserably.'"

The stories of the positive outcomes of others provided a potential story for women who were living with uncertain and difficult situations. In hearing or reading positive stories, women were given access to the best possible scenarios. When their own scenarios did not match the positive stories, they came to understand their stories as negative and were not happy with their outcomes. Even when infants who were born early had good long-term results, women still compared themselves to others and cast the story of their pregnancies in a negative light, as they continued to wish they could change the stories of the births of their children. In these cases, upward comparison resulted in women experiencing negative emotions, such as guilt or sadness.

Downward Comparisons

In addition to being told positive stories, women were often told stories about other women or infants who had more serious complications or poorer outcomes. Women saw these stories as attempts to help them reappraise their situations by making them feel thankful their situations were not worse when they were. There were some women who found these stories effective in helping them feel gratitude for the positives of their situations. However, there were times when women found themselves experiencing negative emotions as a result of hearing these stories. Some women found themselves overwhelmed with guilt as they wondered why their infants were born at 35 weeks' gestation and only needed minimal medical interventions while other infants were born at 26 weeks' gestation. Additionally, some women found that, rather than acknowledging their feelings, the stories shared to promote downward comparisons sometimes made them feel as if their feelings were negated. The implied message to some women was that they should not feel bad about their situations because it could be much worse. Women felt that these stories took away their permission to grieve their own situations. At times women only wanted to complain and feel bad about their circumstances, and being asked to make a downward comparison did not allow for this.

Fear was one of the most common negative emotional reactions women experienced as the result of a downward comparison. Women who were still unsure about the outcome of their own story looked to other stories to see potential outcomes, and those outcomes were often frightening. Prior to becoming pregnant with triplets, Catt worked as an ICU nurse at a children's hospital and had met several sets of triplets. Due to the nature of her work, the triplets she met had been very ill. She explained how the stories she had seen and heard caused immediate fear once she learned she was carrying triplets.

> It terrified me. Like my initial feeling was, "Am I going to have three severely damaged babies?" And then I was like, "What if they are all handicapped? How does that work? Am I going to have to take on most of that?" Not take it on, but emotionally … And then it wasn't fair to bring them into the world that way.

Seeing the worst possible outcomes of a triplet pregnancy scared Catt and transformed her story into one of fear and one in which she even questioned if she should continue the pregnancy with all three infants.

Others also heard and read stories that frightened them. Nikki learned at 18 weeks that her identical twin girls suffered from twin-to-twin transfusion syndrome, a potentially fatal condition in which one twin takes nutrients from the other. After learning of her diagnosis she went on the Internet and found stories posted on the Twin-to-Twin Foundation website. She explained the fear some of the stories aroused in her:

> Well, the woman who created the foundation, she lost a baby to twin-to-twin. So reading her story was really scary and I tried, I tried to tell myself all of the measurements were coming out good and they were monitoring me very closely.

The stories she read gave her several negative possibilities that she tried to erase with the positives of her own situation, but the fear never completely subsided.

Other women feared an extensive hospital stay or being on bed rest for an extended time. For example, Astrid, mother of triplets, read several stories of women who had been hospitalized for several weeks due to preterm labor and was frightened by the idea; she did not want to be on heavy medications or away from the comforts her own home. The fear of having a similar experience as the women she had read about prompted her to be extra cautious in her bed rest regimen. She found as many ways as possible to minimize the strain on her cervix such as getting a bedside commode to limit the number of steps she took each day and lying in the back seat on the way to her doctor's appointments to reduce pressure on her cervix. The fear her downward comparisons sparked prompted her to understand her situation as dangerous and transformed her story into one of being extra cautious as she fought to stay at home and keep her infants inside her as long as possible.

Often, stories of those with poor outcomes, such as very premature infants or the loss of a child, evoked sadness and grief in the women. Many of the women felt deeply connected to other women who had experienced high-risk pregnancies and premature birth and were able to empathize with their pain and grief. Women knew they could have had similar outcomes and, although they were grateful for their better situations, they were profoundly sad for the women and families who had not been as fortunate. Maggie, a mother of twins born at 33 weeks recalled routinely being sad for other infants and families in the NICU. She said,

> Yeah, and you just feel really sad. I have great admiration for those nurses. I was there one evening when a baby died and that was obviously so hard for them. Just the whole atmosphere was just kind of somber for a while. I remember being so emotional. I think that was the hormones and everything. I was just a wreck.

Hearing the stories with negative outcomes often reminded women of just how dangerous their pregnancies were and gave them a glimpse of what could happen. These stories helped them to understand the gravity of having a premature infant and knew that it easily could have been them with the very sad story to tell.

Even as women recognized the positives in their situations, they still experienced emotional distress over the sad stories they heard. Marie, mother of triplets born at almost 35 weeks, described being in the NICU and observing some of the other more critical infants in the unit.

> To be honest, I was just so grateful that ours were so healthy compared to many of the babies that were in there … I think I was just literally looking at, wow, some of these babies are near a pound and I worry about them, but I was just so blessed and grateful for where we were and the doctors were telling us they're great, they are healthy.

Encountering and observing stories of other infants who were born too early led Marie to a dual emotional reaction as she felt both happy for herself and worried for others.

At times, hearing or reading the story of another woman with a poor outcome for her pregnancy evoked guilt. Some women described sitting in the NICU and seeing infants and families worse off than their own and being filled with guilt over their good outcomes. Amy, mother of twin girls, described feeling guilty for complaining about her situation when she saw other sick infants in the NICU.

> You know, one of the other babies, you know other people were over with it crying and then … And you know, I would feel guilt at the same time, we would be like, "Oh my god, we are so grateful." You know, because these other people are experiencing, you know unhealthy babies, going through whatever.

Another mother of triplets, Ambrosia, echoed this guilt. She saw herself with three relatively healthy infants next to families who had one infant who died or with one infant who was just over a pound. She recalled hearing Kate Gosselin, mother of sextuplets, describe her guilt that she had six infants who were born at 30 weeks and were doing well while other families in the NICU went home without a child. After Ambrosia's triplets were born she understood Gosselin's feelings. Women felt guilt over their good fortune compared to others with lesser fortune. This guilt also prompted women to lessen their complaining and feelings of self-pity as they tried to appreciate the positives of their situations.

Due to the open format of many NICUs, women were easily able to observe and hear the stories of the other patients in the NICU. When they encountered a particularly sad or troubling story, many of the women found themselves saddened and concerned, wishing they could do something to help. A situation that frequently troubled women was infants who appeared to have no or limited visits from their parents. Women described being in the NICU day after day and seeing infants who never had a parent by their bedside or who had a mother who came once a week for an hour. Jessica, mother of triplet boys, described her concern for other infants in the NICU: "there were babies where no one ever came to visit and I would ask, like can I hold this baby? It was heartbreaking."

Women who had stories with poor outcomes, such as losing one or more of their infants or giving birth prior to 30 weeks, recognized that those who were experiencing a high-risk pregnancy or were having signs of premature labor might be upset by their stories and tried not to frighten another woman unnecessarily. Helene, whose triplets were born at 28 weeks, described how she avoided sharing too many details of her pregnancy with those who were still pregnant with twins or triplets. She felt that her story would be upsetting and instead she chose to encourage women by telling them of other women she knew who had carried their infants for a long time.

Conclusions and Implications

Social comparisons seemed to be inevitable in these women's pregnancies and early motherhood experiences. Another way women integrated the stories they heard and read into their own stories was through the process of narrative comparison. Women were constantly comparing their own experiences to those they heard and read about and assessing how their pregnancies were progressing based on those comparisons. The ways their stories compared to the stories they heard or read influenced the stories they told. Women's roles changed as they saw themselves as heroes, protagonists, victims, and even villains. The overall tone of their stories changed as well. The experience of having a high-risk pregnancy was novel to most of the women, and many were unsure what to expect. Comparing themselves to others' stories about high-risk pregnancies allowed women to better gauge how their pregnancies were progressing as well as make sense of what they were experiencing.

Many of the comparisons women made to the other stories they heard and read assisted them in characterizing themselves and defining their role in the story. Often it was important for women to see themselves and have others see them as the "good mother" character. When women's bodies struggled to carry their infants to a safe gestation, they felt less like a good mother and more as their responsibility to provide a safe and healthy start for their infants. These feelings often were exacerbated when they were referred to the stories of other women who were able to carry their infants longer. For example, many of the mothers of triplets mentioned hearing stories about women who delivered close to 36 weeks and were able to bring their infants home from the hospital. This kind of story caused women to question why their own bodies were struggling and they often judged themselves harshly for what they saw as their personal failure. Women struggled to see themselves as good mothers when their infants were born too early and often cast themselves as villains in the stories finding fault with themselves and blaming themselves for their outcomes. Women cast themselves as villains because they believed they should have been stronger or more in control of their bodies to keep their infants gestating longer.

Women who deliver prematurely need constant reassurance that they did all they could to keep their infants as healthy as possible. This reassurance can come from medical staff, spouses, family, and friends. Physicians or nurses could take time to explain to women why they delivered early and during the explanation reiterate that it was not women's fault. Additionally, the exemplar stories should be prefaced as that—exemplars. These stories do represent the best possible outcomes, but they are rare stories. For every story that women pregnant with triplets heard or read of a woman delivering triplets at 36 weeks, there were dozens more of women delivering triplets at earlier gestations. Women may need help to keep their situations in perspective and assistance in understanding the physical factors that led to their early deliveries. Many women tended to find fault with themselves, even when forces outside their control were responsible for their early deliveries.

Interestingly, none of the women judged other women whose outcomes were not as positive as their own. Instead they expressed feelings of sorrow and pity for women whose infants were born at very early gestations. Women did not fault other women for their weak cervixes or irritable uteri; however, women did not have the same nonjudgmental attitude when they considered their own situations. When telling their own stories, women cast themselves in a villain role as they placed the blame for their situations on themselves. Women should be encouraged to consider how they positively judged others in similar situations and to apply the same understanding and sympathy to themselves. This encouragement could come from family, friends, and medical personnel. In addition, books written about high-risk pregnancies and premature births should include a section about the need for self-forgiveness.

Throughout the interviews, it was interesting to note the mixed reaction women had to downward comparisons. Often, hearing or reading stories about situations that were worse than their own led to feelings of gratitude, and women were able to recognize some of the positives in their own situations and put their own struggles in perspective. At the same time, though, women felt a profound sense of grief when they encountered stories of those who had worse outcomes than they. Having faced similar fears and challenges, women could empathize with other mothers who had poor or tragic outcomes and could easily put themselves into these mothers' places. Women could easily imagine having similar experiences and at times this made it difficult to hear or read others' stories. Many women also knew how close they had been to being involved in a tragic story, and this added to their grief. Women had a difficult time feeling more positive about their situation because someone else had not been as fortunate as they.

Another reaction to hearing downward comparison stories was a sense of guilt. Women felt guilty that their own situations were not as bad as others. Women also felt guilty for their negative feelings regarding their own situations. For some women, negative stories felt like an implication that they should not feel sorry for themselves because it could be much worse. Other women wanted to concentrate on their own stories and wanted or needed tacit permission to complain about their situations from those around them. Women knew it could be worse, but, in most cases, they also knew it could have been better, and they needed the time and space to mourn what could have been. Women wanted space to tell their stories in the ways they wanted to tell those stories without having to always acknowledge how things could have been more tragic. There were times when women just wanted to complain and feel victimized. Women understood the benefits of acknowledging what was good in their situations, but they also needed to be able to tell their stories with raw and honest emotions.

Those who support women through these difficult experiences, such as medical personnel, family, and friends, need to recognize this need and give women the space and freedom to tell their stories in the way they want. Although the tendency might be to remind women of how much worse their situations might be to help them gain perspective, these reminders might not always be helpful and welcome. Often women need someone to listen and nod as they complain because their main desire is for someone to acknowledge the difficult time they are having. For example, when a woman is in the hospital on bed rest and starts to complain to the nurse about how stir crazy she is, the nurse should listen and acknowledge the woman's frustrations rather than responding with a story about someone who had a more difficult time on bed rest. When women are spending long days with their infants in the NICU, friends should acknowledge their fatigue and sadness and not include reminders of how infants could be more ill or more frail. Medical personnel and friends and family might also encourage women to write their stories in a journal or a private blog. This gives women a way to tell their stories without fear of judgment.

Specifically, medical personnel need training to make them aware of the mixed reactions patients may have to hearing the stories of other patients. Because women have both positive and negative reactions to stories that spark comparisons, it is impossible to indicate whether storytelling should be done. Perhaps medical personnel simply listening to women talk about their experiences and reactions to stories would allow the medical professionals to be more cautious about sharing stories with their patients.

Appraisal support can be a valuable form of support as it helps an individual think about their situation in a new way. Encouraging social comparisons is one way to spark the appraisal process. Individuals should be cautious, though, about encouraging social comparisons, as the upward and downward comparisons may lead to negative rather than positive affect. Upward comparisons may lead to feelings of guilt, failure, and anxiety, particularly when women have little control over their situations. And downward comparisons can invoke the same feelings.

References

Armentraut-Brazee, C., & Mattson, M. (2004). Clash of subcultures in an on-gate community. In M. A. Turney (Ed.), *Tapping diverse talent in aviation: Culture, gender, and diversity* (pp. 207–220). Hampshire, UK: Ashgate.

Barlow, J. H., Hainsworth, J., & Thornton, S. (2008). Women's experiences of hospitalisation with hypertension during pregnancy: Feeling a fraud. *Journal of Reproductive & Infant Psychology, 26*(3), 157–167.

Boyatzis, R. E. (1998). *Transforming qualitative information.* Thousand Oaks, CA: SAGE Publications.

Burleson, B., & Goldsmith, D. J. (1998). How the comforting process works: Alleviating emotional distress through conversationally induced reappraisals. In P. A. Anderson & L. K. Guerrero (Eds.), *Handbook of communication and emotion: Research, theory, applications, and contexts* (pp. 245–280). San Diego: Academic Press.

Burleson, B., & MacGeorge, E. (2002). Supportive communication. In K. L. Knapp & J. A. Daly (Eds.), *Handbook of interpersonal communication* (3rd ed., pp. 374–472). Thousand Oaks, CA: SAGE Publications.

Buunk, B. P., Zurriaga, R., Paira, J., Nauta, A., & Gosalvez, I. (2005). Social comparisons at work as related to a cooperative social climate and to individual differences in social comparison orientation. *Applied Psychology: An International Review, 54*(1), 61–80.

Dias, L., & Lobel, M. (1997). Social comparison in medically high-risk pregnant women. *Journal of Applied Social Psychology, 27*(18), 1629–1649.

Festinger, L. A. (1954). A theory of social comparison processes. *Human Relations, 7,* 117–140.

Finnstrom, B., & Soderhamn, O. (2006). Conceptions of pain among Somali women. *Journal of Advanced Nursing, 54*(4), 418–425.

Jones, S. M., & Wirtz, J. G. (2006). How does the comforting process work? An empirical test of an appraisal-based model of comforting. *Human Communication Research, 32*(3), 217–243.

Lindlof, T. R., & Taylor, B. C. (2002). *Qualitative communication research methods* (2nd ed.). Thousand Oaks, CA: SAGE Publications.

March of Dimes. (2007). Coping with the NICU experience: Understanding your feelings. Retrieved from www.marchofdimes.com/prematurity

Mattson, M., Petrin, D. A., & Young, J. P. (2001). Integrating safety in the aviation system: Interdepartmental training for pilots and maintenance technicians. *Journal of Air Transportation World Wide, 6,* 37–64.

Mattson, M., & Stage, C. W. (2003). Contextualized conversation: Interviewing exemplars. In R. P. Clair (Ed.), *Expressions of ethnography: Novel approaches to qualitative method* (pp. 107–118). Albany, NY: State University of New York Press.

McDermott-Perez, L. (2007). *Preemie parents: Recovering from baby's premature birth.* Westport, CT: Praeger.

Michinov, N. (2007). Social comparison and affect: A study among elderly women. *Journal of Social Psychology, 147*(2), 175–189.

O'Reilly, R., Peters, K., Beale, B., & Jackson, D. (2009). Women's experiences of recovery from child-birth: Focus on pelvis problems that extend beyond the puerperium. *Journal of Clinical Nursing, 18*(14), 2013–2019.

Padden, T., & Glen, S. (1997). Maternal experiences of preterm birth and neonatal intensive care. *Journal of Reproductive & Infant Psychology, 15*(2), 121–139.

Petersen, S., & Ritz, T. (2010). Dependency of illness evaluation on the social comparison context: Findings with implicit measures of affective evaluation of asthma. *British Journal of Health Psychology, 15*(2), 401–416.

Stage, C. (1999). Negotiating organization communication cultures in American subsidaries doing business in Thailand. *Management Communication Quarterly, 13*, 245–280.

Taylor, S. E., & Lobel, M. (1989). Social comparison activity under threat: Downward evaluation and upward contacts. *Psychological Review, 39*, 19–40.

Tough, S., Newborn-Cook, C., Johnston, D., Svenson, L. W., Rose, S., & Belik, J. (2002). Delayed child-bearing and its impact on population rate changes in lower birth weight, multiple birth, and preterm delivery. *Pediatrics, 109*, 399–403.

Ventura, S. J., Martin, J. A., Curtin, S. C., Menacker, F., & Hamilton, B. E. (2001). Births: Final data for 1999. *National Vital Statistics Reports, 49*, 1–99.

Wills, T. A. (1981). Downward comparison principles in social psychology. *Psychology Bulletin, 90*, 245–271.

Chapter 8

Assessing Baseline Cultural Sensitivity Among Employees at a Hospital System: A Mixed-Methods Approach

Jay Baglia, Anthony Nerino, Judith N. Sabino, and Jarret R. Patton

Introduction

International and national organizations both public and private have thoroughly documented that health disparities are experienced by racial and ethnic minorities (Meyers, 2007; Nelson, 2002; Wilkinson & Marmot, 2003). These disparities occur in an alarming number of contexts across healthcare disciplines including pediatrics (Hahn, 1995), paramedic and ambulatory medicine (Ebell & Smith, 1995), cardiology (Croft et al., 1999; Daumit, Hermann, Coresh, & Powe, 1999), nursing (Orque, 1983), and oncology (Barber et al., 1998). Furthermore, disparities have been identified in analyses of patient satisfaction (Auslander, Thompson, Dreitzer, & Santiago, 1997), access to services (Flores, Abreu, Olivar, & Kastner, 1998), message design (Engleberg & Flora, 1997), health literacy (Bernhardt & Cameron, 2003), and environmental design (Tucker et al., 2003). The variety of these contexts indicates that members of racial and ethnic minorities experience health disparities beyond the patient-physician dyad.

There is little doubt that the causes of health disparities are deep-rooted and are ingrained in the U.S. health system. Consequently, attempts to counteract some, and ultimately all, these differences are imperative. Because race, ethnicity, class, gender, religious preference, sexual orientation, and age have all been shown to influence medical decision making and/or outcomes, it is essential that healthcare institutions exert significant effort toward training and educational programs to address these issues. Many of these efforts involve improving cultural competency. Betancourt, Green, Carrillo, and Ananeh-Firempong (2003) define a culturally competent healthcare system as one that "acknowledges and incorporates—at all levels—the importance of culture, the assessment of cross-cultural relations, vigilance toward the dynamics that result from cultural differences, expansion of cultural knowledge, and adaptation of services to meet culturally unique needs" (p. 294). In the *New England Journal of Medicine*, Fox (2005) emphasizes the importance of cultural competency training for physicians. Purnell and Paulanka (1998) note that communicating health and treatment information requires cultural sensitivity if a provider's recommendations are to be culturally congruent. Ulrey and Amason (2001) assert that culturally sensitive members of a healthcare institution are culturally competent communicators, able to provide better care to their patients, in addition to reducing stress and improving coping behaviors.

Intercultural communication theory posits that intercultural sensitivity represents the affective component of intercultural communication competence (Chen & Starosta, 2000), which is composed of affective, cognitive, and behavioral components deemed instrumental in all cross-cultural interactions. Intercultural sensitivity refers to "an individual's ability to develop a positive emotion toward understanding and appreciating cultural differences that promote effective and appropriate behavior in intercultural communication" (Chen & Starosta, 1997, p. 5). These affective elements of intercultural sensitivity include characteristics such as empathy, open-mindedness, self-esteem, self-monitoring, and nonjudgment.

A systematic review of healthcare systems deemed "culturally competent" suggests that attaining a baseline assessment of existing employees' cultural sensitivity is a crucial component in addressing educational and training needs (Anderson et al., 2003) and working toward cross-cultural healthcare. This chapter, in part, outlines the process of one hospital system's efforts to establish baseline measures of cultural sensitivity in order to develop educational programs and ultimately provide effective cross-cultural healthcare for its diverse patient population. The results of this baseline assessment have implications for the ongoing local phases of the project—the development of education and training for hospital employees—as well as for the application of the Intercultural Sensitivity Scale (Chen & Starosta, 2000) to large professional populations. Intercultural communication is inevitable in today's healthcare process; therefore, it is imperative to understand how hospital systems can employ communication more effectively to improve the health of communities.

Study Context

The region represented in this study, the Lehigh Valley of eastern Pennsylvania, has a population of over 800,000 and has changed significantly in the last 25 years. In the region's largest city, Allentown, the Latino population has nearly tripled since 1990 and it grew to over 40 percent percent of the total population in 2010 (U.S. Bureau of the Census, 2010). In fact, an early 1990s cover story in the *New York Times Magazine* highlighted the significant demographic and cultural changes to this formerly farming and manufacturing community (Stains, 1994).

The region's Middle Eastern and Southeast Asian populations are also growing. The long-established Amish and Mennonite communities contribute to the area's diverse residents.

Lehigh Valley Health Network comprises three hospitals, with nearly 1,000 beds and almost 10,000 employees, including a physician group of close to 500 physicians and 1,100 medical staff members who are board certified in over 90 specialties. The system serves urban, suburban, and rural patients through nine community health centers. Pharmacies, imaging centers, labs, and health management services (including Hospice) round out the full-service nature of this network. The increasing diversity of the population served, as well as the system's size, requires employees to be both comfortable and competent when interacting with patients and families whose backgrounds are different from their own.

This chapter describes one aspect of this large hospital system's efforts to increase the cultural competence of its employees. In 2007, Lehigh Valley Health Network established a Cultural Awareness Implementation Team (CAIT) that was charged with developing a comprehensive plan to enhance cultural competence and improve patient healthcare experiences. Six key tasks were identified by CAIT: (1) standardizing collection of race, ethnicity, and language preference data; (2) expanding language-appropriate services; (3) developing educational programs to increase knowledge and skill of network employees; (4) recruiting and retaining diverse employees; (5) assembling a repository of patient education resources pertaining to health and well-being among culturally distinct groups; and (6) collecting a baseline measure of cultural sensitivity among hospital employees (Gertner et al., 2010). This chapter reports the results of that baseline assessment.

Methodology

Using Chen and Starosta's (2000) Intercultural Sensitivity Scale and supplementing it with both menu questions and open-ended questions, we reveal two key findings: (1) an alternative set of three domains (contrasted with the five originally reported in the validation study of this instrument) that may be indicative of results stemming from the professional health context in which they were administered (rather than, for example, a university student sample) and (2) a typology culled from the open-ended questions that roughly equates lower scale scores with responses that reflect resistance, separation, and marginalization attitudes and higher scale scores with responses that reflect accommodation and integration attitudes. These responses, in a word, *operationalize* previously abstracted numerical scores and are significant for the ways in which they can be employed in education and training materials.

Instrument: The Intercultural Sensitivity Scale (ICSS)

The 24-item Intercultural Sensitivity Scale (ICSS) is intended to measure respondents' ways of thinking about interacting with people who have cultural backgrounds different from their own. Chen and Starosta (2000) argue that intercultural competence requires intercultural sensitivity as a precondition. As a five-option Likert-type scale, the ICSS asks respondents to convey the extent to which they agree/disagree with an attribute (see Appendix 8.1). Using an undergraduate college student convenience sample in a validation study, Chen and Starosta proposed the ICSS as a five-factor model, measuring (1) Interaction Enjoyment, (2) Interaction Engagement, (3) Interaction Confidence, (4) Interaction Attentiveness, and (5) Respect for Cultural Differences. The instrument achieved a Cronbach's *alpha* of 0.88. The number of replication and validation studies, however, has been limited and has provided varied results (see, for example, Dong, Day, & Collaco, 2008; Fritz, Graf, Hentze, Mollenberg, & Chen, 2005; Peng, 2006). Using the scale with a Malaysian university student population, Tamam (2010) reported a reliable three-factor model, measuring (1) Interaction Attentiveness and Respect, (2) Interaction Openness, and (3) Interaction Confidence. The results reported here include a similar (although by no means identical) three-factor model (see Appendix 8.1). Furthermore, the significantly larger population surveyed as well as this professional context help answer our first research question: How does Chen and Starosta's Intercultural Sensitivity Scale function in a healthcare environment?

The decision to use a generic instrument to assess intercultural sensitivity (rather than one designed specifically for a medical environment) was in part guided by the scope of the project. The team implementing the baseline assessment wished to survey the entire employee population and not limit the measure to healthcare professionals (e.g., nurses, nurse practitioners, physicians, physicians' assistants) and/or only those with patient contact. Because our goal was to measure sensitivity as part of the baseline and because hospital employees have limited time to participate in surveys, we identified the ICSS as the most appropriate tool.

We employed an innovative mixed-method approach to data collection. We supplemented the ICSS with three open-ended questions. By supplementing the quantitative scale with open-ended questions, we hoped to operationalize the concept of cultural sensitivity. In other words, by looking for corroboration within the results, the quantitative scores provided by the ICSS would be enhanced by the qualitative representation. Our three open-ended questions were: (1) "What do you think our organization can do to become more culturally responsive among our employees?" (2) "What do you think our organization can do to become more culturally responsive to our patients and community?" (3) "Please share any other comments about LVHN's cultural awareness education." Both the Chen and Starosta quantitative survey data and the qualitative open-ended questions were collected simultaneously (Tashakkori & Teddlie, 1998). For this chapter, only the responses to the first question are analyzed. For our purposes, the first open-ended question was designed to solicit qualitative feedback to gauge both individual and organizational readiness concerning cultural sensitivity within the network as well as to operationalize the ICSS factors. Eight demographic questions were also included to help the baseline assessment team understand individual responses to the survey relative to age, gender, education, position, organizational and community history (tenure), racial and ethnic minority status, and previous cultural awareness training. Other closed-ended questions asked for preferences from a menu with regard to preferred learning environment modalities (e.g., e-learning, role playing, workshops) and topic information (e.g., diet, religious practices, attitudes about death and dying). These menu-driven items would enhance educational efforts for particular occupations within the network, whether nurse, receptionist, or pastoral care representatives, for example. Finally, it is important to note that all the additional questions followed the 24-item ICSS to maintain integrity of the original instrument. The full questionnaire was designed to measure knowledge, attitudes, and behaviors, assess training needs, measure immediate and longitudinal impact of training, and compare scale scores among professions and between those staff members who had received cultural awareness training in the past with those who had not.

After securing IRB approval, the survey was administered electronically to all employees (n = 9,731) using an intranet web-based survey program called Ultimate Survey v.4®.

Sample

All members of the population were invited by email and provided with a link to the survey. Respondents were assured anonymity in the text of this email invitation. Follow-up reminders were sent after the first and second week, and the survey was closed after the third week with a final response rate of 35 percent (n = 3,446).

The highest percentages of survey respondents were nurses, followed by technical support and office support. These three occupation designations accounted for 63 percent of all respondents. Of the total population of the health system staff, nearly 36 percent of all nurses, 27 percent of all physicians, and 42 percent of technical and office support partners participated in the survey.

Comparing the age groupings of the actual nursing staff (RN, LPN) provided by human resources and the respondent sample suggests a high degree of correspondence. This pattern also holds for both technical support staff and for mid-level healthcare providers. Across all positions, the ages of the respondent sample mirror the age distribution of the health system population. Approximately 85 percent of survey respondents were female, nearly identical to the gender composition of the health system staff. Based on these comparisons, we argue that our sample, while not random, is representative of the health system population.

Analytic Method

Survey analysis included two distinct analytic phases. The first, a quantitative phase, provided descriptive characteristics of the respondent sample, baseline scale scores, and validation analysis of the instrument scales. The second, qualitative phase, consisted of analysis of the responses for the open-ended questions to understand staff perceptions about intercultural sensitivity and to ascertain training needs. Sorting responses by the instrument's subscales provided context for the open-ended questions.

Quantitative Analysis. The initial analytic step involved performing a reliability analysis of the five subscales identified by Chen & Starosta (2000). Cronbach's *alpha* testing suggested that the ICSS performed reasonably well; in fact, the Cronbach's *alpha* was nearly identical to the original validation sample (0.89), providing some evidence of external validity.

The next step involved validating the five-factor structure of the instrument. A principal components analysis (PCA) with a varimax rotation was employed, replicating both the initial Chen and Starosta (2000) analysis and Tamam's (2010) confirmatory analysis. Although structural equation modeling is an appropriate approach in confirmatory factor analysis, the primary concern was grouping the open-ended responses into relevant categories. PCA was selected because it generates solutions that explain the total variance of the scores, rather than limiting the solution to the common variance, and it was the method previously employed to develop and confirm the scale structure. Through an oblique rotation, however, the five-factor structure was reduced to three factors representing three intuitively similar constructs. In addition to this more efficient solution, the results of the ICSS application provided stronger valid measures of intercultural sensitivity and further support the utility of this readily available instrument for broader use.

Qualitative Analysis. The second major analytical aspect of the project was reviewing and coding the open-ended responses. Following the validation and reliability testing of the ICSS, we turned to the coding and analysis of the qualitative portion of our data. This process prompted our next research question: How will high and low scores be reflected in the responses to the open-ended questions?

To answer that question we first had to code the responses. We began by looking at a random sample of responses to our first two open-ended questions: What do you think our organization can do to become more culturally responsive among our employees? and What do you think our organization can do to become more culturally responsive to our patients and their families? Initially our codebook included four broad categories that became more refined further along in the process. As a data management tool (Crabtree & Miller, 1999), a codebook need not be too refined and should be created for both "ease in interpretation" as well as providing a mechanism for determining inter-observer agreement (Viera & Garrett, 2005). These four initial coding categories were: (A) responses having to do with education, (B) responses having to do with community interventions, (C) responses having to do with language, and (D) responses having to do with administrative/leadership interventions.

Examples of responses having to do with education include formal education (e.g., Require all employees to attend a cultural awareness class), information (e.g., Somewhere on the Intranet have reference material available for caregivers), and informal education (e.g., Have a heritage day of the week in which everyone can participate). Examples of responses having to do with community include external collaboration (e.g., We can seek partnerships with other community-oriented organizations) and interpersonal communication (e.g., Treat everyone the same, and Listen). Examples of responses having to do with language include clinical interpreter services (e.g., Have in-house interpreters 24 hours a day), translation (e.g., Have signs throughout the hospital in Spanish), language classes (e.g., Seminars, especially Spanish for the Medical Professional, would be valuable), and the primacy of English (e.g., Don't put people on phones that can't speak or understand English). Responses having to do with administration include accountability (e.g., Rules have to be put in place on how to deal with others who discriminate), hiring and retention (e.g., Increase our African-American and Hispanic physician pool), and a category we called status quo (e.g., I don't think undue time should be spent concerning how we become more responsive).

Two of the authors (the first and third) undertook the task of independently coding each of the open-ended responses. The second author then cross-tabbed the responses to determine the level of agreement. We achieved a Cohen's *kappa* of 0.76 on the question What do you think our organization can do to become more culturally responsive among our employees? and a Cohen's *kappa* of 0.78 on the question What do you think our organization can do to become more culturally responsive to our patients and their families? These *kappa* scores indicate substantial agreement (Viera & Garrett, 2005). Even with a substantial *kappa* agreement, the first and third authors met to discuss those responses for which we did not concur and, through discussion (and sometimes debate), ultimately reached agreement on 100 percent of the responses, fine-tuning our codebook in the process.

Our original analytic plan was to compare high and low scorers of the complete ICSS with their open-ended responses. However, with the discovery of the three-factor solution, we decided instead to compare high and low scorers within each of the three domains, arguing that the type of responses provided by someone who scored low on Interaction Confidence might be different than someone who scored low on Intercultural Esteem. This more nuanced approach would ultimately provide more finely tuned educational and training materials. After all, someone who has low confidence has different educational needs from someone whose survey results indicate a lack of respect for cultural differences.

Results

Principal components analysis performed on this large sample of a hospital network staff indicates that the ICSS demonstrated moderate external validity. Interestingly, the results of the survey indicated that both high and low scores ran the gamut of demographic indicators with the only moderately predictive outcome being that more education was likely aligned with higher scores. What is more interesting was that, similar to Tamam's (2010) study, this sample produced what we believe to be a more parsimonious, three-factor solution. Furthermore, this three-factor solution appears to reflect affective, behavioral, and attitudinal components of communication.

The Three-Factor Solution

From Chen and Starosta's construction sample, only one factor replicated exactly; the structure of the other two scales suggests that the items organized in a different, but theoretically coherent fashion. The Cronbach's *alpha* coefficients for the subscales are moderate to strong and the factors explain a greater portion of the common variance than the five factors identified in the origination study.

The first factor, Interaction Confidence, is a straightforward measure of self-assessed competence and, more important, a willingness to engage in intercultural exchanges. Successful communicators are confident in their ability to both listen to others and simultaneously engage in respectful self-expression. Interaction Confidence replicates precisely from the original survey structure and represents an attitudinal component of intercultural sensitivity. With a Cronbach's *alpha* for Interaction Confidence of 0.78 this factor has acceptable reliability.

The second factor, which we title Intercultural Esteem, appears to encompass those items that capture respect for differences and open-mindedness. In this solution, Intercultural Esteem suggests an affective component of intercultural sensitivity and reflects a level of regard for another person's cultural background and differences. The Cronbach's *alpha* for Intercultural Esteem in our sample is 0.87, indicating a good reliability.

The third factor, which we call Communication Presence, includes items that assess perceived interpersonal dynamics and appears to reflect a capacity to engage in crucial self-monitoring. Items that comprise this scale include all three items from the original scale construction factor called Interaction Attentiveness and four items from Interaction Engagement. Self-awareness and awareness of others in intercultural exchanges is, of course, necessary for fostering successful communication. This factor represents a behavioral aspect of intercultural sensitivity and is important for communicators who must adapt and monitor effective communication interactions. The Communication Presence Cronbach's *alpha* is 0.74, indicating an acceptable reliability.

Thematic Analysis of Open-Ended Responses

It is important to report that just over half the participants provided responses to the first open-ended question. The only difference—although not a statistically significant difference—was that those with more education were more likely to compose responses. Therefore, our claims must be tempered with the recognition that we were analyzing the responses of only that subgroup. The first open-ended question gauged respondents' assessment of organizational readiness and revealed a correlation of those scoring at the lower end of the scale with ethnocentric attitudes and cultural defensiveness as well as a correlation of those scoring at the higher end with attitudes revealing acceptance and sensitivity. Furthermore, those scoring at the lower end of the scale were far more likely to include attitudes that unmasked what we term an *external locus of control*; that is, their suggestions indicated a prevalence for solutions to the problem of a diverse patient population as coming from others, whether from management decisions, hiring more interpreters, or having culturally distinct counterparts change their behavior (e.g., Speak English). Conversely, those scoring at the higher end of the scale made suggestions that indicated far more individual agency or what we term an *internal locus of control*. This group tended to encourage perspectives that would result in understanding and empathy with a goal of improved perspective-taking.

The following section provides an overview of the responses of our first open-ended question for the entire survey population as well as specific examples of the kinds of responses representative for both the low and high scorers in Intercultural Esteem and Interaction Confidence, both of which reflected significant differences. The third factor—Communication Presence—had no statistical significance between high and low scorers of the ICSS (See Table 8.1)

Table 8.1

Summary of Coded Responses by Overall Survey Population in Addition to High-Scoring and Low-Scoring Population Subgroups

	Responses having to do with Education[1]	Responses having to do with Community[2]	Responses having to do with Language[3]	Responses having to do with Administration[4]
Overall Population	53%	18%	11%	18%
Top 10% Overall	57%	17%	7%	19%
Bottom 10% Overall	36%	23%	19%	22%
Intercultural Esteem				
Top 10%	63%	10%	10%	20%
Bottom 10%	40%	21%	21%	18%
Interaction Confidence				
Top 10%	54%	16%	16%	22%
Bottom 10%	58%	12%	12%	14%
Communication Presence				
Top 10%	62%	11%	11%	19%
Bottom 10%	51%	19%	19%	20%

notes:

1. Responses having to do with Education include formal education (workshops, classes, e-learning), information (fact sheets, websites), and informal education (cultural heritage days, holidays, food fairs).

2. Responses having to do with Community include listening, respecting differences, and being open minded, as well as Us vs. Them discourse.

3. Responses having to do with Language include language classes, requests for more interpreters, signage and literature translation, and the primacy of English (Speak English).

4. Responses having to do with Administration include hiring/retention initiatives, accountability, institutional food offerings, leadership, and "status quo" responses (We're already doing enough).

Despite the overall survey population naming educational initiatives (whether formal, informational, or informal) at a rate of 53 percent, those scoring in the lowest 10 percent recorded a response having to do with education only 36 percent of the time. Compared to the overall bottom 10 percent of the ICSS scores, those scoring low in Interaction Confidence were considerably more likely to suggest educational solutions than those scoring low in Intercultural Esteem. While the overall survey population suggested responses having to do with language only 11 percent of the time, those scoring low in both Intercultural Esteem and Communication Presence, as well as those with an overall score in the lowest 10 percent, recorded responses having to do with language at a rate almost double the overall survey population. This finding suggests that for many with low scores on the ICSS, language is a barrier to sensitivity. In the following section, we share some of the most interesting results of this mixed-methods analysis. We begin by explaining some of the results in the factor Intercultural Esteem followed by a closer look at the results of Interaction Confidence. Because the differences between top and bottom scorers in the Communication Presence were not statistically significant, we do not share those results.

Intercultural Esteem. By looking more closely at the responses within each of the four coding categories, we discovered that the particular responses varied considerably between the top scorers and the bottom scorers. For example, in the Community code, those scoring higher were far more likely to suggest collaborative solutions (such as dialogue and opportunities for interaction) than those scoring low, who suggested assimilation often in the form of Us/Them phrasing, a tendency that didn't occur in the top-scoring group at all. Likewise, in the Language code, those scoring high in Intercultural Esteem were twice as likely to suggest Spanish classes (an indication of agency, or an internal locus of control) as those scoring in the lowest 10 percent. Most conspicuous, however, was the fact that those scoring lowest in Intercultural Esteem were strikingly intolerant of languages other than English; fully half of those in this group whose responses were coded as Language included a comment urging the primacy of English (e.g., I feel we are in America and as such English and our cultures should be first or more bluntly Speak English). Finally, responses having to do with administration also varied considerably between the two groups. While top scorers in Intercultural Esteem strongly encouraged hiring and retention practices to add to the diversity of the employee population (e.g., Hire more people of color to reflect our changing community landscape) as well as pointedly suggesting that an initiative of cultural competence must start at the top (e.g., Ideas seem to trickle down from the top. Please train upper management), those scoring in the lowest 10 percent strongly maintained a status quo perspective (e.g., We've done enough).

Interaction Confidence. While the differences between high and low scorers in the Interaction Confidence factor were not as pronounced as the differences found in Intercultural Esteem, there were some aspects of the open-ended responses that are noteworthy. Both high and low scorers in the Interaction Confidence factor had their responses coded as "Education" at more than twice the rate as any other code. This was not true of the lowest scoring respondents in the Intercultural Esteem factor. One important difference is that those scoring in the lowest 10 percent in the Interaction Confidence factor are more than twice as likely to prefer their educational materials in the form of "fact sheets" or informational websites as those scoring in the top 10 percent. On the other hand, high scorers were more than three times as likely as their low-scoring counterparts to choose informal educational opportunities (e.g., Celebrate different cultures with days of the week devoted to learning more about a culture's food, dress, and history). In the coding category of Community, high scorers were more than twice as likely to point out the need to respect differences. And while the percentages of the two groups who were compelled to recommend the need to remain open-minded were identical, the quality of the responses was dissimilar. For example, those in the top 10 percent included feedback in the form of active agency (e.g., Become more open-minded) while those in the bottom 10 percent assigned responsibility to "others" (e.g., Have employees share their beliefs or Ask them).

Discussion

Although only the Interaction Confidence factor from the original validation sample replicates on our sample; the structure of the other two factors suggests that the items organized in a theoretically coherent fashion and these new scales make intuitive sense. The three factors measure similar constructs as the original five factors and address knowledge (Intercultural Esteem), skills (Interaction Confidence), and awareness (Communication Presence). According to Sue, Arredondo, and McDavis (1992), knowledge, attitudes, and skills are necessary for the delivery of cross-cultural care to diverse patient populations. The open-ended responses—including those from the overall population sample along with those explored more thoroughly in this chapter—provide a much-needed operationalization of otherwise abstract scale scores.

Items from the Intercultural Esteem subscale encompass respect for differences, an open-minded attitude, and a willingness to engage in intercultural exchanges. Intercultural Esteem suggests a knowledge component of intercultural sensitivity and reflects a level of regard and respect for cultural differences as a result of this knowledge. When a respondent recommends that the hospital system "Recruit employees from other cultures who help us educate ourselves," she/he recognizes that delivering cross-cultural healthcare must reflect the community it serves through the makeup of the system's personnel (Anderson et al., 2003).

Interaction Confidence measures self-assessed competence and willingness to engage in intercultural exchanges. Successful communicators are confident in their ability to both listen to others and engage in respectful self-expression. Interaction Confidence represents a skills component of intercultural sensitivity. When a respondent remarks that "I am very interested in different cultures but am hesitant and untrusting of myself to deal with issues that come up. What I may consider normal may be offensive to another culture," she/he acknowledges the importance of applying communication skills that, for her/him, still require development.

The last scale—Communication Presence—reflects the capacity to engage in crucial self-monitoring. For successful communication to occur, self-awareness and awareness of others in intercultural exchanges is essential. This factor represents the awareness aspect of intercultural sensitivity and is important in adapting and monitoring effective communication interactions. When a respondent urges leadership to "Make it clear that there will be zero tolerance with negative remarks directed toward people of different cultures," she/he is stressing the implications of self-monitoring, both for staff and patients alike.

The findings from our study suggest that the ICSS is somewhat generalizable to this nonstudent sample. The alternative three-factor structure appeared to capture similar, if somewhat scaled down, *constructs*. The three-factor structure and the five-factor structure are consistent in theme in that they tend to measure affective, behavioral, and cognitive levels of intercultural sensitivity. However, the three-factor structure may have successfully "unpacked" original subscales that were not reliably measuring unidimensional constructs (Tong & Chen, 2008).

Several dynamics could explain these findings. First, the original factors were constructed with college undergraduates. The communication demands in a college arena, including a broader exposure to different cultures and the similar socioeconomic levels that serve as the backdrop to most of these exchanges, differ significantly from the demands of a professional community. Medical professionals not only have greater demands in terms of the purpose, content, and outcome of intercultural communication, but the risks are greater for failing to communicate effectively.

Second, the mean age of our sample is significantly older than the construction sample and may reflect both maturity and experience. Possibly, experience has contributed to greater *integration* of affect, awareness, and confidence as reflected in the new scales.

Many of the constructs used in the measurement of intercultural sensitivity are themselves questionably correlated and others are poorly defined. As an example, suspended judgment is identified as a component of a culturally sensitive person. In most instances, however, this term describes a behavior or a choice, not a characteristic. Measurement of this behavior is difficult, as humans make rapid and complex judgments of others in interactions, particularly those interactions that require adaptations and modifications to communication.

The largest limitation inherent in this study involves the nature of the sample. Although a large percentage of the hospital staff took the survey and reasonable inferences may be attempted, participation in the survey was by self-selection and was, therefore, not random, limiting somewhat the validity of both baseline measures, findings on instrument validity, and the quantity and quality of the open-ended responses.

Another limitation is that there are no mechanisms to assess for the presence of a social desirability effect. Overall, institutional scores for the hospital are reasonably positive. Scores in this range suggest that there may be an effort on the part of employees who participated in the survey to inflate responses to appear more interculturally sensitive. The anonymous nature of the survey and the sheer size of the sample suggest that if a social desirability effect is present, however, it may be modest. After all, the blunt statements (e.g., "As long as certain segments of the population do not wish to mainstream, what is the sense in trying to integrate them? Let them have separate but equal) indicate that for a sizable portion of respondents, there was no effort to impress. It is possible that the recent implementation of widely disseminated cultural diversity training may have also inflated scores.

The final limitation of this study is that it does not in any way incorporate the perspectives of patients. Polacek and Martinez (2009) included patient focus groups in their exploration of a hospital system and Ahmed and Bates (2007, 2010) included patient perspectives of healthcare interactions in a clinic.

With regard to the ICSS, given the findings and the limitations inherent in attempting to measure this construct, it may be both realistic and feasible to re-think the scales and adopt these more parsimonious domains. That said, the ICSS appears to be a reasonably valid instrument for assessing intercultural sensitivity across a wide range of employment positions and, given the results of this analysis, may have broad application in large healthcare or educational settings. These findings may be especially important since it has been demonstrated that the existing instruments specific to the healthcare profession make some problematic assumptions or have significant shortcomings (Kumas-Tan, Beagan, Loppie, MacLeod, & Frank, 2007).

Conclusions and Implications

The purpose of a baseline assessment was to establish a measure of intercultural sensitivity, to inform educational programming, and to assess impact of educational, training, and cultural competence interventions. We promoted the use of a validated instrument rather than attempting to construct a survey based on local predilections. Although scale scores provide some information to assess institutional climate, we strongly encourage open-ended questions be included in any survey. Despite the obvious weakness of having only half of our participants provide responses to the open-ended questions, these supplementary components "fit together to enhance description" (Morse, Niehaus, Wolfe, & Wilkins, 2006, p. 281). As Morse (2006, p. 96) further elucidates, inference from qualitative data in mixed-method research "is used in the initial stages of constructing a conceptual framework." Analysis of these responses greatly informs educational and training initiatives, and provides a deeper understanding of employee scores.

With this three-factor solution for the ICSS, we can also look more strategically at both individual and demographic-specific scores in conjunction with the responses to our open-ended questions. We conclude this chapter with an overview of this hospital system's educational program.

Educational Interventions

Because our nation comprises people from many cultures, healthcare providers and support staff must understand the cultural background of patients relative to their health and well-being. In response to increasing diversity in what were traditionally homogeneous populations, many community hospitals are recognizing inequities in both health quality and healthcare within these new patient populations. As a result, some hospital networks are systematically strengthening and improving services that address the cultural needs of patients to assure delivery of quality, equitable care.

Research has shown that educational interventions can improve the cultural competency knowledge, attitudes, and behaviors of healthcare professionals (Beach et al., 2005). Several reports and organizations recommend the provision of cultural competency education for healthcare professionals. For example, the Institute of Medicine's *Unequal Treatment* recommended that all healthcare professionals receive training in cross-cultural communication as a strategy to reduce healthcare disparities (Smedley, Stith, & Nelson, 2003). Likewise, the Office of Minority Health's (2000) *National Standards for Culturally and Linguistically Appropriate Services (CLAS) in Healthcare* recommend that healthcare organizations provide education on culturally and language-appropriate services to staff members in all disciplines and at all levels. Similarly, the inclusion of cultural awareness education is required by the Association of American Medical Colleges Liaison Committee on Medical Education and the Accreditation Council for Graduate Medical Education, among other accreditation organizations (see Bates & Ahmed, 2012).

Kleinman (1980) points out that a medical system is, itself, a cultural system. And the hospital system featured in this chapter is "a system of symbolic meanings anchored in particular arrangements of social institutions and patterns of interpersonal interactions" (p. 24). So, as we conclude, it is important for us to describe the various education interventions, both internal and external, as paradigmatic of meaningful culture change within this system. We begin by describing internal, provider-focused educational interventions.

Education is a key strategy to assure the delivery of cross-cultural healthcare at this and other healthcare systems. The objective of this education is to inform employees of the knowledge, attitudes, and skills that facilitate communication with and care for culturally different peers and patients. The delivery of language-appropriate cross-cultural healthcare will assure the provision of high quality services for all patients. For two years, FY10 and FY11, this system's senior management adopted a network-wide goal that every employee complete at least one cultural awareness educational event per year.

Since conducting this baseline assessment, Lehigh Valley Health Network has developed more than 16 educational programs related to diversity and cultural awareness. Key educational themes include a patient-based approach to cross-cultural care as well as fostering of diversity and acceptance of difference. In addition, skills-based education programs on how to participate in interpreter-facilitated conversations as well as educate multicultural audiences are also available. These programs were developed, in part, due to the menu-driven questions on the survey that asked for learning preferences and content preferences.

For instance, the most popular learning preferences were cultural "fact sheets" (especially popular among nurses) and diversity workshops. The most requested content categories include religious practices, attitudes about healthcare institutions, attitudes about death and dying, gender roles, and attitudes about pain.

Eight "live" educational programs are featured among these 16 programs available for system employees. Some programs offer general overviews of cross-cultural healthcare, while others provide specific skill-building opportunities (such as how to work with a language interpreter or how to teach others about cross-cultural healthcare). Audience-specific workshops are also available. For example, a session on "fostering diversity" is offered for management staff and a 40-hour interpreter program is available for staff members with demonstrated competency in two languages. Finally, customized presentations are also delivered on request. In preparation for a disparity reduction initiative, leaders of the cancer center requested a workshop on the "concept of race" so that all team members had a foundation of knowledge about and sensitivity for race, including screening, delivery of bad news, and treatment options relative to cancer.

While live presentations are the ideal format for cross-cultural healthcare education, online instruction is used to provide background information in this area. Currently eight programs are available within the health network's e-learning system. These programs include basic overviews as well as specific topics (such as generational diversity). Four of these online programs were developed by Lehigh Valley Health Network staff members.

In addition to the live and online education options, specific strategies were taken to embed cultural awareness education within existing instructional venues. For example, cross-cultural healthcare has been a topic in several departmental grand rounds presentations, within the new resident orientation program and medical school curricula, a topic of the quarterly patient safety newsletter (which is required reading for clinical staff members), and a component of clinical services orientation. This strategy to weave these topics within existing educational programming ensures that this information reaches more staff members and demonstrates the alignment of cultural competence within other organizational tenets.

In addition, a web-based, user-friendly, cross-cultural information resource (and decision support tool) was made available to all health network staff members in July 2010. Provided with funding to the patient-centered experience initiative from a local health trust, the Quality Interactions® Cultural Competency Resource Center features succinct background information, short vignettes/case studies, and skill-based tips to deliver cross-cultural healthcare. This tool was developed by nationally known physician experts on cross-cultural healthcare and was based on a "patient-based approach" to cultural competency (that is, the patient is the best source of his or her cultural information). The content of this resource complements the content of live presentations provided by hospital system educators. We conclude with two external examples that serve as representative anecdotes for the promise of patient- and community-focused, cross-cultural healthcare.

A Native American man is hospitalized for gall bladder surgery. Prior to surgery, he and his wife request permission to perform a smudging ceremony, a cleansing ritual. The ceremony involves burning herbs (sweet grass and sage) to cleanse the body physically and spiritually. After consultation with risk management and fire safety colleagues, the nursing leadership on the unit created a place where the smudging ritual could be provided safely without jeopardizing other patients or staff members. "We give so much credit to our caregivers," the man said. "We felt comfortable knowing they were open to our culture. They accepted us, and that made us feel wonderful."

One of the best examples of the incorporation of cultural preferences into the delivery of the system's services occurred within the planning and development of the Health Center at Moselem Springs. Lehigh Valley Health Network purchased the Inn at Moselem Springs in 2010 with the intent to convert this historic meeting place into a state-of-the-art healthcare facility to serve patients at the far rural end of the region. To understand the healthcare needs of this population, several members of the physician hospital network development team met with local community leaders, physicians, EMT teams, and other stakeholders in focus groups and individual meetings. Among those who participated were Old Order Mennonite leaders, who were interested in knowing how the new facility would be able to meet their health concerns, accommodate their schedules, and be respectful of their limited communication access and travel preferences. By engaging these leaders in open dialogue, health network leaders at Moselem Springs were able to incorporate plans for walk-in hours in the early morning and evenings, and discussed plans for ongoing communication with Old Order Mennonite leadership. In addition, after harvest in December, Old Order Mennonite workmen held a "barn-raising" at Moselem Springs, building a shed (made from ash wood) that accommodates four horse-drawn carriages, as well as a bicycle stand, so members of this community can feel welcome as they come for services at the new health center.

Future research for this hospital system will include an analysis of the open-ended questions that address what the system can do to become more responsive to patients and community. Plans also include analysis of patient satisfaction survey data to better inform our cross-cultural healthcare delivery. We will also conduct a follow-up assessment of employees to evaluate the impact of our initiatives. Another fruitful analysis of this data set is to more thoroughly analyze the relationship between learning preferences and content preferences across a variety of the demographic information collected and endeavor to create educational opportunities that promise significant impact based on those specifics. While not without its hurdles, the pathway created to foster organizational transformation regarding cross-cultural healthcare in our network might be useful to other healthcare organizations on similar journeys.

References

Ahmed, R., & Bates, B. R. (2007). Patient gender differences in patients' perceptions of physicians' cultural competence in healthcare interactions. *Women's Health & Urban Life: An International and Interdisciplinary Journal, 6,* 58–80.

Ahmed, R., & Bates, B. R. (2010). Patients' ethnocentric views and patients' perceptions of physicians' cultural competence in healthcare interactions. *Intercultural Communication Studies, 19,* 111–127.

Anderson, L. M., Scrimshaw, S. C., Fullilove, M. T., Fielding, J. E., Normand, J., & Task Force on Community Preventive Services. (2003). Culturally competent healthcare systems: A systematic review. *American Journal of Preventative Medicine, 24*(3S), 68–79.

Auslander, W. F., Thompson, S. J., Dreitzer, D., & Santiago, J. V. (1997). Mothers' satisfaction with medical care: Perceptions of racism, family stress, and medical outcomes in children with diabetes. *Health and Social Work, 22,* 190–199.

Barber, K. R., Shaw, R., Folts, M., Taylor, D. K., Ryan, A., Hughes, M. et al. (1998). Differences between African American and Caucasian men participating in a community-based cancer screening program. *Journal of Community Health, 23,* 441–451.

Bates, B. R., & Ahmed, R. Introduction to medical communication in clinical contexts. In B. R. Bates & R. Ahmed (Eds.), *Medical communication in clinical contexts* (pp. 1–16). Dubuque, IA: Kendall Hunt.

Beach, M. C., Price, E. G., Gary, T. L., Robinson, K. A., Gozu, A., Palacio, A. et al. (2005). Cultural competence: A systematic review of healthcare provider educational interventions. *Medical Care, 43,* 356–373.

Betancourt, J., Green, A., Carrillo, J. E., & Ananeh-Firempong, O. (2003). Defining cultural competence: A practical framework for addressing racial/ethnic disparities in health and healthcare. *Public Health Reports, 118,* 293–302.

Bernhardt, J., & Cameron, K. (2003). Accessing, understanding, and applying health communication messages: The challenge of health literacy. In T. Thompson, A. Dorsey, K. Miller, & R. Parrott (Eds.), *Handbook of health communication* (pp. 583–608). Mahwah, NJ: Lawrence Erlbaum Associates.

Chen, G., & Starosta, W. (1997). A review of the concept of intercultural sensitivity. *Human Communication. 1,* 1–16.

Chen, G., & Starosta, W. (2000). The development and validation of the intercultural sensitivity scale. *Human Communication, 3,* 1–15.

Crabtree, B., & Miller, W. (1999). *Doing qualitative research* (2nd ed.). Thousand Oaks, CA: SAGE Publications.

Croft, J. B., Giles, W. H., Pollard, R. A., Keenan, N. L., Casper, M. L., & Anda, R. F. (1999). Heart failure survival among older adults in the United States: A poor prognosis for an emerging epidemic in the Medicare population. *Archives of Internal Medicine, 159,* 505–510.

Daumit, G. L., Hermann, J. A., Coresh, J., & Powe, N. R. (1999). Use of cardiovascular procedures among Black persons and White persons: A 7-year nationwide study in patients with renal disease. *Annals of Internal Medicine, 130,* 173–182.

Dong, Q., Day, K., & Collaco, C. (2008). Overcoming ethnocentrism through developing intercultural communication sensitivity and multiculturalism. *Human Communication, 11*, 27–38.

Ebell, M., & Smith, M. (1995). Effect of race on survival following in-hospital cardiopulmonary resuscitation. *Journal of Family Practice. 40*, 571–577.

Engleberg, M., & Flora, J. (1997). AIDS knowledge: Effects of channel involvement and interpersonal communication. *Health Communication, 3*, 71–79.

Flores, G., Abreu, M., Olivar, M. A., & Kastner, B. (1998). Access barriers to healthcare for Latino children. *Archives of Pediatric and Adolescent Medicine, 152*, 1119–1125.

Fox, R. (2005). Cultural competence and the culture of medicine. *New England Journal of Medicine, 353*, 1316–1319.

Fritz, W., Graf, A., Hentze, J., Mollenberg, A., & Chen, G. (2005). An examination of Chen and Starosta's model of intercultural sensitivity in Germany and the United States, *Intercultural Communication Studies, 14*, 53–65.

Gertner, E., Sabino, J., Mahady, E., Deitrick, L., Patton, J., Grim, M. et al. (2010). Developing a culturally competent health network: A planning framework and guide. *Journal of Healthcare Management, 55*, 190–204.

Hahn, B. (1995). Children's health: Racial and ethnic differences in the use of prescription medications. *Pediatrics, 95*, 727–732.

Kleinman, A. (1980). *Patients and healers in the context of culture*. Berkeley, CA: University of California Press.

Kumas-Tan, Z., Beagan, B., Loppie, C., MacLeod, A., & Frank, B. (2007). Measures of cultural competence: Examining hidden assumptions. *Academic Medicine, 82*, 548–557.

Meyers, K. S. H. (2007). Racial and ethnic health disparities: Influences, actors, and policy opportunities. Oakland, CA: Kaiser Permanente Institute for Health Policy.

Morse, J. (2006). Insight, inference, evidence, and verification: Creating a legitimate discipline. *International Journal of Qualitative Methods 5*, 93–100.

Morse, J., Niehaus, L., Wolfe, R., & Wilkins, S. (2006). The role of the theoretical drive in maintaining validity in mixed-method research. *Qualitative Research in Psychology, 3*, 279–291.

Nelson, A. (2002). Unequal treatment: Confronting racial and ethnic disparities in healthcare. *Journal of the National Medical Association, 94*, 666–668.

Office of Minority Health, U.S. Department of Health and Human Services. (2000). National standards for culturally and linguistically appropriate services (CLAS) in healthcare. Federal Register, 65 (247), 80865–80879. Retrieved from http://www.omhrc.gov/clas/finalcultural1a.htm

Orque, M. (1983). Ethnic nursing care: *A multicultural approach*. St. Louis: C. V. Mosby.

Peng, S. Y. (2006). A comparative perspective of intercultural sensitivity between college students and multinational employees in China. *Multicultural Perspectives, 8*, 38–45.

Polacek, G., & Martinez, R. (2009). Assessing cultural competence at a local hospital system in the United States. *The Healthcare Manager, 28*, 98–110.

Purnell, L., & Paulanka, B. (1998). Transcultural health care: *A culturally competent approach*. Philadephia: F.A. Davis.

Smedley, B., Stith, A. Y., & Nelson, A.R. (Eds.). (2003). *Unequal treatment: Confronting racial and ethnic disparities in healthcare*. Washington, DC: National Academies Press.

Stains, L. (2004, May 15). The Latinization of Allentown, PA. *New York Times Magazine*. 56–62.

Sue, D. W., Arredondo, P., & McDavis, R. J. (1992). Multicultural counseling competencies and standards: A call to the profession. *Journal of Counseling and Development, 70*, 477–486.

Tamam, E. (2010). Examining Chen & Starosta's model of intercultural sensitivity in a multiracial collectivist country, *Journal of Intercultural Communication Research, 39*, 173–183.

Tashakkori, A., & Teddlie, C. B. (1998). *Mixed methodology: Combining qualitative and quantitative approaches*. Thousand Oaks, CA: SAGE Publications.

Tong, Y., & Chen, G. M. (2008). Intercultural sensitivity and conflict management styles in cross-cultural organization studies. *Intercultural Communication Studies, 17*, 149–161.

Tucker, C. M., Herman, K. C., Pedersen, T. R., Higley, B., Montrichard, M., & Ivery, P. (2003). Cultural sensitivity in physician-patient relationships: Perspectives of an ethnically diverse sample of low-income primary care patients. *Medical Care, 41*, 859–870.

Ulrey, K. L., & Amason, P. (2001). Intercultural communication between patients and healthcare providers: An exploration of intercultural communication effectiveness, cultural sensitivity, stress, and anxiety. *Health Communication, 13*, 449–463.

Viera, A., & Garrett, J. (2005). Understanding interobserver agreement: The kappa statistic. *Family Medicine, 37*, 360–363.

Wilkinson, R., & Marmot, M. G. (Eds.). (2003). *The solid facts: Social determinants of health* (2nd ed.). Copenhagen: World Health Organization.

Appendix 8.1:
Intercultural Sensitivity Scalee

1   I enjoy interacting with people from different cultures.

2   I think people from other cultures are narrow-minded.

3   I am pretty sure of myself in interacting with people from different cultures.

4   I find it very hard to talk in front of people from different cultures.

5   I always know what to say when interacting with people from different cultures.

6   I can be as sociable as I want to be when interacting with people from different cultures.

7   I don't like to be with people from different cultures.

8   I respect the values of people from different cultures.

9   I get upset easily when interacting with people from different cultures.

10 I feel confident when interacting with people from different cultures.

11 I tend to wait before forming an impression of culturally distinct counterparts.

12 I often get discouraged when I am with people from different cultures.

13 I am open-minded to people from different cultures.

14 I am very observant when interacting with people from different cultures.

15 I often feel useless when interacting with people from different cultures.

16 I respect the ways people from different cultures behave.

17 I try to obtain as much information as I can when interacting with people from different cultures.

18 I would not accept the opinions of people from different cultures.

19 I am sensitive to my culturally distinct counterpart's subtle meanings during our interaction.

20 I think my culture is better than other cultures.

21 I often give positive responses to my culturally different counterpart during our interaction.

22 I avoid those situations where I have to deal with culturally distinct persons.

23 I often show my culturally distinct counterpart my understanding through verbal or nonverbal cues.

24 I have a feeling of enjoyment towards differences between my culturally distinct counterpart and me.

Chen & Starosta (2000)

Interaction Engagement	Items #1, 11, 13, 21, 22, 23, 24
Respect for Cultural Differences	Items #2, 7, 8, 16, 18, 20
Interaction Confidence	Items #3, 4, 5, 6, 10
Interaction Enjoyment	Items #9, 12, 15
Interaction Attentiveness	Items #14, 17, 19

Tamam (2010)

Interaction Attentiveness and Respect	Items #8, 13, 14, 16, 17, 21, 23
Interaction Openness	Items #2, 4, 7, 9, 12, 15, 18, 22
Interaction Confidence	Items #1, 3, 5, 6, 24
Did not load	Items #10, 11, 19, 20

Baglia, Nerino, Sabino, & Patton (2012)

Intercultural Esteem	Items #2, 7, 8, 9, 12, 13, 15, 16, 18, 20, 22
Interaction Confidence	Items #3, 4, 5, 6, 10
Communication Presence	Items #11, 14, 17, 19, 21, 23, 24
Did not load	Item #1

Chapter 9

Physicians' Views of Interpersonal Communication Training, the Importance of Communication in Their Medical Practices and the Delivery of Bad News

Patricia Amason, Cortney Smith,
Samantha Romanin, and Melissa Horvath

Introduction

Communication in medical contexts can be verbal, written, or electronically de-livered; however, interpersonal communication remains the most vital form of communication in medical practice (Makoul, 2003). Medical communication comprises a complex set of behaviors used to carry out the functions of the medi-cal interview: eliciting information, building relationships, and educating patients about a health issue or ways to manage an issue. Medical communication also involves explaining the meaning of a diagnosis, making treatment recommenda-tions, and describing prognoses, while also informing patients and loved ones of how the medical concern will affect their lives (Barrier, Li, & Jensen, 2003; Keller & Carroll, 1994; O'Keefe, 2001; Street, Kurpat, Bell, Kravitz, & Haidet, 2003). Thus, physician-patient communication is a fundamental aspect of medical care (Back, Arnold, Baile, Tulsky, & Fryer-Edwards, 2005). In this chapter we analyze physicians' views of the role communication plays in their medical practices and their preparedness for effective communication with patients, as well as how they perceive the ways in which they communicate bad news to patients and family members/caregivers.

Patient-Physician Communication

Good patient-physician communication leads to positive influences on myriad out-comes such as "patient recall and understanding, adherence, symptom resolution and physiological outcomes, patient and physician satisfaction, and the frequency of malpractice claims" (Laidlaw, MacLeod, Kaufman, Langille, & Sargeant, 2002,

p. 115). Increased patient satisfaction is related to their generating better questions, enhanced compliance with treatment recommendations, a decreased need for prescribed medications, and a briefer recovery time from illness (Barrier, Li, & Jensen, 2003; Fallowfield, Jenkins, & Beveridge, 2002; Greenfield, Kaplan, & Ware, 1989; Hook & Pfeiffer, 2007). Thus, higher quality communication between patient/caregiver and provider establishes a more effective partnership (Street, 2001).

When examining patient-provider interactions we can look to Accommodation Theory as a framework (Giles, Coupland, & Coupland, 1991; Giles, Mulac, Bradac, & Johnson, 1987). This theory proposes that, when speakers from different social groups interact, they adjust or modify their verbal and nonverbal communication to accommodate others. Street (1991) offers that persons attempt to adapt their communication when conversing with persons they perceive as similar to or different from themselves. Thus, they willingly converge by adjusting their communicative styles viewed as more similar to those with whom they wish to gain approval from, establish rapport, and become affiliated. The outcome typically is positive when such convergences occur. Diversities among patients and providers may include education, training, socioeconomic status, medical experiences as well as beliefs, values, and ways of communicating acquired from their cultural backgrounds. Adapting the ways in which individuals communicate based on perceived similarities results in convergence, e.g., when physicians avoid the use of medical jargon and adapt by using understandable language to fulfill their own and their patients' mutual goals of providing and receiving quality healthcare.

Conversely, divergence is the outcome of emphasizing differences, such as when physicians focus more on their social status or their medical expertise. For example, a physician might firmly adhere to an opinion simply because the physician holds a more elevated position. In these cases, physicians may use their titles as leverage with patients or against other healthcare professionals to imply that they are "better informed" because they have a higher level of informational control. Additionally, when physician power and control are more present, divergence is common (Street, 1991). This may be the case when physicians interrupt patients presenting their illness narratives or when presuming a diagnosis before the patient adequately has presented all relevant matters (e.g., making a diagnosis based strictly on physiological symptoms without consideration of potential socioemotional or psychological contributors). Divergence also is present when physicians fail to consider cultural differences in values and beliefs. This often is the case when physicians attempt to impose their values of western medical practices on persons who do not share those cultural values or who distrust western medical practices.

Ineffective Communication

Physicians with poor communication skills may be more likely to exhibit signs of divergence when their behaviors may be attributed to one, if not all, of the following outcomes: blocking, lecturing, collusion, or providing premature reassurance. *Blocking* occurs when a patient raises a concern or question, but the physician fails to respond or redirects the conversation (Maguire, Faulkner, & Booth, 1996) and, thereby, fails to "elicit the range of patient concerns and consequently [is] unable to address the most important concerns" (Back et al., 2005, p. 165). *Lecturing* occurs when a physician delivers a large amount of information all at once without giving the patient a chance to respond or ask questions (Siminoff, Ravdin, Colabianchi, & Sturm, 2000), often leaving a patient unable to follow the pace of information delivery (see Back et al.). *Collusion* occurs when patients fail to reveal information to their physician because it is a difficult topic to discuss or the patient assumes it is not pertinent because the physician did not ask about it directly (The, Hak, Koeter, & van Der Wal, 2000). Finally, physicians may participate in *premature reassurance* by responding to a patient's concerns with reassurance before exploring and understanding the real concern (Faulkner, Maguire, & Regnard, 1994).

Implications for Health Outcomes

A physician's willingness or unwillingness to adapt their communication style could affect a patient's participation in medical consultations. Street (2002) found that 84 percent of active participation behaviors in medical encounters were patient-initiated rather than prompted by a physician's attempt to build a partnership through supportive communication. Street (1991) reviews literature examining how physicians accommodate in their interactions; he found the dyads were characterized by greater verbal convergence and more information-giving when the patients were perceived as more similar socially and in regard to education by the physician. Physicians often have difficulty converging with persons from alternative cultural backgrounds, negatively affecting health-related decision making (Kreps, 2006). Differences in patient and provider race and sex also contribute to divergent barriers in patient-physician communication. However, how differences are managed often contributes to the valence of health outcomes resulting from patient-physician interactions.

Cultural Differences

It is important for providers to be sensitive to cultural differences as they play "a large role in shaping health related values, beliefs, and behavior" (Betancourt, 2004, p. 953). Cultural competence is a key element in increasing the quality of medical care and is important for improving patient-physician communication (Ahmed, 2007; Ramirez, 2003). In the United States, the number of immigrants has nearly tripled since 1970 and, as a result, physicians can expect to care for new patients from a variety of ethnic backgrounds during their careers (Kundhal & Kundhal, 2003). Language barriers, cultural values and practices, differences in beliefs about causes of disease, and treatment options present myriad potential errors and other limitations in the medical field (Cisneros, 2007; Ramirez, 2003). Clinicians should be skilled in accessing and understanding their patients' cultural values (Kundhal & Kundhal, 2003); however, these and other sociodemographic factors such as race and socioeconomic status often contribute to discrepancies in physician attitudes toward their patients and, ultimately, the quality of the care provided (van Ryn & Burke, 2000). From interview studies with persons from African American, Hispanic, Asian, and Caucasian groups, members of the nonwhite groups indicated they believed they would have received more attentive medical care, respect, and fair treatment if they were members of a different racial group (Johnson, Saha, Arbelaez, Beach, & Cooper, 2004; van Ryn & Burke, 2000).

Ahmed (2007) argues for providers to demonstrate greater cultural competence as they attempt to accommodate cultural differences through convergence. Ethnocentric patients often are suspicious of modern medical practices and fear their providers. Ahmed continues that accommodation to cultural differences may improve increased patient participation with their providers (see also Street, 1991, 1992, Street et al., 1995) as well as greater patient autonomy and protection of their personal rights (see also Beisecker & Beisecker, 1993), ultimately resulting in a more positive partnership with providers (Roter & Hall, 1993, Street, 1992). Ahmed and Bates (2010) argue for a more holistic view of culture by emphasizing the integration of

> patterns of beliefs, values, assumptions, attitudes, history, norms, traditions, customs, lifestyles, and institutions shared by a group of people within a community, organization, or nation, who have a common nationality, race, ethnicity, language, religion, or socio-economic status, or a combination thereof. (p. 112)

Thus, healthcare providers and their patients demonstrate their cultural competency through their recognition of relevant differences and their efforts to adapt to differences with the ultimate goal of providing the types of medical services needed.

Each patient has a different reaction to and outlook on life as well as employs individualized coping mechanisms. Therefore, healthcare providers also must be able to adapt their messages to the unique communication needs of their patients by interpreting patient behaviors and converging communicatively particular situations (Skilbeck & Payne, 2003). It also is important to consider whether patients prefer to have information given addressing their needs as individuals or if they are more comfortable receiving information associated with persons among the same groups to which they identify (Ahmed & Bates, 2010).

Cultural Competence Training

Research demonstrates that formal intercultural training improves the cultural competence of healthcare professionals; however, formal training only occurs in a limited number of undergraduate premedical programs (Flores, Gee, & Kastner, 2000) and a few medical schools' curricula (Crandall, George, Marion, & Davis, 2003). Medical educators need to stress to students the importance of demonstrating concern for fulfilling *all* patient needs—social and cultural. Moreover, medical education should show through its objectives a commitment to providing medical students the means to acquire intercultural communication skills, identify how and where in the curricula such skills are included, and demonstrate the extent to which the objectives are achieved (LCME, 2011). Despite the curricular standards established by the LCME, Ramirez (2003) asserts that more effective cultural competence training should be integrated into medical school curricula, interactive workshops could be used before the medical students begin clinical rotations, and refresher courses could be given during residency and fellowships. While training opportunities would be useful, it also is important for healthcare systems to place greater diversity in the workforce. This may be accomplished by hiring more translators, specialists in producing language-sensitive health education materials (Betancourt, Green, Carrillo, & Ananeh-Firempong, 2003), and providers from myriad cultural backgrounds. Accommodating cultural differences presents many challenges. Perhaps the most challenging, yet most important context in which effective communication skills must be employed is in the delivery of bad news (Barclay, Blackhall, & Tulsky, 2007; Amiel et al., 2006).

Delivering Bad News

Communication plays one of its most important roles when providing negative information. The most crucial objectives in delivering bad news are acquiring information from the patient or family member/caregiver, providing medical information, offering support to the recipient, and setting the stage for collaborative efforts in establishing a treatment plan (Baile et al., 2000). Many times an attempt is made to present prognoses in the most hopeful and even optimistic manner, even when the physician knows it is fatal (Doyle, 1994).

As not all patients react to bad news in the same way, it is important for physicians to recognize the differences in how persons perceive and react while receiving such news. Physicians who are of the same sex as their patient or the family member(s)/caregiver(s) report fewer communication barriers and offer more comfort (Gjerberg, 2002). Ethnicity also impacts how bad news is given and received (Ishikawa, Hashimoto, Roter, Yamazaki, & Takayama, 2005; Johnson, Roter, Powe, & Cooper, 2004; Sleath, Rubin, & Huston, 2003; Sung, 1999; Tse & Chong, 2003). When bad news is delivered without considering the patient's or family member's needs, or cultural differences are not considered, the result may be long-term consequences such as poor psychological adjustment for patients (Ngo-Metzger, August, Srinivasan, & Mevskens, 2008; Kagawa-Singer & Blackhall, 2001).

Even though informing patients about bad news across all patient-physician contexts is an important communicative task, physicians across four medical career stages feel they are not trained extensively enough in this area of communication (Barclay et al., 2003). Many studies find physicians deficient in communication skills (Baile et al., 2000; Buckman, 1984; Eggly et al., 1997; Girgis & Sanson-Fisher, 1995). Poor communication training leads to physicians delivering bad news poorly. This, in turn, leads to stress for the physician and a distressing impact on the recipients of the poor communication—the patients and relatives/caregivers (Fallowfield, 1993)—and impacts the quality of the actual healthcare delivered (Lambert et al., 1997).

Some intense training programs are offered for post-graduate Continued Medical Education credit emphasizing the skills most useful in helping improve physicians' confidence in providing bad news with patients and family members and providing hands-on training with a simulated dialogue with a patient (Wilkinson, Leliopoulou, Gambles, & Roberts, 2003). Several studies investigate the ways in which bad news may be delivered (Baile et al., 2000; Buckman, 1992; Fallowfield, Jenkins, & Beveridge, 2002; Rosenbaum & Kreiter, 2002; Sparks, Villagran, Parker-Raley, & Cunningham, 2007; Ungar, Alperin, Amiel, Beharier, & Reis, 2002; Viadya, Greenberg, Patel, Strauss, & Pollack, 1999).

Implications of Poor Communication in Healthcare Delivery

Effective communication is necessary for quality healthcare delivery. The first ingredient necessary for effective communication is the development of a trusting relationship between patient and provider (Perloff, Bonder, Ray, Ray, & Siminoff, 2006). When physicians build rapport and gain trust through convergence with patients, the communication leads to positive influences on myriad outcomes, such as "patient recall and understanding, adherence, symptom resolution and physiological outcomes, patient and physician satisfaction, and the frequency of malpractice claims" (Laidlaw et al., 2002, p. 115). Increased patient satisfaction is related to their ability to generate better questions, enhanced adherence to treatment recommendations, a decreased need for prescribed medications, and a briefer recovery time from illness (Barrier, Li, & Jensen, 2003; Fallowfield, Jenkins, & Beveridge, 2002; Greenfield, Kaplan, & Ware, 1989; Hook & Pfeiffer, 2007; Stewart et al., 1999). Moreover, patients and caregivers who trust providers and feel their thoughts and feelings were recognized are less likely to pursue litigation even under the most unpleasant outcomes (Adamson, Tschann, Gullion, & Oppenberg, 1989; Levinson, Roter, Mullooly, Dull, & Frankel, 1997; Moore, Adler, & Robertson, 2000). When trust is high, the quality of communication between patient and provider emerges and greatly enhances a more effective partnership (Street, 1992).

It is evident that effective communication is vital for quality medical care. Much research is published examining patient perspectives on the importance of communication in their relationships with healthcare providers. After reviewing the literature, we find that little exists from the physicians' perspectives. Thus, there is a need for evaluation of physicians' views of the role communication plays in their practices, the importance of communication training for practicing medicine, how physicians received training for effective interpersonal communication, and ways in which physicians describe perhaps the most difficult context in while they share information—delivering bad news to their patients and their family members and caregivers. This lack of research into the doctors' perspectives of these communication issues led us to answer the following research questions:

- RQ1: What are the physicians' attitudes toward the importance of communication in their practices?
- RQ2: What perceptions do physicians have of how effectively their formal medical training in communication prepared them for the communication that occurs in their practice?
- RQ3: How do physicians describe the ways in which they convey bad news to patients and their family members?

Methods

After obtaining approval from the Institutional Review Board, a purposive sampling method was used to identify practicing physicians to serve as participants. They were among a group of physicians practicing in three metropolitan areas in the southeastern United States. Physicians from both sexes with different educational experiences and medical expertise were solicited by letter and asked to contact the researchers to arrange for data collection. Seventy-three physicians representing a wide range of medical specialties positively responded and agreed to be interviewed. Due to scheduling constraints, 60 physicians actually met with a member of the research team (see Table 9.1 for a breakdown of specialties represented). Forty-eight of the physicians were male, 12 were female. The average age of the participants was 48 years with an average length in practice of 16.5 years. To accommodate as many participants as possible, nine of the participants responded to the questions in written form while the remaining participants were queried face-to-face. Data were analyzed using a grounded theory approach to identify patterns in physicians' responses (Glaser & Strauss, 1967).

Table 9.1

Medical Specialities of Participants

Specialty	Number of Participants
Family Practive	10
Pediatrics	8
Radiology	7
Internal Medicine	6
Obstetrics/Gynecology	6
Gastroenterology	4
General Surgery	4
Orthopedic Surgery	4
Colo-Rectal Surgery	4
Oncology	3
Hematology	3
Ophthalmology	3
Cardiology	3
Pulmonary Medicine	3
Otolaryngology	3
Plastic Surgery	2
Allergy Immunology	1
Neurology	1
Urology	1

Results

The first research question focused on the attitudes physicians have toward the importance of communication in their practices. The results indicate that physicians see communication as important in their daily interactions with the most important interactions being with their patients. A number of reasons were provided for why communication is important. A 52-year-old physician stated that it is "hard to imagine practicing medicine without it because a doctor deals with relationships on multiple levels." Other physicians described effective communication as making a difference between a patient being satisfied or unsatisfied. Effective communication was identified as playing a critical role in working with patients and families specifically when dealing with patients' problems, taking medical histories as well as in explaining diagnoses and treatment plans. Moreover, good communication was identified as playing an important role in achieving a correct diagnosis and ensuring that patients and families understand what the physician was saying and vice versa. One physician used the analogy of the communication used in the medical field to that of a used car salesperson, "communication builds their confidence, otherwise, the patient doesn't buy it. Communication is essential." One 36-year-old female pediatrician's description of communication as "everything" signifies its importance in the medical field. She stated that it is an integral aspect of practicing medicine and that "it is key and if there is bad communication nothing else works."

All the physicians stated that miscommunication between themselves and a patient has occurred in their practices. The reasons attributed to the miscommunication were different among the physicians, such as patient agendas, the patient only hearing the worst scenarios possible or hearing information incorrectly, and cultural or ethnic differences between the physician and the patient. Eighteen of the physicians provided that societal issues (i.e., insurance companies, the fast pace of today's existence, etc.) impact efforts to maintain good patient relationships. Difficulty in building rapport with patients was cited when physicians perceive that patients will be dissatisfied with the services they receive or have problems with their insurance carriers ultimately resulting in their seeking another provider.

In the effort to improve their relationship with their patients, many of the physicians indicate they try to sit down on the patient's eye level during their meetings as it enhances patients' perceptions that the physician is spending more time with them. A 42-year-old male allergy and immunology specialist noted, "it is important to sit during consultations so patients see you as more approachable and get the sensation that you really care." Many physicians concurred as they described how they sit during the initial history taking part of the exam and stand only during the physical part of the exam. Several physicians also commented on how they must use both open- and close-ended questions to get to the medical problem of a patient. The more standard use of all open-ended questions typical of medical interviews (What can I do for you today?) was cited as not as useful as a combination of question types to adequately identify all patient needs.

The second research question focused on physicians' views of the extensiveness to which they were trained in the communication skills needed to effectively practice medicine. While the majority of physicians responded that communication is important in their practices, most indicated their communication skills training while an undergraduate and medical student was minimal at best. A physician practicing family medicine for 22 years stated that courses in communication "would be nice … It would be a benefit if taught appropriately." When asked if they had any type of formal training in communication while undergraduates, 12 physicians responded, "yes," they were required to take a communication course. Four of the physicians mentioned that the only communication training was in their required freshman-level communication class.

The majority of physicians indicated they had no training or no significant communication training while in medical school, but some stated they had a class focused on patient history-taking. Six of the physicians discussed how the required course on history-taking did not focus on communication skills or how to accommodate those skills to the demands of particular situations or in the presence of cultural differences. Five physicians replied they had more extensive communication skills training, but typically in courses with titles unrelated to communication skills. Some mentioned receiving more communication training while in psychiatry rotations and after completing their medical school training in continuing medical education (CME) courses focused on bioethics. Only one physician interviewed (the youngest in age) spoke about his intensive communication training during medical school.

The physicians practicing the fewest number of years were required to interact with standardized patients to practice skills in the interviewing process. They were each evaluated during their third year on their clinical communication skills. Most of the physicians interviewed were not taught with these methods. Several of these physicians remembered shadowing mentoring physicians during internships and residencies. These physicians stated their formal communication training only occurred by observation and critique during their rotations. Mentors who valued communicating effectively critiqued their mentees' communication skills; however, one physician commented that training consisting of only following a mentor is a gamble as there are good communication role models and bad ones. If medical students do not see the good communication techniques demonstrated, they are at a disadvantage for being equipped to eventually implement those techniques.

The third research question focused on the methods physicians report using to convey bad news. The older physicians indicated that breaking bad news was much more difficult at the beginning of their medical practice. As the years passed, they learned to adapt their communication behaviors to what seemed to work the most effectively for them. Several physicians admitted that delivering bad news is more difficult than it seems or they have difficulty breaking bad news to their patients. Several physicians expressed the importance of showing empathy toward their patients' situations.

The physicians indicated that certain behaviors were necessary when giving a patient bad news. One physician stated, "I do not mince words and under no circumstance will I allow the discussion to not include the patient." Others answered that they speak directly and always make sure the patients understand what is being said. Additionally, some physicians indicated that the best way to explain a negative diagnosis is in a private room, face to face with the patient, straightforward and directly with the bad news first. An oncologist described his method for communicating bad news. He stated, "I sit down in person, lean forward (which shows interest), touch the patient on their shoulder and hand and am straightforward." He also described the importance of ending the consultation on a positive note by giving hope to the patient. Practicing convergence by using words a patient will understand and answering all questions were other techniques the physicians described. One radiologist stated that while addressing patients diagnosed with cancer, he shows the images to the patient and describes exactly where the cancer is and what is being seen. Another stated that he begins by acknowledging there is a problem and the need to accurately diagnose the problem in order to identify the best treatment plan. The main objective of the session most physicians revealed was to give all the facts, allow as much time as needed for questions from the patient or family members, and make sure the information is understood.

Timing of the bad news delivery is also important. One oncologist stated that if a biopsy returns on a Friday afternoon, he should call the patient on Saturday or Sunday so patients and family members do not have to spend unnecessary time worrying. Another physician indicated he designated these meetings for the end of the day to allow more time for discussion and questions, and he provides a comfortable environment in which to break the news. While each physician described his or her own way of breaking bad news, each indicated he or she learned their method for breaking bad news from observation and experience rather than from formal training. One physician indicated that the main priority was to use terms that the patient could understand. Another physician admitted in his response that delivering bad news is more difficult than it seems. In regard to training in bad news delivery, all physicians stated they had received inadequate formal training. One stated, "I had very little training through medical school; my sense is that most physicians do a terrible job of giving bad news to their patients."

Conclusions and Implications

The Need for Convergence

Extant research stresses the positive impact of effective communication between physicians and patients. The results of the present study show that most physicians rate communication an integral part of practicing medicine. Physician responses demonstrated their efforts to accommodate their communication with patients and family members by engaging in convergent communication. They attempted to use more understandable and compassionate language rather than using a divergent method of overuse of medical jargon or being overly direct. However, the physicians interviewed indicated they were inadequately trained or not trained at all except "on the job" for effectively converging. Several physicians perceived that their training focused mainly on how to extract information from a patient and how to conduct a physical exam. Many of these physicians did not perceive receiving adequate training from courses that demonstrated how to communicatively accommodate patients and family members in complex and sensitive situations, such as when confronted with cultural differences in beliefs and attitudes, language differences, or in giving bad news. For the most part, the participants stated that communication used in their practice was either learned by observation or experience rather than from formal training. They also revealed that communication is an extremely important aspect of their professional lives, yet believe they were inadequately trained.

Many of the physicians attempted to be more accommodating in their communication with patients. For example, they indicated their choice to sit down when visiting with a patient to be eye level with them. This simple convergent behavior should reduce patient feelings of physician superiority and increase feelings of equality and should be encouraged. Patients perceive physicians to be more professional and caring when they are more immediate and at eye level (Creagan, 1994). Some physicians commented on how each patient is different; therefore, physicians must accommodate their communication behaviors to the unique characteristics of their patients, particularly those who are from different age and sex groups or other cultural backgrounds (McKinlay, Lin, Freund, & Moskowitz,

2002). In the same vein, Epstein (2006) stated that in every physician-patient relationship the context of the situation must be factored into the medical encounter to understand the complex dynamics of the interaction because "no one theory of communication or set of communication guidelines can account for the diverse situations in which communication occurs in healthcare" (p. 273). Due to variations in cultural values, persons trust and place value in modern western medical practices differently. Additionally, persons often have dissimilar knowledge and understanding of medical jargon, as well as comfort in discussing personal issues. Thus, cultural sensitivity is necessary when attempting to accommodate to any cultural difference.

Several physicians commented on how they must use open- and close-ended questions to fully identify patients' medical problems. Andrews (2000) stresses that open-ended questions, such as "How can I help you?" or "What's the problem?" is the best method of opening the medical interaction. However, after beginning the interview with an open-ended question, a physician then should become as precise as possible by using more close-ended questions for making correct diagnoses and treatment options. Interestingly, of the physicians interviewed, no clear pattern emerged as to how they open the medical interview.

Communicating Bad News

In regard to delivering bad news, many physicians stated experience as their means of training rather than any formal mechanism for learning how to *effectively* communicate bad news. One physician admitted to having "very little training in medical school" and continued, "My sense is that most physicians do a terrible job of giving bad news to their patients." In other words, they were unprepared until they actually were in practice for a number of years. Several physicians listed residency as the place where they learned to communicate with patients. This statement further illustrates the need for communication skills to be taught much earlier in the education process. The physicians in the present study indicated they were ill-prepared when it came to delivering bad news. One physician stated that he believed the main objective was to use information that the patient could understand. While this is an important aspect, it may cause the patient to feel that she is less significant to the physician than the disease. Thus, other strategies may be more beneficial to patients and their family members/caregivers receiving upsetting news about a diagnosis or prognosis. Bad news is devastating, regardless of the manner in which it is delivered. However, sensitivity is key in presenting the news or as stated by Johnson, Siegler, and Winslade (1986), "the truth may be brutal, but the telling of it should not be" (p. 53). The patient's psychosocial needs as well as the physiological needs must be met in order to provide the best experience possible during this difficult time. Taking these needs into account is crucial for the patient's overall well-being. Research shows a direct relationship between physician empathy and support, and positive health outcomes, patient satisfaction, and overall life quality. The skills necessary for doing so are teachable (Baile & Aaron, 2005).

The Need for Training

The physician-patient and physician-family member/caregiver relationship must be based on trust and openness for quality care to result. There is a strong need for more precise training for physician skillsets in interpersonal communication and knowledge of cultural differences necessary for establishing and maintaining these relationships. The ultimate outcome is that patient and caregiver needs are met in the most effective way possible. Physicians who are ineffective communicators often overlook crucial issues or misdiagnose patients, because they did not ask the right questions or ignored other concerns that needed to be addressed. Other misdiagnoses or inappropriate treatment plans emerge because physicians fail to ask about or notice psychiatric and psychosocial problems underlying patients' chief complaints (Barrier, Li, & Jensen, 2003). Over 40 years ago it was stated that "care to doctor-patient relation has for too long been left to chance; because of its importance to general practice it must now be examined, defined and taught, for only then can it be practiced efficiently" (Korsch, Gozzi, & Francis, 1968, p. 855). However, it was not until 2007 that the National Board of Medical Examiners began assessing medical students on their ability to effectively communicate with patients prior to receiving their licenses to practice medicine. The results from this study suggest the need not only for enhanced communication training for students in medical training, but also for postprofessional opportunities for practicing physicians through workshops or seminars.

Limitations and Strengths

There were several limitations to the study. First, the sample was purposive as opposed to random, which may have led to skewed results. Additionally, the data might be more representative of the training and experiences of physicians as a whole with a larger number of participants and from a national rather than regional population. It may be the case that physicians trained and practicing outside of the southeastern United States have received additional training in communication skills as a whole and in delivering bad news in particular. Also, the physicians self-selected to participate in the study. By doing so, they demonstrated they value communication. Their willingness to sit down with the researchers and talk or write about communication in their practices may have skewed the results, since they likely may be among those physicians who are *most* concerned with communication among their peers. The results might have been far different had we obtained information from a number of physicians who do not prioritize communication. Another limitation would be the physicians' inherent social desirability to answer questions in a more positive manner.

Regardless of the study's limitations, several strengths of the present research are evident. First, a number of physicians representing a wide range of medical specialties participated in this in-depth examination of their beliefs about the role communication plays in their professional practice. Most of the physicians agreed that effective communication is vital to their best serving their patients' needs. There also was general agreement that most of the training they received in how to effectively communicate has occurred "on the job" rather than from formal instruction while in their medical training, and that they entered their medical practices ill-prepared for the communication accommodation demands they experienced. There also were shared views about the challenges they faced in communicating with persons from different cultural backgrounds and that delivering bad news was particularly difficult.

Future Research

Future research is needed to examine the specific interpersonal communication skills physicians need to demonstrate and how they best manage the cultural differences they confront. Studies focused on patient-provider communication should consider ethnic, cultural, sex, and age differences between patients and physicians to determine how these differences affect communication patterns. Additionally, it would be beneficial to examine the perceived effectiveness of both physician and patient communication skills and whether patient-provider pairs share similar levels of satisfaction in the outcome of their medical encounters. Such a study would be helpful in identifying areas where training would assist all parties to increase levels of satisfaction with communication encounters. Moreover, it is clear from the physicians' remarks that more extensive communication training is essential for medical students while they are in training, particularly in giving bad news.

The physicians who participated in the present study viewed communication as the key to effective healthcare delivery. They see it as an integral part of the patient-physician relationship, and, if it is not adequately present, the relationship likely will be damaged and result in inadequate healthcare delivery. Therefore, medical schools should focus on and require communication training throughout the four-year curriculum. It is not enough to call a course "Interacting with Patients." Medical schools must focus on the social science of communication and integrate it as a necessary part of the medical school curriculum. Moreover, persons pursuing medical careers would benefit from communication skills training in their premedical training, as well. The results of this study indicate that those who design the premedical and medical school curricula must focus on including the communication skills that test the communication competence that all graduating medical students must demonstrate.

Ahmed, R. (2007). *Assessing the role of cultural differences on healthcare receivers' perceptions of healthcare providers' cultural competence in healthcare interactions.* (Doctoral dissertation, Ohio University) .

Ahmed, R., & Bates, B. R. (2010). Patients' ethnocentric views and patients' perceptions of physicians' cultural competence in healthcare interactions. *Intercultural Communication Studies, 19,* 111–127.

Adamson, T. E., Tschann, J. M., Gullion, D. S., & Oppenberg, A. A. (1989). Physician communication skills and malpractice claims: A complex relationship. *Western Journal of Medicine, 150,* 356–360.

Amiel, G. E., Ungar, L., Alperin, M., Baharier, Z., Cohen, R., & Reis, S. (2006). Ability of primary care physician's to break bad news: A performance based assessment of an educational intervention. *Patient Education and Counseling, 60,* 10–15.

Andrews, W. C. (2000). Approaches to taking a sexual history. *Journal of Women's Health and Gender-Based Medicine, 9,* 21–24.

Back, A. L., Arnold, R. M., Baile, W. F., Tulsky, J. A., & Fryer-Edwards, K. (2005). Approaching difficult communication tasks in oncology. CA: *A Cancer Journal for Clinicians, 55,* 164–177.

Baile, W. F., & Aaron, J. (2005). Patient-physician communication in oncology: Past, present, and future. *Current Opinion in Oncology, 17,* 331–335.

Baile, W. F., Buckman, R., Lenzi, R., Glober, G., Beale, E. A., & Kudelka, A. P. (2000). SPIKES—A six-step protocol for delivering bad news: Application to the patient with cancer, *Oncologist, 5,* 302–311.

Barclay, J. S., Blackhall, L. J., & Tulsky, J. A. (2007). Communication strategies and cultural issues in the delivery of bad news. *Journal of Palliative Medicine, 10,* 958–977.

Barclay, S., Wyatt, P., Shore, S., Finlay, I., Grande, G., & Todd, C. (2003). Caring for the dying: How well prepared are general practitioners? A questionnaire study in Wales. *Palliative Medicine, 17,* 27–39.

Barrier, P. A., Li, J. T. C., & Jensen, N. M. (2003). Two words to improve physician-patient communication: What else? *Mayo Clinic Proceedings, 78,* 211–214.

Beisecker, A. E., & Beisecker, T. B. (1993). Using metaphors to characterize doctor-patient relationships: Paternalism versus consumerism. *Health Communication, 5,* 41–58.

Betancourt, J. R. (2004). Becoming a physician: Cultural competence? Marginal or mainstream movement? *New England Journal of Medicine, 351,* 953–955.

Betancourt, J. R., Green, A. R., & Ananeh-Firempong, O. (2003). Defining cultural competence: A practical framework for addressing racial/ethnic disparities in health and healthcare. *Public Health Reports, 118,* 293–301.

Buckman, R. (1984). Breaking bad news: Why is it still so difficult? *British Medical Journal, 288,* 1597–1599.

Buckman, R. (1992). *How to break bad news—A guide for healthcare professionals.* Baltimore: Johns Hopkins University Press.

Cisneros, L. (2007). Studies show importance of language services on reducing disparities, increasing quality of patient. *University of California, San Francisco Newsletter*. Retrieved from http://www.ucsf.edu/news/2007/11/7362/studies-show-importance-language-services-reducing-disparities-increa

Crandall, S. J., George, G., Marion, G. S., & Davis, S. (2003). Applying theory to design cultural competency training for medical students: A case study. *Academic Medicine, 78,* 588–994.

Creagan, E. T. (1994). How to break bad news—and not devastate the patient. Mayo *Clinic Proceedings, 69,* 1015–1017.

Doyle, D. (1984). *Palliative care: The management of far advanced illness.* Beckenham, UK: Croom Helm.

Eggly, S., Afonso, N., Rojas, G., Baker, M., Cardozo, L., & Robertson, R. (1997). An assessment of residents' competence in the delivery of bad news to patients. *Academic Medicine, 71,* 397–399.

Epstein, R. M. (2006). Making communication research matter: What do patients notice, what do patients want, and what do patients need? *Patient Education and Counseling, 60,* 272–278.

Fallowfield, L. (1993). Giving sad and bad news. *The Lancet, 341,* 476–478.

Fallowfield, L. J., Jenkins, V. A., & Beveridge, H. A. (2002). Truth may hurt but deceit hurts more: Communication in palliative care. *Palliative Medicine, 16,* 297–303.

Faulkner, A., Maguire, P., & Regnard, C. (1994). Breaking bad news—a flow diagram. *Palliative Medicine, 8,* 145–151.

Flores, G., Gee, D., & Kastner, B. (2000). The teaching of cultural issues in U.S. and Canadian medical schools. *Academic Medicine, 75,* 451–455.

Giles, H., Coupland, J., & Coupland, N. (1991). *Contexts of accommodation: Development in applied sociolinguistics.* Cambridge: Cambridge University Press.

Giles, H., Mulac, A., Bradac, J. J., & Johnson, P. (1987). Speech accommodation theory: The next decade and beyond. *Communication Yearbook, 10,* 13–48.

Girgis, A., & Sanson-Fisher, R. W. (1995). Breaking bad news: Consensus guidelines for medical practitioners. *Journal of Clinical Oncology, 13,* 2449–2456.

Gjerberg, E. (2002). Similarities in doctors' preferences—Gender differences in final specialization. *Social Science & Medicine, 54,* 591–605.

Glaser, B. G., & Strauss, A. L. (1967). *The discovery of grounded theory: Strategies for qualitative research.* Hawthorne, NY: Aldine de Gruyter.

Greenfield, S., Kaplan, S. G., & Ware, J. E. (1989). Assessing the effects of physician-patient interaction on the outcomes of chronic disease. *Medical Care, 27,* 110–127.

Hook, K. M., & Pfeiffer, C. A. (2007). Impact of a new curriculum on medical students' interpersonal and interviewing skills. *Medical Education, 41,* 154–159.

Ishikawa, H., Hashimoto, H., Roter, D. L., Yamazaki, Y., & Takayama, T. (2005). Patient contribution to the medical dialogue and perceived patient-centeredness: An observational study in Japanese geriatric consultations. *Journal of General Internal Medicine, 20,* 906–910.

Johnson, A. R., Siegler, M., & Winslade, W. J. (1986). *Clinical ethics: A practical approach to ethical decisions in clinical medicine* (2nd ed.). New York: MacMillan.

Johnson, R. L., Roter, D. L., Powe, N. R., & Cooper, L. A. (2004). Patient race and the quality of patient-physician communication during medical visits. *American Journal of Public Health, 94,* 2084–2090.

Johnson, R. L., Saha, S., Arbelaez, J. J., Beach, M. C., & Cooper, L. A. (2004). Racial and ethnic differences in patient perceptions of bias and cultural competence in healthcare. *Journal of General Internal Medicine, 19,* 101–110.

Kagawa-Singer, M., & Blackhall, L. J. (2001). Negotiating cross-cultural issues at the end of life: 'You got to go where he lives.' *Journal of the American Medical Association, 286*, 2993–3001.

Keller, V. F., & Carroll, J. G. (1994). A new model for physician-patient communication. *Patient Education and Counseling, 23*, 131–140.

Korsch, B. M., Gozzi, E. K., & Francis, V. (1968). Gaps in doctor-patient communication: Doctor-patient interaction and patient satisfaction. *Pediatrics, 42*, 855–871.

Kreps, G. L. (2006). Communication and racial inequities in healthcare. *American Behavioral Scientist, 49*, 760–774.

Kundhal, K. K., & Kundhal, P. S. (2003). Cultural diversity: An evolving challenge to physician-patient communication. *Journal of the American Medical Association, 289*, 94.

Laidlaw, T., MacLeod, H., Kaufman, D., Langille, D., & Sargeant, J. (2002). Implementing a communication skills programme in medical school: Needs assessment and programme change. *Medical Education, 36*, 115–124.

Lambert, B. L., Street, R. L., Cegala, D. J., Smith, D. H., Kurtz, S., & Schofield, T. (1997). Provider-patient communication, patient-centered care, and the mangle of practice. *Health Communication, 9*, 27–43.

Levinson, W., Roter, D. L., Mullooly, J. P., Dull, V. T., & Frankel, R. M. (1997). The relationship with malpractice claims among primary care physicians and surgeons. *Journal of the American Medical Association, 277*, 553–559.

Liaison Committee on Medical Education (LCME). (2011). Standards for accreditation of medical education programs leading to the M.D. degree. Retrieved from http://www.lcme.org/functions2011may.pdf

Maguire, P., Faulkner, A., & Booth, K. (1996). Helping cancer patients disclose their concerns. *European Journal of Cancer, 32*, 78–81.

Makoul, G. (2003). The interplay between education and research about patient-provider communication. *Patient Education and Counseling, 50*, 79–84.

McKinlay, J. B., Lin, T., Freund, K., & Moskowitz, M. (2002). The unexpected influence of physician attributes on clinical decisions: Results of an experiment. *Journal of Health and Social Behavior, 43*, 92–107.

Moore, P. J., Adler, N. E., & Robertson, P. A. (2000). Medical malpractice: The effect of doctor-patient relations on medical patient perceptions and malpractice intentions. *Western Journal of Medicine, 173*, 244–250.

Ngo-Metzger, Q., August, K., Srinivasan, L. S., & Mevskens, F. L. (2008). End of life care: Guidelines for patient-centered communication. *American Family Physician, 77*, 167–174.

O'Keefe, M. (2001). Review article: Should parents assess the interpersonal skills of doctors who treat their children? A literature review. *Journal of Pediatric Child Health, 37*, 531–538.

Perloff, R. M., Bonder, B., Ray, G. B., Ray, E. B., & Siminoff, L. A. (2006). Doctor-patient communication, cultural competence, and minority health. *American Behavioral Scientist, 49*, 835–852.

Ramirez, A. G. (2003). Consumer-provider communication research with special populations. *Patient Education and Counseling, 50*, 51–54.

Rosenbaum, M. E., & Kreiter, C. (2002). Teaching delivery of bad news using experiential sessions with standardized patients. *Teaching and Learning Medicine 14*, 144–149.

Roter, D., & Hall, J. A. (1993). *Doctors talking to patients/patients talking to doctors: Improving communication in medical visits*. Westport, CT: Auburn House.

Siminoff, L. A., Ravdin, P., Colabianchi, N., & Sturm, C. M. (2000). Doctor-patient communication patterns in breast cancer adjuvant therapy discussions. *Health Expectations, 3*, 26–36.

Skilbeck, J., & Payne, S. (2003). Emotional support and the role of clinical nurse specialists in palliative care. *Journal of Advanced Nursing, 43*, 521–530.

Sleath, B., Rubin, R. H., & Huston, S. A. (2003). Hispanic ethnicity, physician-patient communication, and antidepressant adherence. *Comprehensive Psychiatry, 44*, 198–204.

Sparks, L., Villagran, M. M., Parker-Raley, J., & Cunningham, C. B. (2007). A patient-centered approach to breaking bad news: Communication guidelines for healthcare providers. *Journal of Applied Communication Research, 35*, 177–196.

Street, R. L. Jr. (1991). Accommodation in medical consultations. In H. Giles, N. Coupland, & J. Coupland (Eds.), *Contexts of accommodation: Developments in applied sociolinguistics* (pp. 131–156). Cambridge, MA: Cambridge University Press.

Street, R. L. Jr. (1992). Communicative styles and adaptations in physician-parent consultations. *Social Science and Medicine, 34*, 1115–1163.

Street, R. L. Jr. (2001). Active patients as powerful communicators: The linguistic foundation of participation in healthcare. In W. P. Robinson & H. Giles (Eds.), *The new handbook of language and social psychology* (2nd ed., pp. 541–560). West Sussex, UK: John Wiley & Sons.

Street, R. L. Jr. (2002). Gender differences in healthcare provider-patient communication: Are they due to style, stereotypes, or accommodation? *Patient Education and Counseling, 48*, 201–206.

Street, R. L. Jr., Cauthen, D., Buchwald, E., & Wiprud, R. (1995). Patients' predispositions to discuss health issues affecting quality of life. *Family Medicine, 27*, 663–670.

Street, R. L. Jr., Kurpat, E., Bell, R. L., Kravitz, R. L., & Haidet, P. (2003). Beliefs about control in the physician-patient relationship. *Journal of General Internal Medicine, 18*, 609–617.

Sung, C. L. (1999). Asian patients' distrust of western medical care: One perspective. *The Mount Sinai Journal of Medicine, 66*, 259–320.

The, A. M., Hak, T., Koeter, G., & van der Wal, G. (2000). Collusion in doctor-patient communication about imminent death: An ethnographic study. *British Medical Journal, 321*, 376–381.

Tse, C. Y., & Chong, A. (2003). Breaking bad news: A Chinese perspective. *Palliative Medicine, 17*, 339–343.

Ungar, L., Alperin, M., Amiel, G. E., Beharier, A., & Reis, S. (2002). Breaking bad news: Structured training for family medicine residents, *Patient Education and Counseling, 48*, 63–68.

van Ryn, M., & Burke, J. (2000). The effect of patient race and socio-economic status on physicians' perceptions of patients. *Social Science and Medicine, 50*, 813–828.

Viadya, V. U., Greenberg, L. W., Patel, K. M., Strauss, L. H., & Pollack, M. M. (1999). Teaching physicians how to break bad news: A 1-day workshop using standardized parents. *Archives of Pediatric Adolescent Medicine, 153*, 419–422.

Wilkinson, S. M., Leliopoulou, C., ambles, M., & Roberts, R. (2003). Can intensive three-day programmes improve nurses' communication skills in cancer care? *Psycho-Oncology, 12*, 747–759.

Chapter 10

Effective Health Communication in the Management of Chronic Conditions: Theoretical Considerations for a Multicultural Framework

Zhenyi Li, Elizabeth Dean, and Jennifer Walinga

Introduction

Chronic lifestyle-related conditions, such as ischemic heart disease, smoking-related conditions, high blood pressure, stroke, type 2 diabetes mellitus, obesity, and cancer, are at critically high levels worldwide (Dean, 2009a, 2009b). These conditions are associated with substantial social as well as economic burdens with the potential to bankrupt economies in the years ahead. Although the World Health Organization (WHO) has long proclaimed that lifestyle-related conditions are largely preventable and, in part, reversible with healthy living, these conditions are the leading causes of premature death in high-income countries, and increasingly in middle- and low-income countries, commensurate with their economic development (Waxler-Morrison, Richardson, Anderson, & Chambers, 2005).

Despite unequivocal evidence supporting the strong association between lifestyle-related conditions and personal choices about smoking, diet, and exercise, the fact that these conditions constitute the leading causes of death is not acceptable, and has been described as "the ultimate knowledge translation gap" (Dean, Lomi, Bruno, Awad, & O'Donoghue, 2011, p. 2). Clearly, the explanation for "the ultimate knowledge translation gap" is multifactorial, including factors such as government policy, corporate marketing, the roles of health professionals, and individual choice, which are largely culturally influenced. To modify a person's lifestyle choices, effective health education can be a cost-effective means of promoting lifelong health and well-being. This necessitates an understanding and appreciation of cultural diversity by both the healthcare providers and receivers.

In this chapter, we argue for a framework with multicultural considerations to maximize the effectiveness of health communication based on the multiculturalism developed in Canada and elsewhere. We prefer the term multicultural to cross-cultural or intercultural to characterize such a framework because the term multicultural is perceived as being more comprehensive compared with cross-cultural or intercultural.

A framework based on multiculturalism acknowledges the reality and necessity of the coexistence of multiple interpretations of health behaviors. A consideration of these offers a rational basis for targeted management focused on lifestyle behavior change, and potentially superior outcomes, through effective health communication. Arguably, although it may be premature to propose a multicultural framework for effective health education in the management of chronic lifestyle-related conditions, we outline in this chapter a range of theoretical considerations relevant to this topic that could provide a basis for such a framework. To illustrate our central themes, we provide examples of the application of a multicultural framework in health communication research, practical applications of a multicultural framework to enhance health education outcomes, and finally, insights that have emerged from our ongoing research to inform future research directions.

Definitions and Rationale

Our terms are defined as follows. A health communication *framework* refers to a scholarly approach "concerned with the role of human interaction in health and the healthcare process" (Kreps, 1989, p. 11). The general goal of health communication research is "to generate health communication knowledge for directing healthcare policy, practice, and intervention" (Kreps, 1989, p. 15). The nature of culture impact on health communication is complex, diverse, and dynamic (Canadian Nurses Association, 2004; Health Canada, 2003; Leininger, 1991; Wright & Pemberton, 2004); therefore, it is important to explore cultural influences on health communication through certain frameworks. Compelling conceptualizations, frameworks, and approaches are necessary to inform health communication and establish it as a distinct clinical intervention (Dutta, 2007), and to maximize the benefits of such communication in terms of improving the health outcomes of patients (Geiger, 2001; Leininger, 2002). Chronic lifestyle-related conditions are mostly associated with smoking, suboptimal western diet, and inactivity; however, disturbed sleep and stress are also correlates. The benefits of biomedical outcomes for lifestyle-related conditions as well as for other conditions can be compromised without sufficient attention to the quality of concurrent health education (Dean, 2009a, 2009b).

Several assumptions need to be made when articulating and discussing the role of culture in health communication. First, culture is viewed as shared and learned knowledge, behavior, and values of a group of people (Galanti, 2008). Second, everyone, including healthcare providers and receivers, may benefit from an understanding and appreciation of the role of cultural diversity. Third, a framework that reflects such diversity needs to acknowledge that: (a) first and foremost, health communication is cultural; (b) the nature of health communication is inherently multicultural; and (c) health communication can be viewed from a social constructionist perspective. We discuss the relationship and distinctions between a multicultural framework and health communication frameworks such as the culture-centered approach (Dutta, 2007) and the cultural sensitivity approach (Resnicow, Braithwaite, Dilorio, & Glanz, 2002).

Finally, we interpret multiculturalism as an attempt to dynamically balance participation, representation, dialogue, and knowledge exchange opportunities within individuals and across groups regardless of their socioeconomic, cultural, political, regional, professional, educational, religious, or other categorical differences (Belay, 1993; see also Kallen, 1915, 1924/1970; Hollinger, 1995). Theoretically, individuals are entitled to have equal rights. However, in reality people do not have equal accessibility or input into institutional "structure," which is "the organization of social systems, the patterns of distribution of resources, and the patterns of control of these resources" controlled by "the privileged" (Dutta, 2007, p. 317). Promoting multiculturalism will not necessarily eliminate such inequalities. Nor do we anticipate the disappearance of power struggles and conflicts. However, a multicultural framework could help everyone appreciate the need to improve health communication, support everyone to present their thoughts, reasons, and values effectively, and enable everyone to understand that health communication needs to be culturally sensitive and specific. This chapter elaborates these three advantages of multiculturalism through a review of our exploratory research initiatives to date. But, before we do this, we articulate three central claims about the role of culture in health communication.

Health Communication Is Cultural

In general, human communication is embedded in cultural norms and traditions. An exploration of cultural influences on the dynamics of effective health communication can be justified in terms of their impact on health communication from cross-cultural, intercultural, or multicultural perspectives. Scholars have advanced various ways of "linking" culture to health communication (for example, Airhihenbuwa, 1995; Dutta, 2008; Lupton, 2003; Zoller, 2005). Only by "re-acknowledging" the cultural nature of health communication are stakeholders in healthcare likely to improve the outcomes of their patients with chronic lifestyle-related conditions. We concur with Srivastava that "there has been increasing recognition that cultural issues are important in relation not only to the client but also to the healthcare provider and the healthcare system" (2007, p. 5). We argue, however, that such recognition is often partial because the cultural nature of health communication is insufficiently acknowledged. This can be illustrated by two established approaches, the cultural sensitivity approach and the culture-centered approach.

The cultural sensitivity approach highlights that culture is a part of health communication (Resnicow et al., 2002). Cultural sensitivity aims to increase awareness of and sensitivity to the role of culture in health communication. The target group of this approach is mainly healthcare providers (Dutta, 2008). The anticipated goal is to enable them to increase their sensitivity when sending messages to receivers from various cultural backgrounds. The common practice is to translate or tailor-write health-related messages in a culturally appropriate way to the receivers. The outcome evaluation is based on how appropriately and effectively these messages are written, translated, and received. However, to what extent healthcare providers practice in accordance with the cultural sensitivity approach is unclear. Some may view such an approach as an unwanted addition to their heavy workloads or increased demand on scarce resources (King & Wheeler, 2004). Sending culturally sensitive messages to prevent chronic lifestyle-related conditions may also be regarded as transferring the economic burden of diseases from a functionalist view to a "cultural" one (Lupton, 2003, p. 7).

The culture-centered approach proposes that the "privileged" need to emphasize culture as "the core of health communication practices" (Dutta, 2007, p. 304) as a means of better hearing the voices of the "marginalized." The goal of this approach is to promote dialogue between the so-called privileged and the marginalized. From this political economic perspective, health communication can be viewed as a potential power struggle between the one who has or controls the distribution of resources (i.e., the privileged) and the one who receives inadequate services (i.e., the marginalized). Such a seemingly adversarial relationship within the current healthcare "structure," particularly with respect to "the distribution of power," aims, through its understanding, to add "agency and voice" to "communicate culture for health" (Dutta, 2007, pp. 317–325). Despite its intent, the culture-centered approach may not adequately justify or explain why culture needs to be at the core of health communication practices. For example, the role and of other prominent factors such as economic and political ones is not clear, as is whether these should be weighted less than cultural factors in implementing health communication. And, if so, on what grounds?

The seminal work of Edward Hall has helped shed light on the role of culture in health education. He established the tradition to treat "culture in its entirety as a form of communication" (1959, p. 51). Hall suggested that the contents and function of culture are the two indivisible faces of one coin. Consistent with the working definition we use in this chapter, that culture is a collection of meanings shared by a group of people, he argues that the contents of culture are what a culture has and that the function of culture, also known as the reasons we need culture, is for communication. Therefore, in a multicultural framework, culture needs to be conceptualized to include both its contents and function. On one hand, health communication is about meanings and interpretations related to health, illness, and disease (McFarland, 2002). On the other hand, in terms of function, culture facilitates the complex and dynamic process of meaning exchange; or in other words, "culture is communication" (Hall, 1959, p. 119). When content and function intersect, health communication concerns the dynamic construction and exchange of the meanings and interpretations (Nance, 1995), as well as continually changing contexts and interpersonal relationships (Dreher & MacNaughton, 2002). Therefore, overemphasis of either content or function risks misrepresenting the pivotal role of culture in health communication. For example, the cultural sensitivity approach emphasizes varying contents among cultures, but may overlook the function of culture in relation to communication. The culture-centered approach, to the contrary, stresses the function of culture. Thus, culture can be viewed as dynamic and constitutive, and similarly so can health communication.

Health Communication Is Multicultural

In line with Hall's epic notion of communication as culture, health communication can be viewed as a coexistence of multiple interpretations of health-related issues from a multicultural perspective (Barnlund, 1975). Healthcare providers and receivers, no matter how closely their cultures may be related, will inevitably experience situations in which their interpretations of health conditions are different (Street, 2003). This difference emerges because both providers and receivers are "cultured," sometimes sharing commonalities, other times differences. Similar or different, their cultures coexist in the context of health communication. Therefore, health communication is not simply cultural, but more aptly multicultural. The multicultural reality of health communication necessitates a framework that represents the multicultural characteristics in both descriptive and normative ways, namely, a combination of cross-cultural and intercultural approaches.

As described, multiculturalism is a more comprehensive approach compared with cross-culturalism or interculturalism. Cross-cultural research, as the foundation for intercultural and multicultural studies, primarily compares differences across cultures (Gudykunst, 1987). Intercultural studies focus on interactions between people or organizations from different cultural backgrounds and emphasize application to real-life situations (Stewart, 1978). Both Gudykunst and Stewart acknowledge cultural diversity in this globalizing world (Gudykunst, 1987). Neither of them, however, addresses the approach to accommodate multiple conceptualizations and interpretations in healthcare or other professional settings (Brach & Fraser, 2000; Gerrish, 2000; Kendall & Hatton, 2002; Long, Chang, Ibrahim, & Asch, 2004; see also Smedley, Stith, & Nelson, 2002). For example, cross-cultural nursing research has generated a long list of cultural differences with respect to how people deal with birth and death (Waxler-Morrison et al., 2005). Intercultural communication studies of physician-patient interactions provided insights about clinical challenges. Kleinman (1980) provided numerous examples and insights about microlevel, one-on-one physician-patient communication. However, no study has proposed a macrolevel analysis or perspective, which may explain why health disparity "issues persist" (Spector, 2009, p. xv).

The notion of multiculturalism is not only descriptive but also normative. Heywood (2007) differentiated these characteristics of multiculturalism by arguing that descriptive multiculturalism refers to "cultural diversity" and normative multiculturalism implies "a positive endorsement … to the alleged benefits to the larger society of moral and cultural diversity" (p. 313). By emphasizing the dual characteristics of multiculturalism, we can synthesize theories and practices generated from cross-cultural descriptive and intercultural normative health communication studies. This synthesis could enable us to augment management outcomes in a health system hallmarked by complexity, e.g., the complications of one or more risk factors for or manifestations of lifestyle-related conditions (de Savigny & Adam, 2009; WHO, 2007).

Health Communication Is Socially Constructed

In addition to serving as a basis for Hall's cultural communication theory, the elements of a multicultural framework are also grounded in social constructionist theory. First, a multicultural framework recognizes the multiplicity of influences. To claim that only certain people have the power to create the "creed" of biomedical structure is neither sufficient nor fair. Holistic therapies, for example, have been dominant and deeply rooted in many Asian cultures for thousands of years before modern Western medical practices were introduced over the past two centuries. One cannot argue that the healthcare structure changes that have taken place in those cultures were only because of the power of modern Western medical practices, or because of a blatant disregard for heritage. In fact, traditional and Western medical practices often coexist in Asian countries (Aung, Benjamin, Berman, & Jacobs, 1997). A multicultural framework to health communication strives to attribute its derivation from more than a single factor (Cassidy, 1996).

Second, a multicultural framework argues that illness, disease, chronic conditions, and other bodily experiences are culturally constructed to a large extent in some patients: The culture of the person directly experiencing the illness or condition generates meaning by which that person interprets his or her experiences and treatment (Hajela, 1994). At the same time, the cultures of other people also generate similar or different interpretations of that experience and treatment. These people include the patient's relatives, friends, physicians, nurses, and social workers, and researchers, lawyers, and journalists in some cases. The point is not to determine an exhaustive list of participants in an illness experience. Practically, the list cannot be exhausted. In relation to a multicultural framework, we stress the importance of recognizing the coexistence of multiple participants, interpretations, and experiences. For example, biomedical intervention is only one of many cultural practices participating in such a health communication interaction. Also, most people are exposed to and familiar with more than one culture, exposure that is reflected in their lifestyle-related health behavior choices.

We have conducted a range of investigations (viz., Rodrigues, Jongbloed, Li, & Dean, 2007; Wang, Li, Jongbloed, & Dean, 2007, 2008) related to multicultural considerations and health education. Our preliminary results support our contention that a multicultural framework for health education is indicated. Based on cross-cultural survey, our findings support that people tend to negotiate meanings of chronic lifestyle-related conditions based on more than one cultural perspective. Therefore, a multicultural framework advocates meaning negotiation, i.e., communication, for better health education outcomes.

Lastly, a multicultural framework not only proposes to shift and broaden our paradigm for healing the human system, but also proposes to shift and expand our approach to healing the healthcare system. When viewed through a multicultural lens, the biomedical system is one of the many interacting and interdependent parts of the larger system of human health and sustainability. Taking a multicultural view of human health and sustainability translates directly into many aspects of the healthcare system identified by scholars: interaction between care givers and receivers (Zola, 1996); relationships between disease interpretation and culture (Barnes, Powell-Griner, McFann, & Nahin, 2004); values related to healthcare (Astin, 1998); healthcare policy, regulation, system, and practice (Lupton, 1995); and, choices in each person's life (Aday, 1993). Likewise, it is through these aspects of communication that a multicultural framework to health education can be constructed.

To expand the points in the chapter thus far, the remaining sections describe examples of a multicultural framework in health communication research, practical applications for better outcomes based on a multicultural framework, and insights that have emerged from our research.

Examples of a Multicultural Framework for Health Communication Research

Dutta (2007) has observed that a cultural sensitivity approach prevails "within the United States" (p. 307) whereas a culture-centered approach seemed to be more common outside the United States (p. 313). A health communication framework that includes and focuses on the individual may better enable that person to assume responsibility for his or her health and enhance his or her health outcomes. However, the traditional biomedical model is a reductionist approach where a problem is identified and, typically, a drug or possibly surgery is prescribed (Engel, 1977). The association between lifestyle-related conditions and behaviors such as smoking, suboptimal nutrition, inactivity, sleep deprivation, and excessive stress is unequivocal (Dean, 2009a). Further, effective health education can prevent and, in some cases, reverse as well as manage these conditions (Dean, 2009b). The failure of successful implementation over the long term could reflect a lack of attention to cultural diversity.

Ischemic heart disease or IHD is among the most common chronic lifestyle-related conditions that affect people around the world. Like other chronic conditions, IHD is interpreted differently by people, depending on their cultural perspective and, thus, is well suited for analysis from a multicultural perspective. We applied a multicultural framework to three cross-sectional exploratory research projects with the same structured questionnaire as a basis for examining the impact of IHD-related knowledge, beliefs, and behaviors across cultures (Rodrigues et al., 2007; Wang et al., 2007, 2008).

A multicultural framework for health communication studies emphasizes participation or the capacity people have to fulfill their life roles. Therefore, we included people from different cultures, with different experiences and identities. Our target population included (a) 835 Chinese urban residents in four Chinese provinces, specifically Hubei, Liaoning, Hebei, and Shanxi, (b) 102 Chinese Canadians, (c) 102 Indo-Canadians, and (d) 204 Euro-Canadians. Respondents were either from one of the four provinces in China or from the Greater Vancouver, Canada area. By doing so, we included people living in different continents with varying educational and occupational backgrounds who had emigrated or never left their hometowns, and those with or without a diagnosis of IHD. We also had comparable groups of people who were similar ethnically but resident in different places, i.e., Chinese living on Mainland China and Chinese living in Canada. We included people living in the same place but with different cultural backgrounds, i.e., Chinese Canadians and Indo-Canadians living in Vancouver. We studied a large group of Euro-Canadians in our studies to explore the degree to which the responses of the non-Euro-Canadian participants represented the mainstream culture of Euro-Canadians, which would provide insight into the need for and development of health communication in specific groups.

Data Collection

Multicultural distinctions needed to be considered in the design of the questionnaire. The structured questionnaire with closed-ended questions related to IHD-related knowledge, behaviors, beliefs, and sociodemographic information was based on the literature and adapted from existing instruments as described below.

Knowledge of IHD risk factors was assessed by asking subjects to respond "True" or "False" to 10 statements related to risk factors. The possible range of scores was from 0 to 10, with higher scores representing greater knowledge of positive health behaviors and risk factors for lifestyle-related conditions.

Five lifestyle-related behaviors related to IHD risk were assessed: physical inactivity, suboptimal diet, smoking, excessive alcohol consumption, sleep deprivation, and stress. A survey tool previously developed by Al-Mazeedi and Dean was used (personal communication). Multiple choice questions adapted from the Canadian Community Health Survey were used to obtain information about health promotion and perceived barriers and facilitating factors for participating in positive health behaviors. Health beliefs related to stroke were assessed using the Health Belief Model (HBM). This model is based on the belief that individuals will undertake a positive health action if they perceive the disease or condition to be threatening (perceived susceptibility), if they believe it to have potentially serious consequences (perceived seriousness), if they believe the recommended action to be effective (perceived benefits), and if they find barriers to practicing the particular health behavior (perceived barriers) to be minimal.

The IHD health belief scale was based on a validated instrument for assessing beliefs about osteoporosis-related preventive behaviors among women and included the construct of self-efficacy which reflects the individual's confidence in his or her ability to perform a specific task by overcoming barriers. Nine subscales measured the following constructs: perceived susceptibility to develop IHD, perceived seriousness of IHD, perceived benefits about following a healthful low-fat diet (dietary benefits), perceived barriers to following a healthy low-fat diet (dietary barriers), perceived benefits of exercising (exercise benefits), perceived barriers to exercising (exercise barriers), general tendency to engage in health behaviors (health motivation), perceived self-efficacy about following a healthful low-fat diet (dietary self-efficacy), and perceived self-efficacy about exercising regularly (exercise self-efficacy). Items had a five-point response format with anchors at 1 (strongly disagree) and 5 (strongly agree). Items for the exercise self-efficacy questionnaire had a three-point response format ("not at all confident," "confident," or "very confident") that was modified from the original scales. Summary scores were obtained by adding the responses to individual items within each subscale. High scores represented greater susceptibility, seriousness, benefits, barriers, health motivation, and self-efficacy. General health beliefs were measured by asking how important respondents believed certain health behaviors were for them to remain healthy.

The questionnaire was pre-tested on a convenience sample of seven individuals and modifications were made to enhance clarity of certain items. More choices were added for items with multiple response options. To ensure a representative sample, the questionnaire was available in English, Mandarin Chinese, and Punjabi. Four bilingual individuals independently translated the questionnaire into Chinese and Punjabi. The translated questionnaire was tested for clarity and comprehension on a sample of four bilingual individuals and revised accordingly. All these efforts were spent to ensure multicultural inclusiveness and appropriateness based on fundamental notion of coexistence of multiple interpretations of chronic lifestyle-related conditions.

Results

The findings of these three exploratory projects focused on five aspects of communication consistent with a multicultural framework and social constructionist perspective. These were (1) interaction between caregivers and receivers; (2) relationships between disease interpretation and culture; (3) values related to healthcare; (4) healthcare policy, regulation, system, and practice; and (5) choices in every person's life.

Caregivers and receivers. The Chinese are more likely to rely on their families, close friends, and the media for IHD-related knowledge. Physicians and healthcare professionals are not ranked at the top. This reflects the cultural differences between Westerners and the Chinese, and these can be explained based on Hofstede's (2001) work. He argued that the Chinese are more family oriented and collectivistic. They tend to trust family members and close friends rather than authority figures. In addition, Hofstede pointed out that Chinese society is hierarchical, where authority of knowledge tends to be concentrated at the top. This suggests that the distribution of the knowledge via mass media is viewed as being preferable and trustworthy. Media in Western society however is often distrusted by the public.

Disease interpretation and culture. Our studies revealed that respondents have similar knowledge but different lifestyle behaviors associated with chronic, lifestyle-related conditions. In general, Chinese knowledge related to stroke risk factors, nutrition, and healthy lifestyles in general is comparable to Westerners'. However, we observed differences on two major dimensions: knowledge acquisition and behavior change, which are particularly important for health education by healthcare professionals. For example, most Chinese male respondents from China continue to smoke although they know it is a risk for IHD. Many Indo-Canadian respondents reported it was hard to give up heavy fat food although they agreed with the food guidelines issued by Health Canada. Chinese respondents from both China and Canada were engaged in jobs requiring prolonged sitting and reported little motivation to be active during and after work. Cultural traditions tend to be more influential in affecting lifestyle behaviors than educational knowledge disseminated by healthcare professionals. In India, deep-fried food tends to be associated with affluence. In China, physical activity is favored less than passive activities, such as passive massage, for people with higher social status with respect to health and recreation. Based on Confucian teachings, gentlemen or nobles are not supposed to walk or move fast as it is counter to the needs of overall health. Cigarette exchange is a social tradition, especially for government officials and businesspeople in China. Therefore, even when the respondents in our studies were aware of healthy choices, they were challenged to change unhealthy behaviors within their cultural contexts. Change was viewed as easier when they had the opportunity to reside outside their traditional communities. For example, we observed that Chinese immigrants to Canada were more likely to quit smoking, particularly if they had been living in Canada over 10 years. Immigrants perceived that smoking cessation was easier in Canada given their perception of respect for individual decisions in Canadian society. This, however, may also be cultural. Canada ranks higher in individualism than China in Hofstede's national cultural dimensions survey (Hofstede, 1980, 2001; Hofstede & Bond, 1984).

Values. Western biomedical interventions may be subject to being both over- and undervalued depending on culture and ethnicity as well as individual personal factors. People from collectivistic cultures, for example, may not perceive they have as much control over the management of their signs and symptoms as someone from an individualistic culture (Hofstede, 2001). Patients who believe that the "will of God" is paramount may experience less self-efficacy in determining the outcome of his or her IHD and, potentially, be less receptive to health education.

Cultures vary widely with respect to attitudes about smoking and its social acceptability, food, and physical activity. In addition, cultures vary on the acceptability of sleep deprivation and high stress. These differences are not insurmountable. Rather, identification and knowledge of individual distinctions among patients with respect to their knowledge, beliefs and behaviors will better able the health educator including the clinician to tailor and target the health education content consistent with the patient's needs.

Our studies suggest that although Chinese people may be aware of the risks and needs of lifestyle behavior change, their behaviors are not changed. This could be explained by the typical Chinese cultural characteristics proposed by Hofstede (1980, 2001) as well. Being a member of a collectivistic culture, Chinese people focus more on others than themselves. Further, they tend to suppress their personal needs in favor of group preferences. For example, they know that smoking is not healthy. Nonetheless, they may continue to smoke as it is consistent with the cultural "norm," in particular, for men doing business. They may maintain the same unhealthy diet and lifestyles if others are doing so. This group-oriented trend was consistent throughout our results.

Policy. The findings of these studies support the need to culturally modify approaches to health education when counseling clients to change their lifestyles to prevent lifestyle-related conditions such as IHD and stroke. In China, it is probably more appropriate and effective to promote healthy lifestyle from the top through mass media by setting up models of seniors who have adopted healthy behaviors and encouraging group-based changes of lifestyle. It also may be culturally expedient to use family members and close friends for distributing health knowledge. For example, a Chinese smoker may be more apt to quit if in a group that is targeted to quit.

Choices. Other determinants of learning that inform the type of teaching indicated include language, literacy, age, and potentially, gender (Glanz, Rimer, & Lewis, 2002). Learners also vary with respect to such preferences as reading to learn, experiencing change, having someone provide feedback, and interactive learning, or some combination. Thus, a brochure or web-based material, even if translated into a patient's native language, may be ineffective due to these other factors. Although it may appear time consuming to evaluate the learner to such a degree, benefits of a valuable "teachable moment" may be compromised without taking time to evaluate the learner and, specifically, the learner's preferred learning style. Across all learning preferences, however, systematically and predictably conducted follow-up is important if learning about the power of lifestyle behavior change on health, and the behavior change itself, is to be effective and sustained over time.

Conclusions and Implications

Three themes have emerged from our program of research. These are: the benefit of viewing health communication as a cultural issue; the advantage of a perspective based on multicultural considerations with respect to health education; and the reasons why a multicultural perspective may be relatively neglected in Western mainstream healthcare systems.

During the process of the questionnaire design, data collection, and analyses of these three projects, health communication was consistently regarded as cultural. All questions were asked according to the respondents' cultures. Measurements for wine and liquor, for example, were adjusted respectively for Canadians and non-Canadians. Even income was asked in a culturally specific way: Canadians talk about annual income, while Chinese people are used to monthly income. These minor adjustments increased workload for data entry because additional conversions were necessitated for many entries. Not doing so, however, may well have limited the accuracy and validity of the data collected, which would have compromised the findings of the studies.

The advantage of applying a perspective consistent with a multicultural framework in health education becomes apparent from the examples cited above. In general, such considerations acknowledge multiple interpretations of chronic, lifestyle-related conditions. It provides additional possibilities for understanding the contexts of lifestyle behavior changes. Patients can be resistant to or ambivalent about change, particularly when healthcare professionals' messages are inconsistent with patients' values and beliefs. In such situations, healthcare professionals need to acknowledge the inconsistency and help enable the patient to articulate, explore, and resolve such inconsistency. This can be achieved by evoking the patient's intrinsic motivation pertaining to the goals and values of his or her family or community (Britt, Hudson, & Blampied, 2004; Rollnick, Miller, & Butler, 2008; Pollak, Childers, & Arnold, 2011). Therefore, the overarching philosophy for motivating patients' behavioral change is the partnership between the patient (which may mean the patient's family to varying degrees) and the clinician (Dean et al., 2011). This partnership is only possible when cultural values are mutually respected and discussed in a multicultural context.

Possible reasons for the apparent lack of attention to multicultural perspectives in health education include world view differences, educational bias, and lack of systems thinking.

World View Differences

The distinction between the reductionist Newtonian world view and less mechanistic world views such as Taoist logic is apparent. Fang and Faure argued the former one "sets attributes in terms of opposition," while the latter "tends to associate" factors no matter how different they are (2011, p. 324). Our research supported the claim that both Chinese and Indian ethnic groups tend to seek harmony and balance when ill. Euro-Canadians, to the contrary, have less tolerance for the coexistence of health and illness. Healing in Newtonian biomedical culture means to re-establish balance as before. In the Chinese or Indian cultures, healing often refers to a new balance, not necessarily the same as before. Such an interpretation based on the "endless, cyclic, and transforming movement ... relies on the dialectical interaction of yin and yang," Chen explained, "developed into a set of guidelines for Chinese beliefs and behaviors" (2008, p. 9). The image of yin and yang suggests "healthy development of universal phenomenon hinges upon a constant dynamic balance between yin and yang" (Fang & Faure, 2011, p. 325). Therefore, in Chinese culture, contradiction, such as yin and yang, health and ill, birth and death "is a natural way of life" (Fang & Faure, 2011, p. 325). Healing, in that context/culture, is conceptualized as a continuum from illness to dynamic, vibrant, and balanced health. This worldview influences or forms Chinese attitudes, beliefs, and behaviors that are distinct from those of Euro-Canadians.

Education Bias

The need for preparing intercultural-competent medical professionals has long been recognized. Scholarly explorations into the relationship between culture and medicine in academia in the United States began almost 90 years ago (Rivers, 1924). Since that time, numerous articles and books on the topic of culture and health have been published, and many of these by healthcare practitioners and academics. Few Canadian or American medical colleges, however, offer courses on culture-related issues. Emerging trends, including our preliminary exploratory studies, strongly support the need for medical professionals to be culturally competent if they are to be maximally effective practitioners in this era of chronic conditions where education about lifestyle modification inevitably plays a central role. Lum and Korenman (1994) surveyed 126 American medical schools regarding whether they offered cultural-sensitivity courses. Among 98 responses, only

13 schools reporting having such courses, and such a course was only mandatory in one school. Five years later, a survey of medical schools in the United States, Canada, Australia, and the United Kingdom found all but two of the American programs offered optional courses on cultural diversity with no formal assessment component (Loudon, Anderson, Gill, & Greenfield, 1999). These surveys, however, were conducted several years ago, and it is possible that there is greater attention to this important topic at this time.

Flores, Gee, & Kastner (2000) surveyed 126 American and 16 Canadian medical schools. Of these, 118 American and 15 Canadian schools responded. Few schools offered separate courses specifically addressing cultural issues. In the United States, only 8 percent of medical schools offered a separate course. In Canada, there were none. During the 2005–2006 academic year, all 17 medical schools in Canada participated in a survey initiated by McGill University. The investigators concluded that "Canadian medical school curricula are not well positioned to address the need of global health education" (Izadnegahdar et al., 2008, p. 192). This educational need supports our conclusions. For example, in a biomedical framework for health communication, knowledge alone is a poor predictor of behavior change. Health communication based on multicultural considerations, however, could be argued to augment the outcomes of health education behavior change such that valuable resources including time are used most cost effectively.

Lack of Systems Thinking

The healthcare system in Canada can be viewed as a complex, federally supported, provincially governed entity. Such an entity tends to develop an organizational culture consisting of prevailing values, beliefs, and assumptions and communicated through organizational structures, artifacts, and systems (Deetz, 2000; Hofstede, 2001; Schein, 2005).

Consistent across the various healthcare paradigms (biocentric, culturally sensitive, and multicultural) are the principles of organizational culture: Each paradigm reflects a distinct collection of values, beliefs, and assumptions. The biocentric paradigm, at its core, values science, control, and economics. The paradigm is based on a belief that science holds the answers to our healthcare issues, that healthcare, to be sustainable, must operate within the capitalist market model, and that all disease and health conditions are within people's capacity to resolve. The assumptions behind these values and beliefs are that health is an outcome of human intervention, and that disease and injury are constructs independent of environment and social conditions.

The culture-sensitive approach holds at its core the values of inclusion and equal opportunity, yet still in relation to the biocentric paradigm. In the culture-sensitive health paradigm, other cultures are welcomed into the existing biocentric paradigm, and mechanisms are created that enable various cultures to assimilate rather than truly integrate into the overall healthcare system. Though a proponent of diverse values, the culture-sensitive health paradigm remains grounded in biocentric beliefs and assumptions that a human intervention is required to resolve any health challenges.

The multicultural paradigm holds diversity and interdependence as its core values and, therefore, seeks a paradigmatic transformation grounded in the beliefs that there are as many approaches to healthcare as there are individuals; and that our understanding of human health can only be deepened through the contributions and insights offered by multiple approaches to healthcare. The multicultural paradigm stems from the assumption that health is a delicate interaction between the individual and his or her environment, what we consider a more "systems thinking" approach to health systems (de Savigny & Adam, 2009; Leischow et al., 2008; WHO, 2007).

In contemporary healthcare, effective health communication is essential if the tide is to be turned on lifestyle-related conditions. Health communication reflects the adequacy of the dynamic relationship between healthcare provider and receiver, and the cultural perspectives of the receiver in particular. This is likely to be particularly important in multicultural societies such as Canada, the United States, and European countries. The literature, along with our preliminary exploratory studies conducted within and outside Canada, lends support for a multicultural framework on which to construct health education so that it is maximally effective in promoting health and well-being. The multicultural considerations we described in this chapter that can impact the effectiveness of health education could serve as a basis for a multicultural framework specifically designed to augment health through effective health education.

References

Aday, L. A. (1993). *At risk in America: The health and health care needs of vulnerable populations in the United States*. San Francisco: Jossey-Bass.

Airhihenbuwa, C. (1995). *Health and culture: Beyond the Western paradigm*. Thousand Oaks, CA: SAGE Publications.

Astin, J. A. (1998). Why patients use alternative medicine: Results of a national study. *JAMA, 279*, 1548–1553.

Aung, S. H., Benjamin, S., Berman B., & Jacobs, J. (1997). Alternative medicine—Exploring other healthcare systems. *Patient Care Canada, 8*(12), 36–52.

Barnlund, D. (1975). *Public and private self in Japan and the United States*. Yarmouth, ME: Intercultural Press.

Barnes, P. M., Powell-Griner, E., McFann, L., & Nahin, R. L. (2004). Complementary and alternative medicine use among adults: United States, 2002. *Advance Data from Vital and Health Statistics, 343*, 1–19.

Belay, G. (1993). Toward a paradigm shift for intercultural and international communication: New research directions. In S. A. Deetz (Ed.), *Communication yearbook 16* (pp. 437–457). Newbury Park, CA: SAGE Publications.

Brach, C., & Fraser, I. (2000). Can cultural competency reduce racial and ethnic health disparities? A review and conceptual model. *Medical Care Research and Review. 57*(Suppl. 1), 181–217.

Britt, E., Hudson, S. M., & Blampied, N. M. (2004). Motivational interviewing in health settings: A review. *Patient Education and Counseling 53*, 147–155.

Canadian Nurses Association. (2004). *Promoting culturally competent care*. Ottawa: Canadian Nurses Association.

Cassidy, C. M. (1996). Cultural context of complementary and alternative medicine systems. In M. S. Micozzi (Ed.), *Fundamentals of complementary and alternative medicine* (pp. 9–34). New York: Churchill Livingstone.

Chen, G.-M. (2008). *Bian* (Change): A perpetual discourse of *I Ching*. *Intercultural Communication Studies, 17*(4), 7–16.

de Savigny, D. & Adam, T. (Eds.). (2009). *Systems thinking for health systems strengthening*. Geneva: Alliance for Health Policy and Systems Research, and World Health Organization.

Dean, E. (2009a). Physical therapy in the 21st century (Part I): Toward practice informed by epidemiology and the crisis of lifestyle conditions. *Physiotherapy Theory Practice, 25*, 330–353.

Dean, E. (2009b). Physical therapy in the 21st century (Part II): Evidence-based practice within the context of evidence-informed practice. *Physiotherapy Theory Practice, 25*, 354–368.

Dean, E., Lomi, C., Bruno, S., Awad, H., & O'Donoghue, D. (2011). Addressing the common pathway underlying hypertension and diabetes in people who are obese: The ultimate knowledge translation gap. *International Journal of Hypertension,* doi:10.4061/2011/835805

Deetz, S., Tracy, S., & Simpson, J. (2000). *Leading organizations through transitions: Communication and cultural change*. Thousand Oaks, CA: SAGE Publications.

Dreher, M., & MacNaughton, N. (2002). Cultural competence in nursing: Foundation or fallacy. *Nursing Outlook, 50*(5), 181–186.

Dutta, M. J. (2007). Communicating about culture and health: Theorizing culture-centered and cultural sensitivity approaches. *Communication Theory, 17*, 304–328.

Dutta, M. J. (2008). *Communicating health: A culture-centered perspective*. London: Polity.

Engel, G. L. (1977). The need for a new medical model: A challenge for biomedicine. *Science, 196*, 129–136.

Fang, T., & Faure, G. O. (2011). Chinese communication characteristics: A yin yang perspective. *International Journal of Intercultural Relations, 35*, 320–333.

Flores, G., Gee, D., & Kastner, B. (2000). The teaching of cultural issues in U.S. and Canadian medical schools. *Academic Medicine, 75*(5), 451–455.

Galanti, G. (2008). *Caring for patients from different cultures* (4th ed.). Philadelphia: University of Pennsylvania Press.

Geiger, H. J. (2001). Racial stereotyping and medicine: The need for cultural competence. *Canadian Medical Association Journal, 164*(12), 1699–1700.

Gerrish, K. (2000). Individualized care: Its conceptualization and practice within a multiethnic society. *Journal of Advanced Nursing, 32*(1), 91–99.

Glanz, K., Rimer, B.K., & Lewis F.M. (2002). *Health behavior and health education* (3rd ed.). San Francisco: Jossey-Bass.

Gudykunst, W. B. (1987). Cross-cultural comparison. In C. R. Berger & S. H. Chaffee (Eds.), *Handbook of communication science* (pp. 847–889). Beverly Hills: SAGE Publications.

Hajela, R. (1994). Health, behaviour and disease: A bio-psycho-social spiritual perspective. In M. W. Rosenberg (Ed.), *Health and behaviour 1994* (pp. 137–145). Kingston, ON: Queen's University.

Hall, E. (1959). *The silent language*. Garden City, NJ: Doubleday.

Health Canada. (2003). *Access to health services for underserved populations in Canada*. Ottawa: Health Canada.

Heywood, A. (2007). *Political ideologies: An introduction* (4th ed.). New York: Palgrave Macmillan.

Hofstede, G. (1980). *Culture's consequences: International differences in work-related values*. Beverly Hills, CA: SAGE Publications.

Hofstede, G. (2001). *Culture's consequences: Comparing values, behaviors, institutions, and organizations across nations* (2nd ed.). Thousand Oaks, CA: SAGE Publications.

Hofstede, G., & Bond, M. (1984). Hofstede's culture dimensions. *Journal of Cross-Cultural Psychology, 15*, 417–433.

Hollinger, D. A. (1995). *Post-ethnic America: Beyond multiculturalism*. New York: Basic Books.

Izadnegahdar, R., Correia, S., Ohata, B., Kittler, A., ter Kuile, S., Vaillancourt, S. et al. (2008). Global health in Canadian medical education: Current practices and opportunities. *Academic Medicine, 83*(2), 192–198.

Kallen, H. (1915, February 18–25). Democracy versus the melting pot. *Nation*, pp. 190–194, 217–220.

Kallen, H. (1924/1970). *Culture and democracy in the United States*. New York: Arno.

Kendall, J. K., & Hatton, D. (2002). Racism as a source of health disparity in families with attention deficit hyperactivity disorder. *Advances in Nursing Science, 25*(2), 22–39.

King, T., & Wheeler, M. (2004). Inequality in health care: Unjust, inhumane, and unattended. *Annals of Internal Medicine, 141*(10), 815–817.

Kleinman, A. (1980). *Patients and healers in the context of culture*. Berkeley, CA: University of California Press.

Kreps, G. L. (1989). Setting the agenda for health communication research and development: Scholarship that can make a difference. *Health Communication, 1*, 11–15.

Leininger, M. (1991). The theory of culture care diversity and universality. In M. Leininger (Ed.), *Culture care diversity and universality: A theory of nursing* (pp. 5–72). New York: National League for Nursing.

Leininger, M. (2002). Theory of culture care and ethnonursing research method. In M. Leininger & M. R. McFarland (Eds.), *Transcultural nursing: Concepts, theories, research and practice* (3rd ed., pp. 71–98). New York: McGraw Hill.

Leischow, S. J., Best, A., Trochim, W. M., Clark, P. I., Gallagher, R. S., Marcus, S. E. et al. (2008). Systems thinking to improve the public's health. *American Journal of Preventive Medicine, 35*(2 Supplement): S196–S203.

Long, J., Chang, V., Ibrahim, S., & Asch, D. (2004). Update on health disparities literature. *Annals of Internal Medicine, 141*(10), 805–812.

Loudon, R., Anderson, P., Gill, P., & Greenfield, S. (1999). Disparities: Key perspectives and trends. *JAMA, 282*(9), 875–880.

Lum, C. K., & Korenman, S. G. (1994). Cultural-sensitivity training in U.S. medical schools. *Academic Medicine, 69*(3), 239–241.

Lupton, D. (1995). *The imperative of health: Public health and the regulated body*. London: SAGE Publications.

Lupton, D. (2003). *Medicine as culture: Illness, disease and the body in Western societies* (2nd ed.). London: SAGE Publications.

McFarland, M. R. (2002). Selected research findings from the culture care theory. In M. Leininger & M. R. McFarland (Eds.), *Transcultural nursing: Concepts, theories, research and practice* (3rd ed., pp. 99–116). New York: McGraw Hill.

Nance, T. (1995). Intercultural communication: Finding common ground. *Journal of Obstetric, Gynecologic, and Neonatal Nursing, 24*(3), 249–255.

Pollak, K. I., Childers, J. W., & Arnold, R. M. (2011). Applying motivational interviewing techniques to palliative care communication. *Journal of Palliative Medicine, 14*, 587–592.

Resnicow, K., Braithwaite, R. L., Dilorio, C., & Glanz, K. (2002). Applying theory to culturally diverse and unique populations. In K. Glanz, B. K. Rimer, & F. M. Lewis (Eds.), *Health behavior and health education: Theory, research, and practice* (3rd ed., pp. 485–509). San Francisco: Jossey-Bass.

Rivers, W. H. R. (1924). *Medicine, magic, and religion*. New York: Harcourt.

Rodrigues, G., Jongbloed, L., Li, Z., & Dean, E. (2007). Health-related knowledge, beliefs, and behaviours of Indo-Canadians with special reference to heart disease: Implications for physical therapists. *Paper presented at the 15th International World Confederation of Physical Therapy Congress*, University of British Columbia, Vancouver.

Rollnick, S., Miller, W. R., & Butler, C. C. (2008). *Motivational interviewing in health care: helping patients change behavior*. New York: Guildford.

Schein, E. H. (2005). *Organizational culture and leadership* (3rd ed.). San Francisco: Jossey-Bass.

Smedley, B., Stith, A., & Nelson, A. (Eds.). (2002). *Unequal treatment: Confronting racial and ethnic disparities in health care*. Washington, DC: National Academies Press.

Spector, R. E. (2009). *Cultural diversity in health and illness* (7th ed.). Upper Saddle River, NJ: Pearson.

Srivastava, R. (2007). Understanding cultural competence in health care. In R. Srivastava (Ed.), *The healthcare professional's guide to clinical cultural competence* (pp. 3–27). Toronto: Elsevier Canada.

Stewart, E. C. (1978). Outline of intercultural communication. In F. L. Casmir (Ed.), *Intercultural and international communication* (pp. 265–344). Washington, DC: University Press of America.

Street, R. L. (2003). Communication in medical encounters: An ecological perspective. In T. L. Thompson, A. M. Dorsey, K. I. Miller, & R. Parrott (Eds.), *Handbook of health communication* (pp. 63–89). Mahwah, NJ: Lawrence Erlbaum Associates.

Wang, S., Li, Z., Jongbloed, L., & Dean, E. (2007). Stroke and health-related knowledge, beliefs, and behaviours of Chinese-Canadians: Status and implications for physical therapists. *Paper presented at the 15th International World Confederation of Physical Therapy Congress*, University of British Columbia, Vancouver.

Wang, P., Li, Z., Jongbloed, L., & Dean, E. (2008). Health beliefs and behaviors of Mainland Chinese: A pilot study and implications for health education. *Paper presented at the ASPAC Conference*, Victoria, BC: University of Victoria.

Waxler-Morrison, N., Richardson, E., Anderson, J., & Chambers, N. A. (2005). Cross-cultural caring: *A handbook for health professionals* (2nd ed.). Vancouver: University of British Columbia Press.

World Health Organization (WHO). (2007). *People at the centre of health care: Harmonizing mind and body, people and systems*. Geneva: WHO.

Wright, D., & Pemberton, M. (2004). *Risk and protective factors for adolescent drug use: Findings from the 1999 National Household Survey on Drug Abuse*. Rockville, MD: Substance Abuse and Mental Health Services Administration, Office of Applied Studies, U.S. Department of Health and Human Services.

Zola, I. K. (1996). Culture and symptoms: An analysis of patients presenting complaints. *American Psychological Review, 31*: 615–630.

Zoller, H. (2005). Health activism: Communication theory and action for social change. *Communication Theory, 15*(4), 341–364.

Chapter 11

"Diabetes Conversation": A Dialogue Among Métis, First Nations Community Members, and Professionals to Understand Type 2 diabetes

Hasu Ghosh

Introduction

Type 2 diabetes mellitus (also referred as adult-onset or non-insulin-dependent; hereafter, T2DM) is a serious population health concern among increasingly urbanized First Nations and Métis Canadians (Public Health Agency of Canada [PHAC], 2005), whereas the incidence of T2DM among Canadians in general is much lower than the Aboriginal peoples in Canada (PHAC, 2011). Furthermore, the onset of T2DM in this population occurs at a younger age than in most other populations. The combination of early disease onset, increased urbanization of this population, and rapid progression of this preventable disease process calls for improved communication and collaboration among peoples, providers, and policymakers to slow this disease occurrence and progression. Although there are several published investigations of Aboriginal peoples' and providers' perceptions of etiology and prevention of T2DM in reserve or remote settings (Bhattacharyya et al., 2011; Denny, Holtzman, Goins, & Croft, 2005; Minore, Boone, Katt, Kinch, & Birch, 2004; Thompson, Gifford, & Thorpe, 2000; Vukic, & Keddy, 2002; Williamson, Vinicor, & Bowman, 2004), there are few published studies incorporating policymakers' understanding of T2DM as it relates to susceptibility and prevention of the disease in an urban context. The perceptions of susceptibility to T2DM from policymakers alongside the peoples and health service providers are important to understand, both to add a further layer of complexity and because of their responsibility to influence health service delivery. Those who provide services may have a different view from those who undertake a decision-making role surrounding T2DM in non-urban or reserve or remote settings.

This research brings in perceptions of 3Ps—Peoples (diabetic and nondiabetic both), health service providers, and policymakers. Peoples' understanding of T2D may encompass their personal experiences as patients, caregivers, family members, friends, and community members (Kleinman, 1988; Scofield, 1999;

Thompson, Gifford, & Thorpe, 2000). Providers' perceptions are often contextualized in a structured biomedical framework (Bhattacharyya et al., 2011; Denny et al., 2005; Minore et al., 2004). Finally, policymakers understand the issue of a particular disease in light of their respective organizations' mandates and priorities (Gortmaker et al., 2011). Limited awareness and understanding of each other's perception of T2DM may have consequences for potential misinterpretation among peoples, providers, and policymakers (Montague, 2006). This chapter therefore presents a discussion on the current knowledge of T2DM in First Nations, Métis populations, and professionals living in an eastern Ontario urban setting; sheds some light on the existing knowledge gap related to peoples, health service providers, and policymakers' understandings of the issue; and comments on key factors to improve communication among people, provider, and policymakers that align with the concept self-determination of First Nation and Métis people in urban centers as identified by the Royal Commission of Aboriginal Peoples (RCAP) for chronic disease prevention.

Urban Realities: First Nation and Métis People in Urban Context

Presently more than half of Canadian Aboriginal peoples live in urban centers (Statistics Canada, 2006). The 1951 Census of Canada showed that 6.7 percent of Aboriginal peoples lived in urban Canada (Peters, 2002). By 2006, that proportion had increased to 54 percent. Now First Nations people account for 50 percent of urban Aboriginal populations, while 43 percent are Métis (Statistics Canada, 2006). According to the most recent census in 2006, 62 percent of the total Aboriginal population of Ontario live in urban areas. The percentage of Aboriginal people living in urban areas is higher in Ontario than the national average (Ontario Ministry, 2011; Statistics Canada, 2006). In this eastern Ontario setting, First Nation and Métis peoples migrate toward urban areas primarily for better education, employment, and health services, to migrate from poverty, dispossession of land, deterioration of traditional livelihoods, as well as for family reunification. Aboriginal peoples living in urban Canada lag far behind the Canadian average on socioeconomic, education, and life-expectancy indicators, including the rate of high school graduation, homelessness, substance abuse, poverty, and incarceration (Cardinal & Adin, 2005; Kirmayer et al., 2007; Siggner & Costa, 2005). On the other hand, many of urban First Nation and Métis Canadians are well equipped and resourceful enough to navigate through the health, education, and employment systems and are striving towards better education and a healthier family life in these urban centers. These Aboriginal peoples form a significant and visible portion of the urban Canadian landscape (Environics Institute, 2010). These diverse realities of urban Aboriginal life indicate the need to move beyond the quantifiable aspects of their urban life to encapsulate the range of urban experiences, experiences that form the basics of inequitable health outcomes.

Although urban Aboriginal experience is varied across provinces and cities, many of these people share commonalities attributable to the marginalization of Aboriginal residents. First of all, urban centers present challenges to traditional ways of Aboriginal life, including contact with family, native land and nature, cultural practices and ceremonies (Peters, 2002). Secondly, Aboriginal peoples are dispersed all over the urban centers in Canada (Peters, 2006). Moreover, there are unstable residence patterns among urban Aboriginal peoples, which in turn can create different population subgroups in different cities. For example, in this urban Ontario setting, some First Nation and Métis people may face differential access to Aboriginal health services due to distance, transportation issues, and lack of sufficient recognition of Métis and First Nation cultural diversities in available services. Implications of mobility leading to unstable residence patterns in urban centers may create gaps in access to and continuity of providing health programs and services (Canada Mortgage, 2004).

Despite the increased urbanization of Aboriginal peoples in Canada, health services and policy discussions about them tend to focus on the remote and reserve-based population health. Discussions about self-government, housing, economic, treaty, and other issues focus almost exclusively on the status of First Nation communities of rural and reserve areas (Bartlett, Iwasaki, Gottlieb, Hall, & Mannell, 2007; Young, 2003). This oversight marginalizes the needs and realities of Aboriginal peoples of First Nation and Métis origin who live in urban Canada. Policies affecting the systems that exist and operate in urban areas and that impact on realities of urban Aboriginal life are often designed and developed without Aboriginal community engagement and decisions. Consequently, serious challenges for Aboriginal peoples in accessing those services exist (Ponting, 1997). Likely many of these urban First Nation and Métis peoples find themselves at the fringes of society (Letkemann, 2004).

Social Determinants of T2DM: A Conceptual Framework

Although extremely rare prior to the 1950s, the literature reveals a disproportionate prevalence of T2DM in Aboriginal populations compared to non-Aboriginal (PHAC, 2005). In addition, various studies have presented differential prevalence of T2DM within and among the Aboriginal[1] population groups living across the

---

[1] The Constitution Act, 1982, Section 35.1 states that the Aboriginal peoples of Canada are First Nations, Inuit, and Métis peoples. This study is restricted within the First Nations and Métis people only due to lack of response received from Inuit communities for participation in this research.

Canada (Macaulay et al., 2003). Under the rubric of Aboriginal peoples, the First Nations population living off-reserve is most affected by T2DM, followed by the Métis population. Overall, less is known about T2DM among Métis people in Canada, but we are aware that rates are in general comparable to or lower than the rates in First Nations for most age-sex groups, but higher than the general Canadian population. According to the Métis National Council (2006), the rate of T2DM among Métis population as of 2006 is 5.9 percent, compared to 4.3 percent for non-Aboriginal Canadians. Surprisingly, two-thirds of First Nations people with T2DM are women, as opposed to the Canadian population in general, where men and women are equally affected (Statistics Canada, 2006).

Western biomedical models of chronic disease prevention have traditionally focused on fixing the patient by addressing behavioral risk factors (Leandris, Leonard, Sheree, & Pattie, 2005; Schulz et al., 2005). Such approaches have been criticized as blaming the victim, as it is now understood that the individualistic behavioral risk factors are socially and culturally embedded in the collective lives of individuals, families, and communities across regions and nation states (Reading, 2009). Along the same lines, Peterson and Lupton (1996) stated that risk is not a static objective phenomenon; rather, it is constantly created as part of the social interaction. Likewise, attempts to intervene on these risk factors are embedded in social relations that are rarely acknowledged (Angus, 2008). Not surprisingly, programs and services that aim at disease risk modification and self-management tend to have limited outcome as they are affordable and useful to a limited segment of population—namely, those who belong to a higher socioeconomic background (Wharf Higgins, Young, Cunningham, & Naylor, 2006). Similarly, even when biomedical risk factors are controlled by risk-based prevention strategies, people belonging to lower socioeconomic groups are more likely to be inactive, to be obese, to have an unhealthy diet, and to develop T2DM (Mikkonen & Raphael, 2010). Based on such research, a convincing body of evidence now indicates that addressing sociocontextual factors may help eliminate the disparity in chronic disease prevalence and incidence across varied population groups (Kuh, Ben-Shlomo, Lynch, Hallqvist, & Power, 2003; Norris et al., 2002). Overall, the available research is sparse in terms of understanding peoples' and professionals' perspectives about broader sociocontextual factors that shape the biomedical risk factors of chronic diseases among marginalized populations, such as T2DM among First Nation and Métis people. Here, an alternative framework of social determinants of health would be invaluable, not only because it would provide a more in-depth understanding of how multiple determinants intersect and impact on the health outcome of diversely positioned social groups, but also it would set an understanding of the phenomena that create inequities in health outcomes from multiple stakeholders' perspectives. More importantly, the social determinants of health approach can contribute to understanding varied and interrelated determinants, the majority of which are entangled in unique power relations and a history of colonization (Waldram, Herring, & Young, 2006; Adelson, 2005).

To understand the unique situation of First Nations and Métis population health in urban Canada and to address specific health concerns of these population, it is essential to identify the distinct determinants of health specific to urban First Nations and Métis peoples in Canada and that reflect their lives and their stories (Loppie-Reading & Wien, 2009). Moreover, this alternative framework can play a significant role in informing the existing individualistic behavioral risk models and in contributing attention to the holistic exposure to the susceptibility of developing a disease (Reading, 2009; Mattingly, 2000).

Methodology

This study was conducted by the author as her doctoral research in collaboration and engagement with local Aboriginal community partners. This study's governance structure includes the student researcher (author) and her thesis supervisors, thesis advisory committee of professors involved in Aboriginal and population health research, and an Aboriginal community advisory committee composed of the members from supporting local Aboriginal service and research organizations. This community based research aims to address a priority health problem among Aboriginal populations and acknowledged that there is a "need to balance individual and collective interests, respect for Aboriginal values, knowledge, methodologies and decision making processes … that engages the Aboriginal and research communities" (CIHR, 2007, p. 12).

Consistent with OCAP (ownership, control, access, and possession) principles (Schnarch, 2004), and CIHR guidelines (CIHR, 2007) for health research involving Aboriginal peoples, this research emerged from extensive discussions and input from partner Aboriginal organizations. This project undertook number of mechanisms to ensure that community members were meaningfully engaged in this project. These included:

- extensive consultation with members of the various local and national Aboriginal service and research organizations and Aboriginal communities at the initial phase of this study;
- the author's participation as a guest speaker and volunteer at the local Aboriginal service and research organizations and mainstream health centers has given her the opportunity to share research objectives with their clients and fellow community members as a form of member-checking;

- since its inception, the project proposal, including research instruments, were enriched and developed collaboratively by university-based researchers and members of partner organizations;
- a draft letter of understanding was developed and agreed to by all research team members;
- a dedicated Aboriginal community advisory committee composed of the First Nation and Métis members provided guidance in every step of the research.

Adopting a qualitative approach, this study focused on the collection of primary data in the form of narrative interviews with First Nations and Métis community members and health service providers (HSPs), and with policymakers. Between June 2010 and August 2011, community members and professional participants were recruited in two phases. Community participants were recruited at three main sites across the city. Three community-based organizations, including the Native Friendship Center, assisted with participant recruitment. Eligibility criteria for community participants in the study included: self-identifying as First Nation or Métis,[2] living in the urban setting for at least two years, being 18 years of age or older, and being diagnosed with T2DM or having familiarity with T2DM. Professional participants, including service providers (formal or informal) and decision makers or policymakers (national or provincial) working in the field of Aboriginal chronic disease prevention and decision making were purposefully recruited. After transcribing the interviews, the study adopted a narrative analysis method and analyzed data according to emerging themes and categories relevant to the objectives of the study. The organized data are being employed as a basis for author's doctoral dissertation from which some findings of this paper are constructed.

Results

Preliminary analysis of primary and secondary data resulted in various themes and subthemes of interest that reflected current knowledge of susceptibility to T2DM among urban First Nations, Metis, and professionals. In this paper, however, three themes are discussed that were common to all or most of the community and professional participants (see Table 11.1). These themes were: understanding T2DM

---

[2] In Canada, First Nations refers to peoples of Indian origin who were the first occupants of the land (Wotherspoon & Satzewich, 1993). First Nation peoples in Canada registered under the Indian Act can be referred to as either registered or status First Nation peoples); those not registered with the federal government are called nonstatus First Nation people. Métis refers to the mixed-blood descendants of European fur traders and First Nation women. Métis people are however nonstatus Aboriginal people (Sawchuk, 2001).

in urban context; sensitivity to Aboriginal diversities as perceived; and the need to address "urban realities" in health services for First Nation and Métis people.

Table 11.1

Peoples and Professionals' (Providers and Policymakers) Perceptions of T2DM

Themes	People (Métis and First Nation people)	Professionals	
		Providers (health service providers)	Policymakers
Understanding T2DM: causes and consequences	• Based more on the broader discourse than biomedical risk factors of disease. • Their perceptions are present oriented. • Perceived descriptions largely detailed the socioeconomic factors, such as poverty, food insecurity, etc.	• Based on biomedical point of view • Perceived understandings primarily tend to situate the lifestyle changes in the continuum of past and present. • Perceived descriptions largely detailed on lifestyle change from traditional active to modern sedentary life, as well as substance abuse.	• Based on biomedical point of view • Perceived understandings primarily include legacy of colonialism and present urban issues. • Perceived descriptions detail on housing shortages, poverty, differential access to health services among status and nonstatus Aboriginal people etc.
Sensitivity to Aboriginal diversities as perceived	• Health services for Aboriginal Peoples tend to overlook the Métis-specific needs and more often focus on First Nations' needs and priorities. • Culturally relevant preventive health services for Aboriginal people are primarily based on First Nation world views. • Aboriginal health service professionals can better address the Aboriginal diversities in service provisions.	• Health services take Aboriginal (pan-Aboriginal) approach; nothing is particularly geared to First Nations or Métis people. • Métis people are more comfortable accessing mainstream health services than First Nations in urban centers. • There is a need for Aboriginal health service professionals.	• Takes more of a pan-Aboriginal approach, nothing is particularly geared to First Nations or Métis people. • Hold differing views on whether health services for Aboriginal Peoples are more culturally appropriate for First Nations people than that of Métis people. • There is a need for Aboriginal health service professionals.

continued

continued

Need for addressing "urban realities" of First Nation and Métis people	• Status-blind health services are needed to address need-based health priorities. • Health service providers need to be educated on the diverse realities of urban Aboriginal life.	• Need to provide individualized needs-based services. • Training for Aboriginal cultural sensitivity for next generation of health service providers. • Services must include training for urban life-skills, such as lessons for cooking, monthly budgeting, and grocery store visits, etc. • There is a need for better integration among structured social and health services available in the city.	• Need to provide needs-based response of community-identified issues at the program level. • All three groups of Aboriginal peoples should be engaged in health service planning and program development. • Need for more education among professionals and lay people to know about Aboriginal culture.

Theme 1: Understanding T2DM in urban context

Urban diabetic and nondiabetic First Nation and Métis peoples' perceptions of causes and consequences of T2DM were most clearly based on a broader discourse than a biomedical recognition of T2DM risk associated with proximal causal agents. When asked "In your opinion, what factors contribute to the development of T2DM?" community participants attributed T2DM to various sources, including change in diet from traditional to fast food, obesity, alcoholism, family history, the cost of healthy food, cost of living in urban area, employment, lack of education, housing, social isolation, and access to health services. This is to be noted that community members perceive diabetes in the contemporary context. Their perceptions of T2DM are very "present" oriented. For example, one participant said, "I think also as a Métis ... my perspective is that a lot of the traditional like a lot of the food we eat today are not the things that the ancestors were used to." Another agreed, saying, "I think another factor would be, like, a lot of Aboriginal people here are unemployed too ... so they are still not able to afford the better kinds of food."

Diabetes causation was shared by community members not as disease risk factors but through descriptions of challenges, struggles, and successes in peoples' lives. In other words, peoples' perceptions represent biomedical risk factors of T2DM as being embedded within the broader socioeconomic, political, and educational determinants of their everyday livings. More precisely, peoples' description of susceptibility to T2DM largely detailed the socioeconomic factors than standard physiological risk factors as identified in the Western biomedicine. This is reflected when a participant said, "When you're in poverty, so much time is spent struggling, it's just not worth it. That kills you ... your health. Poverty kills your health."

Participants dealing with T2DM or trying to stay away from the disease attempt to take considerable initiative to modify their dietary patterns and food selections. This again seemed to be challenging for them, given the limited resources they possess and the high cost of healthy food. In this line, one community participant said:

> I take a long time grocery shopping ... I go to a grocery store and I read every label on everything. And I try to buy organic food, but it's too expensive. You know, it's funny, what's good for us is expensive, we can't afford to eat it, and that's not fair, you know.

Professional participants, including health service providers and policymakers, primarily view the causal factors of T2DM from biomedical points of view, emphasizing the lifestyle change in the continuum of past to present. For example, a health service provider, who is also of First Nation origin said, "What comes to my mind is a lifestyle change that's affected our people since, well, at least 30, 40 years." Along the same line of thought, a health service provider of non-Aboriginal descent said:

> Yeah, I try to explain it, that it's because of so many changes from the traditional lifestyle to modern day ... that's a lot of the reason why diabetes is so high because, like, activity changed ... you're not on the land, you're in a city where people aren't going to let their kids go play on the sidewalk.

There is an increasing understating and recognition of broader social determinants of T2DM that have been observed among health service providers and policymakers or decision makers as indicated in the following statement.

> When you look at the Aboriginal population in general ... you look at the social determinants of health ... they're more likely to, you know ... face housing crises or not have affordable housing, or to be on the street. They are overrepresented in the street population ... and, you know is an especially urban problem.

Theme 2: Sensitivity to Aboriginal Diversities as Perceived

A prominent theme in both literature and the interviews is the priority of culturally relevant preventive services for both Métis and First Nation peoples. Particularly, Métis people living in urban areas revealed that health services tend to overlook Métis-specific needs and more often focus on First Nations' needs and priorities. A Métis participant said:

> Oh, it [health services] has to be Métis specific. Because .... when we walk in there as Métis, we always don't feel Aboriginal enough, you know? And we're treated differently. Because we look so much like mainstream. ... Well as a second class, like.

Other comments resonated with these thoughts. For example, one participant said, "it still remains the fact that ... we don't have the same culture. So we're, yes, we are three Aboriginal communities [First Nations, Inuit, and Métis], but three very distinct culture." One community participant of First Nation descent similarly said:

> It's like me. I want to like my culture. I don't want to learn about Mohawk. There is Algonquin. I don't want learn about Cree, I'm Ojibway. I want to learn about my own culture ... I am Native all the same, but I am within a cultural group that is Ojibway, I want to learn that specific stuff. I think there is need to acknowledge that uniqueness.

It seems in many cases, contrary to the cultural diversities that community participants discuss, professionals are either not much aware of or ignorant of the cultural diversities within and among Aboriginal populations and how they can impact developing culturally appropriate service delivery. Three comments reflect this theme:

1. So whoever comes to see us that identifies themselves as having, being First Nations or Métis they same ... come in to the same population groups as the other clients, so we don't pinpoint them or identify.
2. Friendship Centre is really status blind. Everyone who comes to access a Friendship Centres is not asked, Métis, Inuit, or whatever.
3. You know when we speak about cultural diversity; it's no different from every other diverse community. The difference for First Nation, for Aboriginal, is ... they are the first people in Canada.

These merging of cultural diversities are true for both Aboriginal health services as well as for mainstream health services. Recognition of Aboriginal diversities in their health service provision is greatly needed. It is expressed that there is also a need for Aboriginal healthcare professionals to understand and communicate culturally competent messaging for both Métis and First Nation peoples. Indeed,

> There are lot of Aboriginal cultural groups … that is FN and then there are Métis, Inuit … we are mixed now, too … FN, Métis, Inuit. … so how are we going to identify. … I think it is bad when it say that you are Aboriginal so you all speak same, eat same.

Theme 3: Need for addressing 'urban realities' in health services for Métis and First Nation people

In urban centers, First Nation and Métis peoples form a diverse subpopulation with varied cultural, linguistic, socioeconomic, and educational backgrounds and Aboriginal statuses. Their need for culturally appropriate health services must acknowledge their varied needs, needs that are to a great extent are shaped by diverse realities of their urban lives. First Nation and Métis community peoples identified that costs of medications and supplies are challenging for some participants. In particular, Métis and other nonstatus First Nation participants had no access to non-insured health benefits that provide health coverage for status registered First Nation and Inuit people (NWAC, 2007). Community participants discussed the need for monetary supports for medications, supplies, and healthy foods. The following statements highlight this issue:

- They could provide the strips … they are very, very expensive … yes, to monitor blood. Well they give at the pharmacy the glucometer … The-that's for blood testing. Ok? They give you … supply of a strips with it but then you have to buy them, that's the expensive thing. But when the strips are there they cost a fortune, again cost and poverty.
- Before my mom wasn't able to pay for her pills sometimes cause she was lower income and … so sometimes she would just not take them for a month or so or whatever because she couldn't afford to, and then the needles now you have to pay for every month so she can test for.

People also suggested flexible participant involvement supports such as longer clinical hours, patient and understanding attitudes from health service providers, flexible hours for physical social activities, support for transportation and child-care services, and programs that accommodate both work schedules as well as stay-home parents' schedules. Each of these supports would make existing services and programs more accessible. For instance, one participant suggested,

> I think the most important thing is transportation. If they have a diabetic van, for instance … and you know that could go around and collect people … and brought them to a, to a centre and teach them how to exercise.

Community participants in this study discussed the barriers and service needs around educational, nutritional, physical, and psychological aspects, as well as time and monetary limitations. They also stated that lack of social support complicates T2DM prevention and management for them. In reality, the prevention and management of T2DM must integrate a range of culturally appropriate services to address various social, economic, behavioral, and educational determinants of health. This need was reflected when a participant said,

> Ya, education, nutrition, alcoholism, substance abuse … probably more access to athletic places so that not only people who can afford big huge gym memberships can go, maybe people like myself who have no income now and who have a child can go to, you know, these sporting events and stuff .

This interaction clearly indicates the importance of recognizing the diversity of approaches in health and allied service provision to avoid one-size-fits-all approaches. The RCAP (1996) highlighted that "present-day lack of access to culturally competent healthcare is as detrimental as other new determinants of health." Lack of cultural competence in the health delivery system results in miscommunication between healthcare providers and stakeholders and, therefore, creates a barrier to access (Lemchuk-Favel & Jock, 2004; Pohar & Johnson, 2007). A community participant said:

> Every doctor should be educated on the Métis, Inuit, Aboriginal people because we are different … our culture is different, our food is different, historically … yes, it's changed over time and we do need to get back to who we are.

Along the same lines, a physician who is a medical school professor and is of Aboriginal descent talked about need for cultural training for health service providers:

> It's one of the things I teach to, is making sure you are looking at the whole person, not just the problem they are there for. And you look at them not only themselves, you look at their family, their home, their community … That's more positive stuff and you can build on that, you can empower the community.

A physician of First Nation origin, who is very much aware of the fact of diversities among First Nations and Métis people, says:

> The fact that these health services, these decisions are made by … people, you know, who may not be as familiar with the actual needs of the population that they're trying to serve … And to appreciate that, I think they have to go back to the roots of that population … once they understand the … social and historical context of those populations, then you can develop those programs with more realistic measures.

Likewise, a health planner and decision maker explains:

> Long history of issues related to the Aboriginal population of how, you know how, we dealt with them in the past, you know there's residential schools of separation from perhaps from people that have moved from reserves to the city, and they feel dislocated … there's all of those different factors that might influence a person's health.

In response to the question, "How do you define good preventive care for diabetes," two policy decision makers provided similar insights. One said,

> We need to consider their, their, the methods and the cultural appropriateness of the programs and services that they can provide. And also to ensure that mainstream providers are culturally aware and sensitive to what will work and what won't so I think that those are major challenges.

"In health service as long as you take holistic approach and you are not exclusionary, be open for all Aboriginal people … don't be closed minded, open your mind." These statements resonate well with the Ontario Federation of Indian Friendship Centre's (2006) statement criticizing the "pan-Aboriginal approach." They argue that the pan-Aboriginal approach "fails to recognize the differences between diverse and distinct Aboriginal cultures, and amalgamates all Aboriginal cultures into a single melting pot, thereby erasing crucial aspects of identity specific to different Aboriginal peoples." Nevertheless, it is vital to keep in mind that urban First Nation and Métis communities are as varied as the recognized nation states, and that their experiences cannot be homogenized through a blanket terminology such as "Aboriginal."

Conclusions and Implications
Communicating Diabetes Knowledge Among the Stakeholders

This research has explored a range of understandings of the causes, consequences, and prevention strategies needed to reduce T2DM among urban First Nation and Métis peoples. We find that both social determinants of health and biomedical perspectives emerged as obvious ways to interpret these understandings. Preliminary findings of this research for urban First Nations and Métis people are consistent with other studies (e.g., Scofield, 1999, Heuer & Lausch, 2006) that describe lay understandings of causes and consequences of T2DM as a complex process situated within multifaceted narratives of their lives. Community participants continued to view T2DM as a response to specific issues or challenges in their lives. They made direct or indirect connection to broader socioeconomic, political, and cultural determinants of health that influence the high incidence of T2DM among them and their fellow community members. Their descriptions of access to healthy food, physical activities, health services, and education are linked to broader structural shortcomings. Professional participants, however, still conform to the view of T2DM as a "disease entity"; a deviation from the normal state, which requires a "cure" (Jutel, 2006). The professional view is consistent with Western biomedical perspectives. Despite the growing recognition in health service providers and policy makers that a disease-focused intervention only is incapable of reducing the T2DM epidemic among Aboriginal peoples, findings of this research suggest that the prevention and management of T2DM is still dominated by a disease-centered approach.

The views of health service providers and policy makers in our study tended to address both biomedical and social determinants of health views about causation, but their solution to this health issue tended to address the biomedical individual risk factors. Most of them viewed T2DM as a physiological malfunction of body that is a result of adverse socioeconomic conditions, often framed within the context of lifestyle modifications. Although professionals recognized the role of socioeconomic determinants of T2DM causation, almost all their discussions of T2DM prevention centered on behavioral change programs. In this sense, they were always more inclined toward individually oriented strategies than structural reforms. More specifically, policymakers or decision makers expressed the need to reduce T2DM via policy and program changes aimed at inducing active living and healthy food intake. They described policy initiatives they believe are working or will work to tackle the range of social and economic health determinants. Surprisingly, at the pragmatic level, professionals' solutions to T2DM tended to address biomedical risk factors, although they sometimes discussed the role of social structures such as poverty, unemployment, and food insecurity in T2DM causation. This reflects the paradigmatic value of policy framing grounded in biomedical notions of disease causation.

Findings of this study reflect the nature of the challenge both people and professionals face in the area of Aboriginal population health. There appears to be substantial a disconnect between those who believe that systemic change is required to halt the current level of T2DM incidence among urban First Nation and Métis peoples and those who find a solution in prevention of individualized biomedical risk factors of T2DM. There is a pressing need to provide First Nation and Métis culturally appropriate, disease-specific solutions in the context of broader systemic change within which T2DM is experienced.

We must remember that the number of both professional and community participants in this study was relatively small, and there may well be varied points of view about this issue. In addition, the divergent perspectives on T2DM causation and its prevention within these two groups of participants are complex; there are overlapping understandings in how these groups see T2DM. Further quantitative or mixed method research may shed more lights on these findings.

Key Factors to Communicate Among Peoples, Providers and Professionals

Preliminary findings of this research indicate that improved communication and understanding among people, providers, and policymakers require a common ground to share their concerns, struggles, and successes surrounding susceptibility to and prevention of diabetes. This sharing will allow them to build on each other's knowledge and expertise. Collaboration should include a partnership with urban First Nations and Métis community members, Elders, community champions, role models, and Aboriginal leaders to reduce the incidence and prevalence of T2DM. Moving toward a collaborative model of health service through an engagement with community partners could be an option (Bhattacharyya et al., 2011). Whereas self-determination has been recognized as the way forward to improve health outcome, the solution to T2DM needs to come from the communities, not imposed by outsiders as has been the case in Aboriginal health. A study by Chandler and Lalonde (1998) provided evidence of this link through an inverse relationship between self-determination and suicide among First Nation people of British Columbia. They also found that cultural continuity can act as protective barricade against suicide. Active engagement of Aboriginal community members and inclusion of their respective community perspectives and voices in the prevention of chronic diseases such as T2DM are critical. The dynamic interplay of people, providers, and policymakers can win the battle against systemic factors that shapes the susceptibility to T2DM among urban First Nation and Métis peoples.

The divergence and convergence in people and professionals' understandings as summarized in Table 11.1 points toward developing culturally appropriate health service delivery that recognizes diverse realities of urban First Nation and Métis people. In addition, there is a pressing need to address biomedical risk factors of T2DM in a culturally relevant and meaningful manner. The whole approach to preventive T2DM care, management, and education must be re-examined in light of the emerging alternative approach of T2DM causation that espouses social determinants of health. Although there have been some localized attempts to address these issues (Macaulay et al., 2003), there does not appear to be a systematic integration of service provision for urban First Nation and Métis people, particularly in mainstream health centers. Concurrently, First Nation and Métis people access Aboriginal urban health centers at low rates because these centers are not easily accessible due to distance or inconvenient hours of operation. The Royal Commission on Aboriginal Peoples (1996) recommended that less emphasis be placed on diabetes as a disease entity and that more emphasis be placed on social, economic, and political factors that influence health. Policies, health programs, and services that address broader social contexts of clients' lives beyond treating the "disease" are most likely to succeed. Along these lines, a meaningful coordination among the players from outside the health sectors who are working for diabetes service delivery is needed. It is clear that meaningful and culturally appropriate translation of knowledge surrounding T2DM causation and prevention requires that First Nation and Métis people, health service providers, and policymakers understand and communicate each other's perspectives and work in partnership.

Way Forward

Preliminary findings of this research provide support to a considerable recognition among both health service providers and policymakers to recognize diversities in Aboriginal peoples while offering services and developing policies. Literature revealed the need for culturally relevant, "good preventive services" for Aboriginal peoples (Anderson et al., 2003). Similarly, research findings indicate that Aboriginal services do not adequately address Métis' needs and, more often but not always, focus on First Nations' needs and priorities. Universalizing and "pan-Aboriginal" discourses and practices have narrowly generalized First Nation and Métis identity in policy (Maxwell, 2011) and heath service programming that blurs the distinct geographical, cultural, historical, linguistic, and socioeconomic experience of particular Aboriginal groups and collectivities. These concurrent phenomena raise questions about balancing emerging urban Aboriginalities and broadly inclusive services for marginalized First Nation and Métis peoples in urban settings. As mentioned before, this research reinforces the need for Aboriginal population-specific prevention and service delivery that recognizes the diverse need of First Nation and Métis peoples who could be diabetic and nondiabetic. To be more specific, the need is for Métis-specific and First Nation-specific programs and services as well as the integration of their respective perspectives into the pan-Aboriginal services (Ghosh & Gomes, 2011). There is a need to address the broad and complex variety of predisposing urban factors, including the issues of employment, housing, safety, and security, as well as language and cultural barriers, to narrow the gap in communication between community members and professionals, and ultimately, to narrow inequities in First Nation and Métis health outcomes.

Acknowledgments

The author gratefully acknowledges the help and guidance she received in conducting this research from her thesis supervisors, Professors Denise Spitzer and James Gomes. Besides her supervisors, the author is grateful to her thesis advisory committee members and Aboriginal advisory committee members for their continued support and guidance in pursuing this study. The author is immensely indebted to the Métis and First Nation peoples, and professional research participants for sharing their stories with her; without their interest and participation this research would not have been possible. This research is funded by the CIHR-IAPH fund, AK-NEAHR (former Ottawa ACADRE) and IHRDP programs, the PHIRN doctoral award, and the University of Ottawa Admission scholarships and Excellence

Adelson, N. (2005). The embodiment of inequity: Health disparities in Aboriginal Canada. *Canadian Journal of Public Health*, *96*, S45–S61.

Anderson, J., Perry, J., Blue, C., Browne, A., Henderson, A., Khan, K. B. et al. (2003). 'Rewriting' cultural safety within the postcolonial and postnational feminist project toward new epistemologies of healing. *Advances in Nursing Science*, *26*(3), 196–214.

Angus, J. (2008). Contesting coronary candidacy: Reframing risk modification in coronary heart disease. In K. A. Teghtsoonian & P. Moss (Eds.), *Contesting illness: Processes and practices* (pp. 90–106). Toronto: University of Toronto Press.

Bartlett, J. G., Iwasaki, Y., Gottlieb, B., Hall, D., & Mannell, R. (2007). Framework for Aboriginal-guided decolonizing research involving Métis and First Nations persons with diabetes. *Social Science & Medicine*, *65*, 2371–2382.

Bhattacharyya, O. K., Estey, E. A., Rasooly, I. R., Harris, S., Zwarenstein, M., & Barnsley, J. (2011). Providers' perceptions of barriers to the management of type 2 diabetes in remote Aboriginal settings. *International Journal of Circumpolar Health*, *70*(5), 552–563.

Cardinal, N., & Adin, E. K. (2005). *An urban aboriginal life: The 2005 indicators report on the quality of life of Aboriginal people living in the Greater Vancouver region*. Vancouver: Center for Native Policy and Research. Retrieved from http://edocs.lib.sfu.ca/projects/chodarr/documents/chodarr0247.pdf

Chandler, M. J., & Lalonde, C. (1998). Cultural continuity as a hedge against suicide in Canada's First Nations. *Transcultural Psychiatry*, *35*, 191–219.

Canadian Institute for Health Research (CIHR). (2007). *Guidelines for health research involving Aboriginal people*. Ottawa: CIHR. Retrieved from http://www.cihr.ca/e/documents/ethics_aboriginal_guidelines_e.pdf

Canada Mortgage and Housing Corporation. (2004). *Effects of urban aboriginal residential mobility*. Ottawa: Canada Mortgage and Housing Corporation.

Denny, C. H., Holtzman, D., Goins, R. T., & Croft, J. B. (2005). Disparities in chronic disease risk factors and health status between American Indian/Alaska Native and White elders: Findings from a telephone survey, 2001 and 2002. *American Journal of Public Health*, *95*(5), 825–827.

Environics Institute. (2010). Urban Aboriginal peoples study: Main report. Toronto: Environics Institute.

Ghosh, H., & Gomes, J. (2011). Type 2 diabetes among Aboriginal peoples in Canada: A focus on direct and associated risk factors. *Pimatisiwin*, *9*(2), 245–275.

Gortmaker, S. L., Swinburn, B. A., Levy, D., Carter, R., Mabry, P. L., Finegood, D. T. et al. (2011). Changing the future of obesity: Science, policy, and action. *Lancet*, *378*, 838–847.

Heuer, L., & Lausch, C. (2006). Living with diabetes: Perceptions of Hispanic migrant farmworkers. *Journal of Community Health Nursing*, *23*(1), 49–64.

Jutel, A. (2006). The emergence of overweight as a disease entity: Measuring up normality. *Social Science & Medicine*, *63*(9), 2268–2276.

Kleinman, A. (1988). *The illness narratives: Suffering, healing and the human condition*. New York: Basic Books.

Kirmayer, L., Brass, G., Holton, T., Paul, K., Simpson, C., & Tait, C. (2007). *Suicide among Aboriginal people in Canada*. Ottawa: Aboriginal Healing Foundation.

Kuh, D., Ben-Shlomo, Y., Lynch, J., Hallqvist, J., & Power, C. (2003). Life course epidemiology. *Journal of Epidemiology and Community Health, 57*(10), 778–783.

Leandris, C. L., Leonard, J. Jr., Sheree, W., & Pattie, T. (2005). Intervening on the social determinants of cardiovascular disease and diabetes. *American Journal of Preventive Medicine, 29*(5S1), 18–24.

Lemchuk-Favel, L., & Jock, R. (2004). Aboriginal health systems in Canada: Nine case studies. *Journal of Aboriginal Health, 1*, 28–51.

Letkemann, P. G. (2004). First Nations urban migration and the importance of 'urban nomads' in Canadian plains cities: A perspective from the streets. *Canadian Journal of Urban Research, 13*, 241–256.

Loppie-Reading, C., & Wien, F. (2009). *Health inequalities and social determinants of aboriginal peoples' health, health inequalities.* Prince George, BC: National Collaborating Centre for Aboriginal Health.

Mattingly, C. (2000). Emergent narratives. In C. Mattingly & L. Garro (Eds.), *Narrative and the cultural construction of illness and healing* (pp. 181–211). Berkeley, CA: University of California Press.

Maxwell, K. (2011). *Making history heal: Settler-colonialism and urban indigenous healing in Ontario, 1970s–2012.* (Doctoral thesis. University of Toronto).

Metis National Council (2006). *Preliminary assessment of diabetes programs for Métis peoples.* Ottawa: Métis National Council. Retrieved from: http://healthportal.metisnation.ca/pdf/Metis_Diabetes_Report

Minore, B., Boone, M., Katt, M., Kinch, P., & Birch, S. (2004). Addressing the realities of health care in northern aboriginal communities through participatory action research. *Journal of Interprofessional Care, 18*(4), 360–368.

Mikkonen, J., & Raphael, D. (2010).*Social determinants of health: The Canadian facts.* Toronto: York University School of Health Policy and Management.

Pohar, S. L., & Johnson, J. A. (2007). Health care utilization and costs in Saskatchewan's registered Indian population. *BMC Health Services Research, 7*, 126.

Ponting, J. R. (1997). *First Nations in Canada: Perspectives on opportunity, empowerment, and self-determination.* Toronto: McGraw-Hill Ryerson Limited.

Montague, T. (2006). Patient-provider partnership in healthcare: Enhancing knowledge translation and improving outcomes. *Healthcare Papers, 7*(2), 53–61.

Macaulay, A. C. Harris, S. B. Lévesque, L., Cargo, M., Ford, E., Salsberg, J. et al. . (2003). Primary prevention of type 2 diabetes: Experiences of 2 aboriginal communities in Canada. *Canadian Journal of Diabetes, 27*(4), 464–475.

Native Women's Association of Canada (NWAC). (2007). *Social determinants of health and Canada's Aboriginal women.* NWAC's Submission to the World Health Organization's Commission on the Social Determinants of Health. Retrieved from http://www.nwac-hq.org/en/documents/NWAC_WHO-CSDH_Submission2007-06-04.pdf

Norris, S. L., Nichols, P. J., Caspersen, C. J., Glasgow, R. E., Engelgau, M. M., Jack, L. et al. (2002). Increasing diabetes self-management education in community settings: A systematic review. *American Journal of Preventive Medicine, 22*(S4), 39–66.

Ontario Federation of Indian Friendship Centres. (2006). *Statement on the 'pan-Aboriginal' approach.* Toronto: Ontario Federation of Indian Friendship Centres. Retrieved from http://74.213.160.105/ofifchome/page/Document/UP_FILE/20070424234846WIL.pdf

Ontario Ministry of Aboriginal Affairs. (2011). *Urban aboriginal people: Ministry of Aboriginal Affairs quick facts*. Retrieved from http://www.aboriginalaffairs.gov.on.ca/english/services/datasheets/urban.asp

Peters, E. J. (2002). Our city Indians: Negotiating the meaning of First Nations urbanization in Canada, 1945–1975. *Historical Geography, 30,* 76.

Peters, E. J. (2006). First Nations and Métis people and diversity in Canadian cities. In K. Banting, T. J. Courchne, & F. L. Seidle (Eds.), *Belonging? Diversity, recognition and shared citizenship in Canada* (pp. 206–246). Kingston, ON: McGill-Queen's University Press.

Peterson, A., & Lupton, D. (1996). *The new public health: Health and self in the age of risk*. St. Leonards, Australia: Allen and Unwin.

Public Health Agency of Canada (PHAC). (2005). *Building a national diabetes strategy: A strategic framework*. Ottawa: PHAC.

Public Health Agency of Canada (PHAC). (2011). *Diabetes in Canada: Facts and figures from a public health perspective*. Ottawa: PHAC.

Ponting, J. R. (1997). *First Nations in Canada: Perspectives on opportunity, empowerment, and self-determination*. Toronto: McGraw-Hill Ryerson Limited.

Reading, J. (2009). A *life course approach to the social determinants of health for Aboriginal peoples*. Ottawa: Senate Sub-Committee on Population Health. Retrieved from http://www.parl.gc.ca/40/2/parlbus/commbus/senate/com-e/popu-e/rep-e/appendixAjun09-e.pdf

Royal Commission on Aboriginal Peoples (RCAP). (1996). *Report of the Royal Commission on Aboriginal peoples*. Ottawa: Supply and Services Canada.

Sawchuk, J. (2001). Negotiating an identity: Métis political organizations, the Canadian government, and competing concepts of aboriginality. *American Indian Quarterly, 25*(1), 73–92.

Schnarch, B. (2004). Ownership, control, access, and possession (OCAP) or self-determination applied to research: A critical analysis of contemporary First Nations research and some options for First Nations communities. *Journal of Aboriginal Health, 1,* 80–95.

Schulz, A., Shannon, S., Odoms- Young, A., Hollis-Neely, T., Nwankwo, R., Lockett, M. et al. (2005). *American Journal of Public Health, 95*(4), 645–651.

Scofield, G. A. (1999). *Thunder through my veins: Memories of a Métis childhood*. Toronto: Harper Flamingo

Siggner, A. J., & Costa, R. (2005). *Aboriginal conditions in census metropolitan areas, 1981–2001*. Ottawa: Statistics Canada.

Statistics Canada. (2006). *Aboriginal peoples in Canada in 2006: Inuit, Métis and First Nations, 2006 census*. Retrieved from http://www12.statcan.ca/census-recensement/2006/as-sa/97-558/p3-eng.cfm

Thompson, S. J., Gifford, S. M., & Thorpe, L. (2000). The social and cultural context of risk and prevention: Food and physical activity in an urban aboriginal community. *Health Education & Behaviour, 27,* 725–743.

Vukic, A., & Keddy, B. (2002). Northern nursing practice in a primary health care setting. *Journal of Advanced Nursing, 40*(5), 542–548.

Waldram, J., Herring, D., & Young, K. (2006). *Aboriginal health in Canada: Historical, cultural, and epidemiological perspectives*. Toronto: University of Toronto Press.

Wharf Higgins, J., Young, L., Cunningham, S., & Naylor, P. (2006).Out of the mainstream: Low-income, lone mothers' life experiences and perspectives on health. *Health Promotion, 7*(2): 221–233.

Williamson, D. F., Vinicor, F., & Bowman, B. A. (2004). Primary prevention of type 2 diabetes mellitus by lifestyle intervention: Implications for health policy. *Annals of Internal Medicine, 140,* 951–957.

Wortherspoon, T., & Satzewich, V. (1993). *First Nations: Race, class and gender relations.* Toronto: Nelson Canada.

Young, T. K. (2003). Review of research on Aboriginal populations in Canada: Relevance to their health needs. *British Medical Journal, 27*(23), 419–422.

Chapter 12

Communicating About Childhood Immunization: New Insights from Aotearoa/New Zealand

Margie Comrie, Elspeth Tilley, Bronwyn Watson, and Niki Murray

Introduction

This chapter discusses an ongoing research project to explore communicative phenomena in the childhood immunization context in Aotearoa/New Zealand. Childhood immunization rates in New Zealand offer a complex and perturbing research problem—to the extent that, in 2010, a parliamentary inquiry specifically investigated how to improve completion rates (New Zealand Parliament, 2010). Globally, immunization is at a record high (UNICEF, 2008), yet within that overall upward trend, some countries, including New Zealand, are experiencing a decline from prior levels. Minority world (affluent or "developed") countries appear particularly affected by fluctuation, with the World Health Organization concerned about "increasing complacency about immunizing children" in Europe (Global Forum, 2008, n.p.), a 2010 study finding immunization rates declining among "comparatively well educated or 'high-information'" parents in the United States (NCQA, 2010, p. 13), and Australian levels at a seven-year low in 2010 (Uplend, 2010). Given these international trends, our chapter offers a timely exploration of immunization communication decision-making processes that may have implications beyond the immediate geographical context described.

Our research, which was jointly funded by the New Zealand Ministry of Health and the Health Research Council of New Zealand, aimed to discover, from an open-ended qualitative investigation, new ways to conceptualize and explain immunization decision making. The research used a collaborative research process to develop and modify illustrated communication resources reflecting participants' design suggestions. Simultaneously, the inquiry process was open and exploratory. It started a conversation with participants about their decision-making influences rather than being designed to test particular attributes of immunization communication processes.

From a detailed qualitative analysis of focus group and in-depth interview transcripts with 107 immunization decision makers, themes were drawn. Specific discoveries about preferences for visual aspects and content of immunization communications were made, and these were applied to develop and/or modify the design of prototype resources (a flipchart and refrigerator magnet) before seeking each further round of feedback.

This chapter documents the research approach and outlines both the practical tools and the theoretical insights that resulted, showing how applying an emic process enabled generation of new ideas that broadened the range of possible solutions considered for immunization communication challenges in Aotearoa/ New Zealand.

Of particular interest was the fact that our research found that when people who were soon to be facing a decision about whether to immunize a child in their care were asked about their information needs, they frequently had strong, clear, and definite ideas about what information they wanted, how they wanted it, and when they wanted it. In particular, caregivers told us they wanted to know far more about possible reactions, the disease being vaccinated against, what happens at the immunization appointment, the vaccination ingredients, and the reasons for the timing or combination of particular vaccinations. Most respondents also told us that they were dissatisfied with the quality or quantity of information they had received to date, and wanted both more information and more balanced and accessible information. This patent articulation of interest in learning more about all aspects of immunization to inform decision making contradicts suggestions by health professionals in prior research that caregivers may be "apathetic" (e.g., in Grant, Petousis-Harris, Turner, et al., 2011; Petousis-Harris, Goodyear-Smith, Turner, & Soe, 2004, 2005a).

In our study, parents and caregivers were also clear about how they wanted to receive this expanded range of information: Most wanted it delivered during a face-to-face talk with a trusted health professional. A smaller number preferred to find it privately on the Internet, but almost as many wanted to use the Internet in combination with a talk with a trusted health professional. Almost none of the caregivers in our study wanted to receive information in written brochure form, yet this was the main way they had found out about immunization (closely followed by written or broadcast media reports). By the second round of interviews following birth, when many people had made an initial decision and encountered more written material during a visit to their health professional, many were reporting "brochure overload." Our participants indicated this caused them to "tune out"—yet they still did not have all their information needs met and wanted to talk things over in more detail with a health professional and ask particular questions about matters not covered in the brochures, such as autism risk levels.

The clarity of participants' insights and the apparent differences between the information they were currently receiving and what they desired led us to appreciate the value of ground-up, exploratory approaches o investigating difficult communication situations. In particular, the action-research-inspired method of using information resources as talking points and modifying them through multiple feedback loops proved valuable in gaining data that not only illuminated the situation from participants' own perspectives, but also resulted in practical and usable resources, designed by those making the immunization decision to assist them in meeting their information needs.

Literature Review

Because our investigation was concerned with issues on the communication of immunization information to parents and caregivers of infants in Aotearoa/New Zealand, the main focus of literature reviewed here is New Zealand research and data. Nevertheless, as mentioned above, the inability to consistently reach immunization levels considered necessary to achieve "herd immunity," particularly in more affluent countries, is an international phenomenon. For this reason, and as international findings were often an important basis informing our own research project, we have drawn on relevant international studies. Here we present an overview of literature that examines barriers to immunization, connections between health literacy and communication, and known attributes of the immunization decision-making process in Aotearoa/New Zealand and internationally.

Known Barriers to Immunization

New Zealand research examining reasons why children are not immunized presents a complex picture with conclusions often varying, according to whether the views presented are those of health professionals or of parents/caregivers. For example, surveys of health professionals, including family physicians and practice nurses, show that they perceive the greatest barriers to immunization to be parental fear (Grant et al., 2011; Petousis-Harris et al., 2004a, 2005a) and parental apathy (Grant et al., 2011; Petousis-Harris et al., 2005a). However, when the views of parents or caregivers are presented, parental apathy is unlikely to be mentioned as a barrier. On the contrary, reports note that parents seek information on immunization from numerous sources regarding immunization safety and efficacy concerns, actively weighing the perceived benefits and risks of immunization before making a decision (e.g., Hamilton, Corwin, Gower, & Rogers, 2004; Watson, Yarwood, &

Chenery, 2007; Wroe, Turner, & Salkovskis, 2004). Watson et al. (2007) argue that regarding immunization "whatever decision is made, parents do not undertake the process lightly. Indeed, decisions regarding their children's wellbeing were made with considerable thought, questioning and discussion" (p. 7).

While the emphasis may shift depending on the respondent group, in general, recent New Zealand research suggests two main categories of reasons why young children may not be completely immunized. The first category, caregiver choice, aggregates reasons for caregivers' "active decisions to forego immunization" (Wroe, Turner, & Owens, 2005, p. 539), while the second category covers systemic issues.

Caregiver choice issues focus on two major areas of concern. First there are concerns about the safety of immunization, such as the safety of particular vaccines and vaccine efficacy; the effects of vaccines on children's immune systems; the possibility of both short- and long-term serious side-effects; whether the risks of the vaccine outweigh the risks from the disease; caregivers' emotional issues; and caregivers' concerns over whether another illness at the scheduled vaccination date is a contraindication to immunization (Hamilton et al., 2004; Jelleyman & Ure, 2004; Ministry of Health, 2007; Petousis-Harris, Goodyear-Smith, Godinet, & Turner, 2002; Petousis-Harris, Turner, & Kerse, 2002; Petousis-Harris et al., 2005; Petousis-Harris, Goodyear-Smith, Ram, & Turner, 2005b; Wroe et al., 2004). The second area of concern for parents is that insufficient or biased information is provided about the benefits or risks of immunization (e.g., Hamilton et al., 2004; Petousis-Harris et al., 2002; Petousis-Harris, Turner, & Kerse, 2002b; Petousis-Harris, Boyd, & Turner, 2004; Petousis-Harris et al., 2005b; Watson et al., 2007; Wroe et al., 2004).

Systemic issues include access barriers, such as transport availability and cost (e.g., Paterson, Percival, Butler, & Williams, 2004; Paterson, Schluter, Percival, & Carter, 2006; Petousis-Harris et al., 2002; 2004a, 2005a); a shortage of general practitioners (Comrie et al., 2010) and knowledge, attitudes, systems, and funding of healthcare providers (e.g., Grant et al., 2011; Grant, Turner, York, Goodyear-Smith, & Petousis-Harris, 2010; Jelleyman & Ure, 2004; Petousis-Harris et al., 2004a, 2005b; Turner, Baker, Carr, & Mansoor, 2000; Turner, Grant, Goodyear-Smith & Petousis-Harris, 2009).

Of particular relevance here is the impact of lack of immunization knowledge and consequent lack of confidence among health professionals responsible for discussing immunization with parents. Despite international research showing that "poor knowledge of immunization by health professionals, rather than attitudes, is the single biggest factor in vaccine uptake" (Petousis-Harris, Boyd, &

Turner, 2004, p. 2343), New Zealand surveys found that physicians (Jelleyman & Ure, 2004; Petousis-Harris, Boyd, & Turner, 2004) and practice nurses (Petousis-Harris et al., 2005b) did not recognize the importance of their own knowledge gaps, and "rated their own lack of knowledge as the least likely factor in low immunization coverage" (Petousis-Harris, Boyd, & Turner, 2004, p. 2343).

However, Jelleyman and Ure (2004) identified low professional certainty and knowledge about whether, for example, the MMR vaccine is implicated in autism or Crohn's disease. This despite the scientific literature available at the time (e.g., Taylor et al., 1999) reassuring providers of the safety of the MMR vaccine and participants' assertions that "quality scientific research was the most important basis for recommending vaccinations and [that they] considered current recommendations to be well supported" (Jelleyman & Ure, 2004, p. 10). This led Jelleyman and Ure to argue for continuing professional education regarding immunization benefits and risks.

Health Literacy and Communication

In recent years the healthcare system in affluent countries has tended to shift "from a paternalistic to a partnership model" (Kerka, 2003, p. 1), with good health increasingly an individual rather than a healthcare system responsibility. This societal move underlines the importance of health literacy and the need for increased communication between health professionals and clients to facilitate informed decision making and consent. Jacobson et al., (1999) argue that more effective communication between patients and health providers is crucial to improving immunization rates. Similarly, Wilson, Brown, and Stephens-Ferris (2006) note that, in view of the expectation in the United States that parents participate more actively in family health decision making, more needs to be done to provide appropriate information: "Parents can only make informed choices when they are presented with information that makes sense to them" (p. 11).

An important consideration is the impact of cultural relevance on how clients understand or respond to healthcare materials and instructions. That is, these materials need to be socially, culturally, and contextually specific. Kerka (2003) cites research showing the problems caused by expecting health literacy to transcend diverse cultural beliefs, social practices, and translation from one language to another. Examples include problems of miscommunication and tensions between a system that requires individual responsibility and social customs that view health as a collective responsibility. As McCray (2005) suggests, readability assessments of communication resources need to acknowledge clients' prior knowledge and motivation. Consideration of cultural and social practices and beliefs is essential during the development phase of health communication resources.

The suggestions of Doak, Doak, and Root (1996) and McCray (2005) for preparing health communication resources most likely to promote patient comprehension, recall, and adherence fall into two major categories: (1) simplifying the language and (2) incorporating "visual strategies," including using at least a 12-point, mixed-case font, presenting information in bullet point format, using a question-and-answer format, minimizing the number of concepts per page and grouping them under headings, including ample white space, and using illustrations that give readers clues to the text.

Combining such visual strategies with appropriate illustrations, Doak, Doak, and Root (1996) claim, is likely to provide multiple benefits for health communication.

- They cater to those with visual learning styles who tend to rely on visual and audio messages.
- They capture attention, prompting readers to decide whether to take notice of the message.
- Where illustrations provide familiar context, they help readers interpret messages, bridging language barriers.
- They simplify complex concepts and reduce words.
- They aid recall by enhancing emotional impact.
- They encourage focus on key messages and actions.
- They motivate action on the information communicated.

With this guidance in mind, Wilson, Brown, and Stephens-Ferris (2006) recommend health clinics overcome deficiencies in immunization communication by (1) identifying low literacy levels among client caregivers; (2) developing easy-to-read health materials; (3) ensuring that written information and instructions are used alongside face-to-face communication; and (4) tailoring education and advice to individual needs.

Further studies (e.g., Audley, Greene, Davis, Koplan, & Cleary, 1998; Pearson & Raeke, 2000) show that, while developing user-friendly resources, we should recognize the value of health professional dialogue with patients and the importance of a trusting and listening relationship. Communication research emphasizes that how messages and advice are given is as important as the content (Feng & MacGeorge, 2010). Further, findings on the effectiveness of mass health communication campaigns indicate that not only should audiences be involved in formulating messages, but also that campaigns that "spark interpersonal exchange and dialogue" are more effective (Noar, 2006, p. 34). Such studies find an echo in long-standing public relations models endorsing dialogue and discussion (stemming from Grunig & Hunt, 1984) and public communication applications such as the sense-making methodology, where "audiences become peers and collaborators—and if there are 'campaigns' involved they are two-way" (Dervin & Frenette, 2001, p. 69).

Known Attributes of Immunization Decision-Making Processes in Aotearoa/New Zealand and Internationally

Research shows that New Zealand caregivers are most likely to make the decision regarding childhood immunization during the antenatal period (Hamilton et al., 2004). For example, Wroe et al. (2004) and Grant et al. (2011) reported that 88 percent and 67 percent of their survey participants, respectively, had decided before the baby's birth whether they would immunize. However, of the parents surveyed by Grant et al. (2011), only 62 percent recalled receiving immunization information antenatally (although, as we note below, our research suggests this may often be a recall rather than a lack of information issue). Moreover, 29 percent of those parents reported the information had actually discouraged them from immunizing their children. This finding is supported by Hamilton et al. (2004) whose study revealed that more than a third of participants decided antenatally not to immunize their children. Turner (2004) argues that to achieve maximum impact from interventions to aid immunization decision-making, communication with parents should occur during the antenatal period because "giving increased information in the antenatal period with a decision-making aid does follow through to a significant increase in timely immunization coverage" (Turner, 2004, p. 2).

A need for improved resources "to more effectively address parental fears and misconceptions" (Petousis-Harris et al., 2004a, p. 2340) and provide more information about immunization benefits and risks has been expressed by family physicians (Petousis-Harris et al., 2004a), practice nurses (Petousis-Harris et al., 2005a), and caregivers (e.g., Bond, Nolan, Pattison, & Carlin, 1998; Wroe et al., 2004; Wroe, Bahn, Salkovskis, & Bedford, 2005; Wroe, Turner, & Owens, 2005). However, Watson et al. (2007) warn against developing information or mass programs based on fear, as that strategy may create feelings of coercion and distrust. Similarly, Petousis-Harris et al. (2002, p. 401) recommend avoiding blame or guilt and instead using "messages that position children as the centre of the family (its *tāonga* or treasure) and stress the importance of the wellness of children for the family" (n.p.). Wroe, Bhan, Salkovskis, and Bedford (2005) found that caregivers who are provided with information that clearly details adverse effects of immunizations and disease risks were less likely to be anxious about perceived adverse impacts, more likely to understand the risks of the diseases, and more likely to immunize their children.

Method

Our project evolved from a collaborative research relationship with several health and community organizations from the Whanganui District Health Board region, researchers from the Adult Literacy and Communication Research Group at Massey University, and the Immunisation Advisory Centre at the University of Auckland. Based in Whanganui, a small city in the North Island of Aotearoa/New Zealand, the study involved eight local agencies including mainstream, Māori (Indigenous), and Pacific Peoples' organizations, across both rural and urban settings. These were Nga Tai O Te Awa Māori Development Organisation; Whanganui Regional Primary Health Organisation; Te Oranganui Iwi Health Authority Primary Health Organisation; Te Kotuku Hauora O Rangitikei—Te Runanga O Ngati Apa; O Taihape Māori Komiti Inc.; the Born and Raised Pasifika Early Childhood Centre; Birthright (Wanganui), a support organization for sole parents; and the Whanganui Hospital Maternity Service. All partners were integrally involved with every step of the research, a process facilitated through regular face-to-face project meetings involving all collaborator groups and a stakeholder consultation email list on which email progress reports were circulated and discussed. Both university and community partners gave dissemination presentations and held feedback discussions with stakeholder groups at each stage of the research, and stakeholder responses were collated through the project meetings and summarized for further feedback in the email updates.

The research design was developed collaboratively and was most influenced by action research processes and ideals in which research is envisaged as an ongoing partnership between researchers and participants (Greenwood & Levin, 2005). It aimed, through multiple feedback and response loops, to be as inclusive of and reactive to participants' worldviews and input as possible; in this research design, the researchers acted as facilitators who shared and exchanged views in a joint learning experience with participants (Adler, Shani, & Styhre, 2004).

The views of childhood immunization decision makers were gathered at three points. First, during a series of focus groups with those who had been responsible for making immunization decisions. These focus groups also provided the information from which we developed prototype communication resources. Second were views of women in the third trimester of pregnancy whose views were gathered during an interview that accompanied pilot testing of the resources. These women were re-surveyed with a phone interview eight weeks after the birth of their child, offering a third point of view collection.

Focus Group Sample and Procedure

The first phase involved seven focus groups (with five to seven participants) and one additional face-to-face interview (conducted with a focus group participant who was the only attendee at a proposed eighth focus group). All participants were clients of and recruited by the Whanganui organizations mentioned above. This community-based recruitment gave participants the ability to contribute to the research in a context with which they were already comfortable and familiar. It also assisted with ensuring anonymity, as the participants were involved in a context in which they participated ordinarily. The 45 participants included parents, caregivers, and extended family members (who are frequently decision makers in Māori and Pacific Island communities). Our aim was to talk with people from groups who had low representation in the immunization statistics and were therefore regarded as "hard to reach." The partner organizations identified people within these groups who had responsibility for making an immunization decision and invited them to participate. Māori and Pacific People, along with young solo mothers, were strongly represented in our sample. Most, 38 of the 45 focus group members, were women; almost half were under 30; a third were responsible for one child, almost as many were responsible for two children, and the remainder were responsible for between three and six children.

Focus group participants were encouraged to discuss their decision making regarding immunization, the types of immunization information they received from all sources, and the usefulness of that information. They were also asked what information they would have liked to receive, and their preferred method of information delivery. Finally, they were shown some cartoon illustrations and the current Ministry of Health resources, and asked for their opinions.

Development of Tools

Following participant recommendations made in the focus groups, we developed a flipchart and refrigerator magnet to communicate key immunization information. The flipchart was designed to be delivered by a health worker in a one-to-one discussion with the client (the preferred mode of delivery). Each flipchart page outlined one key message about immunization drawn from the focus group discussions about information needs, and photographs, bright colors, and simple wording were used as per participants' preferences. The refrigerator magnet, using photographs, simple language and bright colors, contained three key messages from the flipchart, the infant immunization schedule, and contact information in case of questions or an emergency. Focus group members were shown the resources for further comment in a second round of meetings and further changes were made following these and feedback from health professionals.

Interviewee Sample and Procedure

Next, the two resources were piloted with 62 women in their third trimester of pregnancy as part of a semistructured qualitative interview. Interviewees were recruited with the assistance of midwives to gain perspectives from both urban and rural mothers-to-be. Each participant took part in an antenatal interview where the types of immunization information received and preferences for communication and information channels were explored. Interviewees were also asked to reflect on any decision-making process they had taken part in to date for their soon-to-be-born child and the influencing factors on any decision. Following this discussion, 31 women were read an oral presentation based on the information in the flipchart. The remaining 31 women received the oral information plus additional visual and take-home material: They heard the oral presentation at the same time as they were shown the flipchart[1] and were then given the refrigerator magnet to take home.

A second round of semistructured interviews was held with 61 of the same participants at approximately eight weeks post-birth. The interviewer asked about the types of immunization information received since the antenatal interview, the participant's thoughts on the usefulness of that information, and the factors that impacted on the six-week immunization decision (if it had been made). Participants were also asked what they recalled from the oral presentation or from the oral presentation and flipchart combination, and, for those who received a refrigerator magnet, about their use of this tool. Finally, interviewees were asked to rate the likelihood of immunizing their child at three months of age. The National Immunisation Register (NIR) database was also checked to determine immunization uptake rates at six weeks and three months of age.

Coding Procedure

Coding followed the principles of what has been called the constructivist revision of grounded theory (Strauss & Corbin, 1998; Charmaz, 2000). The coding process sought to find, from multiple readings and an open-ended approach to the data,

---

[1] While the flipchart was intended to be used as a discussion tool, the pilot testing process required consistency of delivery across participants. Therefore, the interviewer read an oral presentation to each participant, and referred further discussion points or questions the participant had back to their health worker.

prevailing concepts and patterns that might lead to an explanatory model for the participants' experiences and perceptions. To systematize the coding and assist with generating comprehensive reports from the data and making changes in response to feedback, a computer-assisted qualitative data analysis software package (HyperResearch) was used (see Bringer, Johnston, & Brackenridge, 2006 for discussion of the use of such programs in constructivist grounded theory approaches).

Findings

In the following sections we look at the findings from focus groups, antenatal interviews, and postnatal interviews that reflect concerns our participants had about immunization, about the way they received information, and what information they wanted to receive. We also present details of the focus group recommendations that informed the development of the communication resources and some results from the pilot testing of these resources. We extrapolate the immunization barriers and facilitators in a final section that leads to some broader issues raised by the findings and relates them to communication theory.

Coding of the focus group and interview transcripts was conducted as a corpus analysis (meaning overall or macro themes of the data were gathered at each of the three stages of the project rather than isolating individual contributions). The focus group and interview participants covered a diverse demographic and cultural mix, but because numbers were too small to be extrapolated as representative of a particular population segment, an aggregate picture of the findings is most appropriate.

Focus Groups

Most focus group participants said that when it came to deciding whether to immunize their children, they felt anxious and disaffected despite (or in some cases because of) current communication attempts. Knowledge levels were low and most did not undertake a protracted decision-making process. They generally accepted immunization as something they "should do," but there were strong indications of social and fear pressures. They sought more detailed, factual information that was both accessible and easily understood, and they had many suggestions for how to achieve that balance.

There was consensus around the importance of impartial, nondirective, evidence-based communication, especially opportunities to receive information from trusted sources. They wanted multilayered communication, with clear, simple, top-level visual summaries but with connections to further details or question opportunities.

For the content, the participants wanted balanced factual data on the risks of immunizing versus not immunizing, factual descriptions of what is in vaccines and how they work, and of the diseases being immunized against. They also wanted calendar schedules of immunization due dates; signs of and action steps for adverse reactions; and phone numbers or other sources for more information.

Participants were critical of some official booklets and pamphlets. They needed written material to be much shorter and avoid big words. They wanted summaries of key points, which could be used as a starting point, not a complete solution, for immunization questions. Interestingly, there were comments both for and against graphs as a way of quickly summarizing information, but the overall consensus was that if graphs were clear and simple (such as a basic chart of risks of immunizing versus risks of not immunizing), they were appreciated.

When focus group participants were shown both photographs of people and cartoon pictures, there was a strong preference for photos. They wanted photos of "real people," babies and families they could relate to, that could appeal to young people, were culturally appropriate, and were taken in contexts like doctors' rooms. Photographs and stories about real-life experiences were seen as a way to draw attention to the importance of vaccination. Participants wanted to know more about the diseases, although there was some distaste expressed at fear appeals, not so much because the content was offensive but because they were overly persuasive. People did not want pictures of babies actually getting injections, but were generally in favor of pictures of babies or children with disease symptoms (one participant suggested a picture of the symptoms but showing just a part of the baby's body, not the whole child), as well as healthy children.

These suggestions were incorporated into the flipchart design. As described above, flipchart prototypes were shown in feedback sessions to the focus group participants. In these feedback sessions the "disease pictures" were particularly drawn to attract the attention of the original focus group members who agreed that, while distressing, they were informative.

First Round Interviews: Antenatal. Grounded analysis of 62 interview transcripts from the first round of (pre-decision) interviews found that the majority of mothers-to-be had received a brochure (often not read), seen something in the media, or received some information from their midwife. Yet more than half (34 interviewees) still considered they had not had a specific conversation with anyone about immunization. Half (31 interviewees) felt their information needs about immunization had not been met. The top information need was simply for "more information," and for most participants, the preferred source of that additional information was a face-to-face discussion with a health professional and an opportunity to ask questions. The Internet was also an important source.

Some mothers-to-be felt that health professionals and the information they provided needed to better address both the pros and cons of immunization, so that people were empowered to make their own decisions rather than feeling they were being "told what to do." Some wanted more detailed information about what is in vaccines, what they do to the body, why they are necessary, and a comparison of the probable outcomes of immunizing versus not immunizing. Some participants had concerns about receiving too much written information, but nonetheless wanted more information. Most participants indicated they intended to vaccinate the children in their care, and based their decisions on personal experience or a sense of compunction, because everyone else was doing it. However, there remained prevalent feelings of uncertainty and fear, sparked in particular by new vaccines, vaccines that come in and then are discontinued, the number of immunizations, and the age at which they are given.

Second Round Interviews: Postnatal

Communication Experiences and Concerns. By the second round of interviews, eight weeks after birth, most of the mothers had made the six-week immunization decision. At this stage more participants had taken part in a conversation (outside the research itself) about immunization (an encouraging three-quarters, compared with just half in the antenatal interview). In line with this was the finding that more participants than in the first round reported receiving immunization information from health professionals, fewer mentioned information from the media, and fewer said they felt inadequately informed. However, brochures were still the primary information source, and it was concerning to note that a quarter of the participants described being overloaded with the same (generally written) information multiple times. The number of women expressing concerns about vaccine safety remained the same, but fewer expressed uncertainty about their decision making. Five alluded to the "herd immunity" argument (not mentioned in the first round of interviews).

When asked about their information needs, mothers in this second round still asked for immunization information to be balanced and to give more details on reactions. There was continued insistence on not being "told what to do." They wanted to know what to expect and how best to prepare for the appointment (for instance, whether and when to use pain relief medication). Participants still overwhelmingly indicated a talk with a health professional as the preferred source of further information. The Internet, while still important, was less frequently nominated. Most wanted a reminder the day before their immunization appointment, either by text message or some other method of their choosing, such as email.

Impact of Resources. During the antenatal interview, half the respondents had received an enhanced information session where they were given a scripted talk and shown the flipchart with its visual images, and half were given the scripted talk only. There were some differences that should be seen as qualitative indications, not statistical findings, but which suggest avenues for follow-up research. The aural-only information group had more people with low recall of information and the enhanced (aural plus visual) information group had more people with confident recall. Disease pictures in the flipchart were most often recalled, with several participants saying these had influenced their decision making. Most of the group who received the refrigerator magnet found it useful and well designed. The aural-only group's highest information priorities mentioned in the second interview were about reactions and the immunization appointment, while the aural-plus-visual-information group's highest information priority was for balanced information. The aural-only group tended to see information they had received prior to the current interview itself as mostly helpful, while the aural-plus-visual-information group tended to perceive the information they had received previously as mostly perfunctory (their expectations of the standard of information they could receive had risen). Subsequent database checking showed all participants, except three in the aural-only group, had fully immunized their children up to three months.

Recommendations for Communication Timing. When asked for recommendations about the timing of immunization communication, most participants suggested two discussions, one before and one after birth. This was because of all the other issues expectant parents are thinking about and because mothers felt they suffered from "baby brain" (and clinical research does support the validity of claims of amnesia during pregnancy, see Rendell & Henry, 2008). They suggested an initial session during the third trimester, because early in pregnancy, mothers may not be engaged with postnatal issues or may forget the information by the time the immunization is due, and too late in the pregnancy they are focused intently on the birth. This window made the 28th to 30th week period the preferred time. Participants suggested a second, follow-up and reminder chat with their health professional at about three to four weeks after birth. They said they were too tired and overwhelmed immediately after the birth to consider the information, but needed a couple of weeks to weigh issues before the six-week immunization appointment.

Summary of Impacts on Decision-Making. Prior to making their immunization decision, we asked mothers-to-be to indicate the sources or issues they felt had been particularly influential on their thinking about immunization (positive or negative). Of most impact was personal experience, such as having been immunized themselves or having had particular educational experiences (such as a science or medical background). Official written materials were not mentioned at all, by any respondents, as an influential impact factor in their thinking.

However, the following were highly influential: a sense of uncertainty (particularly around new immunizations, the number of immunizations, and the perceived young age at which children receive them), and a fear of complications, ranging from allergic reactions to fear of a connection with autism. Often participants who expressed these uncertainties and fears as important factors in their thinking said that, nonetheless, they would go ahead with immunizations, and this was usually because of a cultural expectation that everyone will "just do it." Similar barriers came out of focus group analysis; the most frequently mentioned barriers there were the relevance and accessibility of information material, followed by negative experiences in talking with or visiting general practitioners.

Despite the fact that most participants ultimately expressed (to the interviewer) a choice to immunize (and follow-up checking showed they did immunize their children), the research suggested that their feelings of uncertainty were strong and lingering. The high frequency of uncertainty suggested waning trust in the medical profession as an authoritative information source. As one woman said, "I've just always been of a mind that you get it done. Probably have a lot of trust in the medical industry that maybe I shouldn't have." Similar findings emerged from the focus groups, in which we noted likely generational changes in people's levels of trust in authority, including doctors. Younger people were more distrustful of official medical information, which they saw as unhelpfully "biased" in favor of immunization.

Conclusions and Implications

To tackle low immunization rates, New Zealand's Ministry of Health started in July 2009 to set a series of childhood immunization targets, culminating in a target of 95 percent of 2-year-olds fully immunized by mid-2012. District Health Boards have used the newly established National Immunisation Register to follow up with those who have missed any scheduled immunizations. Nurses in general practice have been urged to take advantage of children's surgery visits on other matters; outreach services contact those who are tardy and arrange clinic appointments or home visits; and culturally appropriate programs have targeted Māori and Pacific peoples. At a national immunization conference in August 2011, health officials commended practitioners for helping the country reach its interim target of 90 percent coverage at 2 years old and for reducing discrepancies between Māori and Pacific peoples and other ethnic groups. However, public health workers and officials were aware that to reach the 95 percent herd immunity target would likely require an effort even more substantial than that which had driven figures up over the previous two years. Moreover, the figures for full immunization at six months remain a low 70 percent. These figures raise concern not only because of the vulnerability of young infants but also because New Zealand and international research indicates that delays in immunization are related to not completing the childhood immunization schedule (Grant et al., 2011; Guyer et al., 1994).

Despite better systems for tracking and reaching those not immunizing their children, the underlying causes of low immunization rates are apparently not being addressed. There seems every possibility that with the immediate pressure of targets lifted and ever-competing needs from other health requirements in a time of government restrictions on public spending, immunization rates may slip again. That participants in our research, only a small minority of whom did not immunize children in their care, expressed very similar concerns to those of 83 people selected because they had *not* immunized their children (Ministry of Health, 2011) indicates the fragility of the situation.

While immunization is free in New Zealand, unlike near-neighbor Australia, this country does not offer parents money to immunize their children. There is no compulsion to immunize, although a large proportion of our focus groups thought children "had to have their jabs" before going to pre-school. In fact, while parents must present an immunization certificate (or a certificate of declination) when they enroll children at childcare or school, its purpose is largely to ensure educators can make certain non-immunized children stay home during an epidemic.

With an emphasis on informed consent and a right to conscientious objection (NZ Parliament Health Select Committee, 2010), the stress falls strongly on communication. As the Government Response to the Health Select Committee Report (2011, p. 4) states, "an approach based on stronger advocacy and regulation … creates significant risks and could erode rather than build trust." Despite some concern by our participants about official "propaganda," the Ministry of Health approach has generally been to play down fear appeals and promote the positives of childhood health. Indeed, health professionals who collaborated with or advised our team were concerned about the decision to use disease pictures and were only reassured after the focus group feedback sessions confirmed these were what the audience wanted.

Another request from our participants also created some tensions with the health practitioner community. This was for "balanced" information and our analysis showed this had two aspects. The first, and perhaps predominant, was for a clear outline of the risks of immunization versus the risks of the disease. While this information could not be contained within the restrictions of the simple visual flipchart, it is relatively straightforward to construct a basic chart or set of tables as an extra talking point for educator/practitioners. The other need, for reliable information from "the other side of the debate," is less easy to accommodate. Indications from our participants were quite clear—they wanted to be told about any information they might encounter that was "anti-immunization," and not be left to discover it for themselves. The wisdom of exposing decision makers to clear facts containing opposing as well as supporting information also finds support in both Elaboration Likelihood Model and inoculation communication theories, as we have discussed elsewhere (Tilley, Murray, Watson, & Comrie, 2011). Orthodox medical practitioners and officials are, however, understandably reluctant to be responsible for exposing audiences to information they stigmatize as unscientific and ultimately unhelpful for health outcomes.

Simply condemning anti-immunization material can be counterproductive, and rational arguments do not always work, as they fail to take into account the strong emotional aspect of immunizing your child. Further, there is a dichotomy between the official information—detailed and rigorous with an ever-present danger it may be interpreted as patronizing—and the strongly emotional, but ultimately more accessible, rhetoric of anti-immunization groups. Recent research (Betsch, 2011) indicates that people searching the Internet with less health knowledge use less complex search terms (e.g., "vaccination," rather than "immunization" or "MMR vaccine"), with the result that they are more likely to access anti-immunization websites.

One solution is to work on building parents' trust in the reliability and efficacy of the immunization process as part of ensuring the well-being of their children. It is a considerable task, especially among a younger, less compliant generation of parents. However, our participants' views on the importance of a talk with their trusted health professional (often their midwife) shows they value the partnership model (Kerka, 2003). This discussion to engage and enlighten clients requires health professionals themselves to be knowledgeable. Investigations by Petousis-Harris et al. (2004, 2005) indicate professionals do not recognize the importance of their knowledge gaps, while Jelleyman and Ure's (2004) research indicates those gaps may be considerable. The ambivalence of frontline health professionals' attitudes to immunization is reflected in their own relatively low uptake of recommended influenza vaccines (Jennings, 2006; Personal communication, August 18–20, 2011.)

In relation to childhood immunization, our discussions with midwives who were lead maternity carers (LMCs) revealed that many lacked confidence in their ability to conduct an informed antenatal discussion; they believed mothers-to-be were not interested in the topic at that stage and generally fulfilled their regulatory requirement to provide Ministry of Health information about immunization by merely providing written pamphlets. Our research showed that this may not only be ineffective, it may actually be counterproductive.

Ensuring that mothers-to-be have their information needs fulfilled requires more than simple production of communication tools, it requires a change of attitude and of practice precipitated by education of LMCs and other relevant health professionals. Jelleyman and Ure (2004) argue for recognition of the need for continuing professional education, especially regarding immunization benefits and risks. Moreover, according to UK researchers, "all healthcare professionals involved in immunization provision require training to ensure that parents are provided with accurate and consistent information to allay any concerns or misconceptions about vaccines" (Samad, Butler, Peckham, & Bedford, 2006, p. 6828).

At the pilot stage, our client-based resources have won approval from end-users and midwives in Whanganui, as well as maternity and immunization managers in five DHB regions. The next stage is to trial the resources in the discussion setting to see whether LMCs find them helpful. We plan to work collaboratively so the research team, midwives, and well-child nurses, along with their clients, all increase knowledge as part of the ultimate goal of improving children's health.

Adler, N. B., Shani, A. B., & Styhre, A. (Eds.). (2004). *Collaborative research in organizations: Foundations for learning, change, and theoretical development.* Thousand Oaks, CA: SAGE Publications.

Audley, C., Greene, D. C., Davis, N. A., Koplan, J. P., & Cleary, P. D. (1998). Patients' trust in their physicians: Effects of choice, continuity, and payment method. *Journal of General Internal Medicine, 13,* 681–686.

Betsch, C. (2011). Innovations in communication: The Internet and the psychology of vaccination decisions. *Eurosurveillance, 16*(17), 1–6. Retrieved from http://www.eurosurveillance.org/ViewArticle.aspx?ArticleId=19849

Bond, L., Nolan, T., Pattison, P., & Carlin, J. (1998). Vaccine preventable diseases and immunisations: A qualitative study of mothers' perceptions of severity, susceptibility, benefits and barriers. *Australian and New Zealand Journal of Public Health, 22*(4), 441–446.

Bringer, J. D., Johnston, L. H., & Brackenridge, C. H. (2006). Using computer-assisted qualitative data analysis software to develop a grounded theory project. *Field Methods 18*(3), 245–266. doi:10.1177/1525822X06287602

Charmaz, K. (2000). Grounded theory: Objectivist and constructivist methods. In N. K. Denzin & Y. S. Lincoln (Eds.), *Handbook of qualitative research* (2nd ed., pp. 509–536). London: SAGE Publications.

Comrie, M., Murray, N., Watson, B., Tilley, E., Sligo, F., & Handley, J. (2010). *Communicating infant immunisation information: Resource development and evaluation.* Wellington: Ministry of Health and Health Research Council of New Zealand.

Dervin, B., & Frenette, M. (2001). Sense-making methodology: Communicating communicatively with campaign audiences. In R. E. Rice & C. K. Atkin (Eds.), *Public communication campaigns* (3rd ed., pp. 69–87). Thousand Oaks, CA: SAGE Publications.

Doak, C. C., Doak, L. G., & Root, J. H. (1996). *Teaching patients with low literacy skills* (2nd ed.). Philadelphia: J. B. Lippincott.

Feng, B., & MacGeorge, E. L. (2010). The influence of message and source factors on advice outcome. *Communication Research, 37*(4), 553–575.

Global Forum for Health Research. (2008). *Immunization rates stagnating in Europe.* Retrieved from http://www.globalforumhealth.org/layout/set/print/Media-Publications/Archive-RealHealthNews/News-analysis/Immunization-rates-stagnating-in-Europe

Government Response to the Health Select Committee Report on the Inquiry into How to Improve Completion Rates of Childhood Inmunisation. (2011). Retrieved from http://www.immune.org.nz/site_resources/Govt_response__Health_Committee_Report__20110601.pdf

Grant, C. C., Petousis-Harris, H., Turner, N., Goodyear-Smith, F., Kerse, N., Jones, R. et al. (2011). Primary care practice and health professional determinants of immunization coverage. *Journal of Pediatrics and Child Health, 47*(8), 541–549.

Grant, C. C., Turner, N. M., York, D. G., Goodyear-Smith, F., & Petousis-Harris, H. A. (2010). Factors associated with immunisation coverage and timeliness in New Zealand. *British Journal of General Practice, 60*(572), 180–86. doi:10.3399/bjgp10X483535

Greenwood, D. J., & Levin, M. (2005). Reform of the social sciences and of the universities through action research. In N. K. Denzin & Y. S. Lincoln (Eds.), *The Sage handbook of qualitative research* (3rd ed., pp. 43–64). Thousand Oaks, CA: SAGE Publications.

Guyer, B., Hughart, N., Holt, E., Ross, A., Stanton, B., Keane, V. et al. (1994). Immunization coverage and its relationship to preventive health care visits among inner-city children in Baltimore. *Pediatrics, 94*(1), 53–58.

Grunig, J. E., & Hunt, T. (1984). *Managing public relations.* New York: Holt, Rinehart and Winston.

Hamilton, M., Corwin, P., Gower, S., & Rogers, S. (2004). Why do parents choose not to immunise their children? *New Zealand Medical Journal, 117*(1189), U768

Jacobson, T. A., Thomas, D. M., Morton, F. J., Offutt, G., Shevlin, J., & Ray, S. (1999). Use of a low-literacy patient education tool to enhance pneumococcal vaccination rates: A randomized controlled trial. *Journal of the American Medical Association, 282*(7), 646–650.

Jelleyman, T., & Ure, A. (2004). Attitudes to immunisation: A survey of health professionals in the Rotorua District. *New Zealand Medical Journal, 117*(1189), U766.

Jennings, L. (2006, May). Influenza vaccination among New Zealand healthcare workers: Low rates are concerning. *New Zealand Medical Journal 119*(1233), U1961.

Kerka, S. (2003). *Health literacy beyond basic skills: ERIC Digest.* Retrieved from ERIC database. (ED478948).

McCray, A. T. (2005). Promoting health literacy. *Journal of the American Informatics Association, 12*(2), 152–163.

Ministry of Health. (2007). *The national childhood immunisation coverage survey 2005: Public health intelligence occasional bulletin No. 39.* Wellington: Ministry of Health.

Ministry of Health. (2011). *Immunisation audience research.* Report for the Ministry of Health, Wellington. Ministry of Health.

National Committee for Quality Assurance (NCQA). (2010). *State of health care quality report 2010.* Washington, DC: NCQA.

New Zealand Parliament Health Select Committee. (2010). *Inquiry into how to improve completion rates of childhood immunization.* Retrieved from http://www.parliament.nz/NR/rdonlyres/BADCF722-D377-4451-8602-1E00938BFC74/188894/DBSCH_SCR_5060_Inquiryintohowtoimprovecompletionra.pdf

Noar, S. M. (2006). A 10-year retrospective of research in health mass media campaigns: Where do we go from here? *Journal of Health Communication, 11*, 21–41.

Paterson, J., Percival, T., Butler, S., & Williams, M. (2004). Maternal and demographic factors associated with non-immunisation of Pacific infants living in New Zealand. *New Zealand Medical Journal, 117*(1199), U994.

Paterson, J., Schluter, P., Percival, T., & Carter, S. (2006). Immunisation of a cohort of Pacific children living in New Zealand over the first 2 years of life. *Vaccine, 24*, 4883–4889.

Pearson, S. D., & Raeke, L. H. (2000). Patients' trust in physicians: Many theories, few measures, and little data. *Journal of General Internal Medicine, 15*, 509–513.

Petousis-Harris, H., Boyd, E., & Turner, N. (2004). Immunisation education in the antenatal period. *New Zealand Family Physician, 31*(5), 303–306.

Petousis-Harris, H., Goodyear-Smith, F., Godinet, S., & Turner, N. (2002). Barriers to childhood immunisation among New Zealand mothers. *New Zealand Family Physician, 29*(6), 396–401.

Petousis-Harris, H., Goodyear-Smith, F., Ram, S., & Turner N. (2005a). The New Zealand national immunisation hotline—What are callers seeking? *Vaccine, 23*(42), 5038–5044.

Petousis-Harris, H., Goodyear-Smith, F., Turner, N., & Soe, B. (2004). Family physician perspectives on barriers to childhood immunization. *Vaccine, 22*(17–18), 2340–2344.

Petousis-Harris, H., Goodyear-Smith, F., Turner, T. & Soe, B. (2005b). Family practice nurse views on barriers to immunising children. *Vaccine, 23*(21), 2725–2730.

Petousis-Harris, H., Turner, N., & Kerse, N. (2002). New Zealand mothers' knowledge of and attitudes towards immunisation. *New Zealand Family Physician, 29*(4), 240–246.

Rendell, P. G., & Henry, J. D. (2008). Prospective memory functioning is affected during pregnancy and postpartum. *Journal of Clinical and Experimental Neuropsychology, 30*, 913–919.

Samad, L., Butler, N., Peckham, C., Bedford, H., & Millennium Cohort Study Child Health Group. (2006). Incomplete immunisation uptake in infancy: Maternal reasons. *Vaccine, 24*(47–48), 6823–6829.

Strauss, A. L., & Corbin, J. (1998). *Basics of qualitative research: Techniques and procedures for developing grounded theory.* (2nd ed.). London: SAGE Publications.

Taylor, B., Miller, E., Farrington, C. P., Petropoulos, M.-C., Favot-Mayaud, I., Li, J. et al. (1999). Autism and measles, mumps, and rubella vaccine: No epidemiological evidence for a causal association. *Lancet, 353*, 2026–2029.

Tilley, E., Murray, N., Watson, B., & Comrie, M. [Elaboration Likelihood Model and inoculation communication theories]. Unpublished manuscript.

Turner, N. (2004). Concerns of health providers and parents affect immunisation coverage. *New Zealand Medical Journal, 117*(1189), U766.

Turner, N., Baker, M., Carr, J., & Mansoor, O. (2000). Improving immunisation coverage: What needs to be done? *New Zealand Public Health Report, 7*(3/4), 11–14.

Turner, N., Grant, C. C., Goodyear-Smith, F., & Petousis-Harris, H. (2009). Seize the moments: Missed opportunities to immunize at the family practice level. *Family Practice, 26*, 275–278.

UNICEF. (2008). *The child care transition, Innocenti Report Card 8*, 2008. Florence, Italy: UNICEF Innocenti Research Centre.

Uplend, R. (2010). *Australia's rate of childhood vaccinations at 7-year low*. Retrieved from http://vaccinenewsdaily.com/news/211719-australias-rate-of-childhood-vaccinations-at-7-year-low

Watson, P. B., Yarwood, J., & Chenery, K. (2007). Meningococcal B: Tell me everything you know and everything you don't know: New Zealanders' decision making regarding an immunisation programme. *New Zealand Medical Journal, 120*(1263), U2751.

Wilson, F. L., Brown, D. L., & Stephens-Ferris, M. (2006). Can easy-to-read immunization information increase knowledge in urban low-income mothers? *Journal of Pediatric Nursing, 21*(1), 4–12.

Wroe, A. L., Bhan, A., Salkovskis, P., & Bedford, H. (2005). Feeling bad about immunising our children. *Vaccine, 23*(12), 1428–1433.

Wroe, A. L., Turner, N., & Owens, R. G. (2005). Evaluation of a decision-making aid for parents regarding childhood immunizations. *Health Psychology, 24*(6), 539–547.

Wroe, A. L., Turner, N., & Salkovskis, P. M. (2004). Understanding and predicting parental decisions about early childhood immunizations. *Health Psychology, 23*(1), 33–41.

Rukhsana Ahmed is an Assistant Professor in the Department of Communication at the University of Ottawa, Canada. She has an interdisciplinary background with a Master's in International Relations from the University of Dhaka, Bangladesh, a Master's in International Development Studies, a Master's in Communication Studies, and a Ph.D. in Health Communication from Ohio University, USA. Her research embraces the cross/trans/inter-disciplinary nature of communication scholarship with a specific focus on healthcare sector services for vulnerable populations and an interest in interpersonal, intercultural, and other realms of communication, including gender and development. Dr. Ahmed's presentations and publications have attracted significant audiences from Canada and the United States. In addition, she has been invited to share her research in Japan, Singapore, Poland, Sri Lanka, and Bangladesh. She serves on editorial boards of and reviews papers for journals in the areas of communication, media, and health.

Patricia Amason is an Associate Professor and Associate Department Chair of the Department of Communication at the University of Arkansas, USA. Dr. Amason earned her Ph.D. from Purdue University in West Lafayette, Indiana, USA. Her research primarily focuses on interpersonal communication and health issues, such as the provision of social support to distressed persons; communication and family crises, such as in cases of infertility; and the provision of quality communication in healthcare delivery.

Jay Baglia is an Assistant Professor of Communication Studies at DePaul University in Chicago, Illinois, USA. He teaches courses in Health Communication, Gender and Communication, and Communication Theory. Dr. Baglia earned his Ph.D. from the University of South Florida in 2003. His 2005 book, *The Viagra Ad Venture: Masculinity, Media, and the Performance of Sexual Health*, was the recipient of the Book of the Year in 2006, an award given annually by the Organization for the Study of Communication, Language, and Gender. Dr. Baglia has presented over 60 papers at regional, national, and international conferences and is on the editorial boards of *Health Communication* and *Women and Language*.

Benjamin R. Bates is currently an Associate Professor and Director for Graduate Studies in the School of Communication Studies at Ohio University, USA. Dr. Bates earned his Ph.D. at the University of Georgia, USA, in Speech Communication in 2003. Since then, he has authored or co-authored more than 50 peer-reviewed publications and made more than 80 presentations to learned societies at the intersection of health, communication, and media.

Dr. Bates has also been invited to serve as a visiting professor at Bangkok University, Thailand and Hong Kong Baptist University. Dr. Bates has served on the editorial boards of eight journals in communication and as a reviewer for 21 other journals in communication, health science, and medicine. He currently edits the journal *Communication Quarterly*.

Eva Berger is the Dean of the School of Media Studies of the College of Management–Academic Studies Division in Israel. She is also consultant to public and private organizations, and has written several programs for the study of communication in Israel's elementary and high school systems. Dr. Berger served as a member of the Israel Film Council for six years, is an advisor to Israel's educational television, and comments on media matters for several newspapers, radio, and television stations. She holds a B.A. in Film and Television from Tel Aviv University, and an M.A. and Ph.D. in Media Ecology from New York University. She is currently involved in a research project dealing with Narrative Medicine in the field of pediatrics with her father, a pediatrician.

Isaac Berger, MD is a recently retired pediatrician. He was Head of the Ambulatory Pediatric Services at Meir Medical Center in Kfar Saba, Israel for 30 years. He was in charge of the Pediatric Emergency Room, the Outpatient Clinics, the Daycare Unit, and the Child Development Center there. Dr. Berger studied Medicine at UNAM (National University of Mexico), and did his pediatric training (including a Fellowship in Neonatology) at Michael Reese Hospital in Chicago. He is currently involved in a research project concerning Narrative Medicine in the field of pediatrics, with his daughter, a communication scholar.

Margie Comrie is an Associate Professor in the School of Communication, Journalism and Marketing at Massey University, New Zealand. Dr. Comrie's Ph.D. in Communication came from Massey University, where she investigated the changes in television news. She has been a project and objective leader in publicly funded investigations into adult literacy, media literacy, and health communication. As a member of Massey University's Adult Literacy and Communication Research Group, Dr. Comrie continues to work on collaborative health communication research.

Elizabeth Dean has been a Professor in the Department of Physical Therapy, Faculty of Medicine, University of British Columbia, Canada, and Visiting Professor, Leeds Metropolitan University, Faculty of Health, Leeds, UK since 2005. Her academic/clinical career and experiences have spanned the corners of the globe with invitations to over 25 countries. Her research and publications have increasingly focused on integrating and translating knowledge of cultural relativism and diversity in promoting health and wellness worldwide, and exploiting evidence-based nonpharmacologic interventions to prevent, reverse, as well as manage lifestyle-related conditions. She is co-editor (with Donna Frownfelter) of *Cardiovascular and Pulmonary Physical Therapy: Evidence and Practice*. She served over a year as Senior, Cardiovascular/Cardiorespiratory Team, Kuwait Dalhousie Project in Kuwait, and as a resident Visiting Professor at the Hong Kong Polytechnic University.

Kevin Dew is Professor of Sociology and Programme Director of the Sociology and Social Policy Programme at Victoria University of Wellington, New Zealand. He has a Ph.D. in Sociology from Victoria University of Wellington, and is a founding member of the Applied Research on Communication in Health (ARCH) Group. His research focus has included health professional-patient interaction and health inequalities. A current research project involves tracking newly diagnosed diabetic patients through their first six months of consultation.

Jayson L. Dibble is an Assistant Professor in the Department of Communication at Hope College, Holland, Michigan, USA. He received his Ph.D. in Communication from Michigan State University, USA. His research focuses on communication within and across relationships, social influence, and message processing. His long-standing line of inquiry centers on the interpersonal delivery of bad news, with a special emphasis on the bad news shared in the healthcare provider-recipient context.

Anthony Dowell is Professor of Primary Healthcare and General Practice at the University of Otago, Wellington, New Zealand. He is a qualified medical practitioner and a founding member of the Applied Research on Communication in Health (ARCH) Group. His research interests include the management of chronic conditions such as mental health and diabetes in primary care.

Hasu Ghosh is currently a Ph.D. Candidate in Population Health and a student in the Health Services and Policy Research Diploma Program at the Institute of Population Health at the University of Ottawa, Canada. Ms. Ghosh holds a Master's in Anthropology with special interest in Medical Anthropology from Carleton University, Ottawa. She borrows from her background in both the biological and social sciences and relies on narrative and diversity analysis to explore urban Métis, First Nations, and professionals' understandings of Type 2 diabetes and its prevention. She works as a part-time Research Affiliate with the Population Health Improvement Research Network (PHIRN). Ms. Ghosh is an active member of various academic organizations and steering committees working for marginalized and high-risk population health improvement research and practice.

Franziska Gygax did her first degree (Lic.Phil.) in English and German at the University of Basel, Switzerland and her Ph.D. at the University of Berne, Switzerland, where she was an assistant and senior assistant teaching American literature. In 1996 she completed her Habilitation on Gertrude Stein and became a lecturer at the University of Basel. In 2003 she was appointed Titularprofessorin of English and American literature. Her main interests include Gender Studies, Queer Studies, modernism, and the theory of autobiography.

Jennifer Hall earned her doctorate from Purdue University, USA, where she studied Health Communication. She currently works as an instructor at Purdue University and serves as the Executive Director of the Greater Lafayette Sexual Assault Prevention Coalition. Hall's research and teaching are centered on a fundamental interest in how individuals, groups, organizations, and cultures communicate about their health and use communication to improve health. Her most current research explores how women who have experienced high-risk pregnancies integrate the many narratives around them into the narratives they create to assist them in making decisions, making sense of their experiences, and asserting their identities.

Melissa Horvath earned her Bachelor of Arts in Communication with Honors from the University of Arkansas, USA. She currently works in consumer development for Nestlé USA in Tampa, Florida. Ms. Horvath's research interests are in communication in applied settings, such as healthcare provision and in industry.

Regula Koenig is a Ph.D. student in English Linguistics who is currently employed at the English Seminar of the University of Basel, Switzerland. She is a team member of the Swiss National Science Foundation project "Life (Beyond) Writing: Illness Narratives" (http://illness-narratives.unibas.ch).

Zhenyi Li is an Associate Professor in the School of Communication and Culture at Royal Roads University, Canada. He received his Ph.D. in Intercultural Communication at the University of Jyvaskyla, Finland. Before Royal Roads University, he taught at the University of British Columbia, Simon Fraser University, Queen's University (all in Canada), University of Lille (France), University of Jyvaskyla (Finland), and Fudan University (China). His current area of research is on intercultural health communication, ranging from interpersonal communication in healthcare settings, intercultural competence development for healthcare professionals, intercultural sensitivity development for healthcare organizations, and multiculturalism in healthcare systems. He has published two books, 25 articles or book chapters, and presented at 36 conferences.

Miriam Locher started her position as Professor for English Linguistics at the University of Basel, Switzerland in August 2008. Before this, she worked as Senior Assistant of English Linguistics at the University of Berne and the University of Zurich (both in Switzerland). Professor Locher's work has been in the field of linguistic politeness and the exercise of power and advice-giving in an American Internet health advice column. Together with Sage Graham, she edited the *Handbook of Interpersonal Pragmatics* (2010).

Lindsay Macdonald is a Research Fellow in the Department of Primary Health Care and General Practice at the University of Otago, Wellington, New Zealand. She is a Registered Nurse and holds a post-graduate degree in Nursing and Linguistics. Her current research focuses on how nurses and other health professionals accomplish their work, in part, through everyday conversations and more formal consultations.

Jennifer A. Malkowski is pursuing doctoral work in communication studies at the University of Colorado at Boulder, USA. She earned her Master of Arts degree from San Diego State University, USA. Her research focuses on the rhetoric of health and medicine, paying particular attention to how issues of identity, gender, and inequality influence the healthcare decision-making process. Specifically, she engages in ethnographic methods of data collection paired with rhetorical methods of textual analysis to explore messages that occur at the political, the physician, and the patient level in order to inform how medical curriculum can better prepare medical professionals for successful patient interaction.

Niki Murray is a Senior Research Officer in the School of Communication, Journalism, and Marketing at Massey University, New Zealand. Dr. Murray earned her Ph.D. in Psychology from Massey University. In her dissertation, Dr. Murray investigated educational stress and ways of coping with stress by individuals with low literacy levels in vocational courses. Her main areas of interest are adult literacy, health literacy and communication, and community collaborative research designs. Dr. Murray continues to work in the immunization communication field, building on the work described above.

Anthony Nerino, MA, has worked as a research associate for six years in the Community Health Department and the Division of Population Health Research at Lehigh Valley Health Network in Pennsylvania, USA. His primary responsibilities are to provide data analysis and methodological assistance on survey projects and community based interventions, including addressing homelessness and addiction treatment. He participates on a community health assessment team, gathering and analyzing surveillance data on birth weight, and child abuse. He is a Ph.D. candidate at Temple University and teaches statistics and research methods.

Jarret R. Patton serves as the Medical Director of Ambulatory Pediatrics and the Physician Liaison of the cultural awareness and diversity initiative at the Lehigh Valley Health Network. While taking pride in caring for many of the underserved or uninsured children in Allentown, Pennsylvania, USA and the surrounding Lehigh Valley, he has continued research interest around health equity and health disparities. He received his B.S. in Chemistry from Xavier University of Louisiana, USA and his MD from Case Western Reserve University, Pennsylvania, USA, and completed residency training at New York University/Bellevue Hospitals. Dr. Patton's current academic appointment is with the College of Medicine at the University of South Florida, USA.

Samantha Romanin earned her Bachelor of Arts in Communication from the University of Arkansas, USA. She is currently a project support coordinator for the California Institute for Telecommunications and Information Technology at the University of California–San Diego. Previously, Ms. Romanin served as Associate Director of Programs for the Junior National Young Leaders Conference and the National Youth Leadership Forum on Medicine.

Judith Natale Sabino is Lehigh Valley Health Network's Diversity/Cultural Awareness Liaison. In this role, she is responsible for facilitating the network's cross-cultural healthcare initiatives in this region of Pennsylvania, USA. Her past experience includes holding leadership positions in the health network's Division of Community Health and AIDS Activities Office. Her research interests include cross-cultural healthcare provision, community health improvement, and access to care. Ms. Sabino holds a master's degree in public health from the Yale University School of Medicine, Connecticut, USA and a bachelor's degree in English/Communication from DeSales University, Pennsylvania, USA.

Cortney Smith is a Ph.D. Candidate and Associate Instructor at the Department of Communication and Culture, Indiana University–Bloomington, USA. Ms. Smith earned her Master of Arts in Communication from the University of Arkansas, USA. Her current research interests are in film criticism and history and interpersonal communication between patients and healthcare providers.

Maria Stubbe is an Interactional Sociolinguist working in the Department of Primary Health Care and General Practice, University of Otago, Wellington, New Zealand. She holds a Ph.D. in Linguistics from Victoria University of Wellington, and is a founding member of the Applied Research on Communication in Health (ARCH) Group. Dr. Stubbe's main research interests are microanalysis of health interactions, and institutional and cross-cultural communication. She has a particular interest in multidisciplinary research, and has published widely in the fields of pragmatics, applied sociolinguistics, and health communication.

Elspeth Tilley is a Senior Lecturer in Communication at Massey University, New Zealand. She holds a Ph.D. in postcolonial discourse analysis from the University of Queensland, Australia and is involved in a range of research projects that utilize qualitative discourse analysis methods. She has been a member of the Massey University Adult Literacy and Communication Research Group since its inception in 2004, and has led grounded data analysis in projects on literacy and employment, apprentices' learning, and immunization communication.

Jennifer Walinga is an Assistant Professor and Director of the School of Communication and Culture, Faculty of Social and Applied Sciences, Royal Roads University in Victoria, British Columbia, Canada. Dr. Walinga received her Ph.D. in Organizational Studies from the University of Victoria, School of Public Administration in Canada. Her doctoral studies focused on communication systems to support problem solving in organizations. Dr. Walinga also consults with and keynotes for organizations on issues of workplace health, communication, problem solving and decision making, innovation, leadership, and change. Her current areas of research include organizational communication systems to support a positive transformation of stress appraisal for enhanced workplace health, insight problem solving systems in applied settings, values-based decision making, and neuroleadership.

Bronwyn Watson is researching the impact of life-long learning and literacy on health in relation to aging. A qualitative methods specialist, Dr. Watson obtained her Ph.D. in Sociology from Massey University, New Zealand in 2006 and has subsequently worked on numerous large-scale social research projects as both a researcher and a research manager.